Remembering 1916

D0419833

The year 1916 witnessed two events that would profoundly shape both politics and commemoration in Ireland over the course of the following century. Although the Easter Rising and the Battle of the Somme were important historical events in their own right, their significance also lay in how they came to be understood as iconic moments in the emergence of Northern Ireland and the Irish Republic. Adopting an interdisciplinary approach drawing on history, politics, anthropology and cultural studies, this volume explores how the memory of these two foundational events has been constructed, mythologised and revised over the course of the past century. The aim is not merely to understand how the Rising and Somme came to exert a central place in how the past is viewed in Ireland, but to explore wider questions about the relationship between history, commemoration and memory.

Richard S. Grayson is Professor of Twentieth Century History at Goldsmiths, University of London. He is the author of *Belfast Boys: How Unionists and Nationalists Fought and Died Together in the First World War* (2009) and editor of *At War with the 16th Irish Division: The Staniforth Letters, 1914–18* (2012).

Fearghal McGarry is Reader in Irish History at Queen's University Belfast. He is the author of *The Rising. Ireland: Easter 1916* (2010), *Rebels: Voices from the Easter Rising* (2011) and *The Abbey Rebels of 1916: A Lost Revolution* (2015).

The year 1916 witnessed two events that would profoundly shape both politics and commemoration in Ireland over the course of the following century. Although the Easter Rising and the Battle of the Somme were important historical events in their own right, their significance also lay in how they came to be understood as iconic moments in the emergence of Northern Ireland and the Irish Republic. Adopting an interdisciplinary approach drawing on history, politics, anthropology and cultural studies, this volume explores how the memory of these two foundational events has been constructed, mythologised and revised over the course of the past century. The aim is not merely to understand how the Rising and Somme came to exert a central place in how the past is viewed in Ireland, but to explore wider questions about the relationship between history, commemoration and memory.

Richard S. Grayson is Professor of Twentieth Century History at Goldsmiths, University of London. He is the author of *Belfast Boys: How Unionists and Nationalists Fought and Died Together in the First World War* (2009) and editor of *At War with the 16th Irish Division: The Staniforth Letters, 1914–18* (2012).

Fearghal McGarry is Reader in Irish History at Queen's University Belfast. He is the author of *The Rising. Ireland: Easter 1916* (2010), *Rebels: Voices from the Easter Rising* (2011) and *The Abbey Rebels of 1916: A Lost Revolution* (2015).

Remembering 1916

The Easter Rising, the Somme and the Politics of Memory in Ireland

Edited by

Richard S. Grayson

Goldsmiths, University of London

and

Fearghal McGarry

Queen's University Belfast

CAMBRIDGE
UNIVERSITY PRESS

CAMBRIDGE
UNIVERSITY PRESS

University Printing House, Cambridge CB2 8BS, United Kingdom

Cambridge University Press is part of the University of Cambridge.

It furthers the University's mission by disseminating knowledge in the pursuit of education, learning and research at the highest international levels of excellence.

www.cambridge.org
Information on this title: www.cambridge.org/9781107145900

© Richard S. Grayson and Fearghal McGarry 2016

This publication is in copyright. Subject to statutory exception and to the provisions of relevant collective licensing agreements, no reproduction of any part may take place without the written permission of Cambridge University Press.

First published 2016
Reprinted 2016

Printed in the United Kingdom by Clays, St Ives plc

A catalogue record for this publication is available from the British Library

Library of Congress Cataloguing in Publication data
Grayson, Richard S., 1969– | McGarry, Fearghal.
Remembering 1916 : the Easter Rising, the Somme and the politics of memory in Ireland / edited by Richard S. Grayson (Goldsmiths, University of London) and Fearghal McGarry (Queen's University Belfast).
Cambridge, United Kingdom : Cambridge University Press, 2016.
LCCN 2015045194 | ISBN 9781107145900 (hardback)
LCSH: Ireland – History – Easter Rising, 1916 – Influence. | Somme, 1st Battle of the, France, 1916 – Influence. | Ireland – History – Easter Rising, 1916 – Historiography. | Somme, 1st Battle of the, France, 1916 – Historiography. | Memorials – Ireland. | Collective memory – Ireland. | Memory – Political aspects – Ireland. | Political culture – Ireland. | Ireland – History – 1922– | Northern Ireland – History.
LCC DA962 .R484 2016 | DDC 940.4/272–dc23
LC record available at http://lccn.loc.gov/2015045194

ISBN 978-1-107-14590-0 Hardback
ISBN 978-1-316-50927-2 Paperback

Cambridge University Press has no responsibility for the persistence or accuracy of URLs for external or third-party internet websites referred to in this publication, and does not guarantee that any content on such websites is, or will remain, accurate or appropriate.

Contents

Figures

Tables

Contributors

NICHOLAS ALLEN is Director of the Willson Center and Franklin Professor of English at the University of Georgia. His books include *Broken Landscapes: Selected Letters on Ernie O'Malley* (2011), *Modernism, Ireland and Civil War* (2009), *That Other Island* (2007), *The Proper Word* (2007), *George Russell and the New Ireland* (2003) and *The Cities of Belfast* (2003).

KEVIN BEAN is Lecturer in Irish Politics at the Institute of Irish Studies, University of Liverpool. His research interests include the development of Irish republicanism, contemporary forms of nationalism in Europe and social movement theory. His publications include The New Politics of Sinn Féin (2007), 'The Politics of Fear? Provisionalism, Loyalism and the "New Politics" of Northern Ireland' in G. Spencer and J. McAuley (eds.), *Ulster Loyalism after the Good Friday Agreement: History, Identity and Change* (2011) and 'Civil Society, the State and Conflict Transformation in the Nationalist Community' in M. Power (ed.), *Building Peace in Northern Ireland* (2012).

GUY BEINER is a senior lecturer at the Department of General History of Ben-Gurion University of the Negev and has held senior research fellowships at Trinity College, Dublin, the University of Notre Dame, the Central European University and the University of Oxford. He has authored several publications on Irish memory and forgetting, most notably *Remembering the Year of the French: Irish Folk History and Social Memory* (2007).

WILLIAM BLAIR has been Head of Human History at National Museums Northern Ireland since 2009. He led the development of the new 'TITANICa' exhibition at the Ulster Folk and Transport Museum (2011) and was author of its companion book *Titanic: Behind the Legend*. More recently he curated the new Modern History Gallery at the Ulster Museum, which opened in 2014. Currently a director of the Irish Museums Association, he is also a member of the UK

Government Advisory Committee in Northern Ireland on the Commemoration of the First World War.

DAVID BRUNDAGE is Professor of History at the University of California, Santa Cruz. He is the author of *The Making of Western Labor Radicalism: Denver's Organized Workers, 1878–1905* (1994) and a co-author of *Who Built America? Working People and the Nation's Economy, Politics, Culture & Society* (1989–1992). His articles on Irish-American history have appeared in *The Journal of American Ethnic History, New Hibernia Review* and *Saothar: Journal of the Irish Labour History society*. His most recent book is *Irish Nationalists in America: The Politics of Exile, 1798–1998* (2016).

DOMINIC BRYAN is Director of the Institute of Irish Studies and Reader in Social Anthropology at Queen's University Belfast. He has developed a research agenda exploring rituals, symbols and memory as they influence identity and social space in Ireland. Much of his early research focused upon Orange parades in Northern Ireland but the research now covers a much broader range of rituals and activities including St Patrick's Day, the Lord Mayor's Show and Carnival in Belfast. In addition, he is working on a major project looking at the popular flying of flags in Northern Ireland.

JONATHAN EVERSHED is an AHRC scholar and PhD candidate at the Institute of Irish Studies, Queen's University Belfast. His PhD research focuses on the politics of commemoration, peacebuilding and Ulster Loyalism during Northern Ireland's Decade of Centenaries, examining ethnographically the impact and significance of commemoration, spe cifically of the Battle of the Somme in contemporary 'Protestant/ Unionist/Loyalist' identity politics. He holds a BA in Politics and Development Studies and an MSc in Violence, Conflict and Development, both from the School of Oriental and African Studies (SOAS), University of London.

DAVID FITZPATRICK was Professor of Modern History at Trinity College, Dublin. His works include *Politics and Irish Life: Provincial Experience of War and Revolution* (1977), *Irish Emigration, 1801–1921* (1984), *Oceans of Consolation: Personal Accounts of Irish Migration to Colonial Australia* (1994), *The Two Irelands, 1912–1939* (1998), *Harry Boland's Irish Revolution* (2003), *'Solitary and Wild': Frederick MacNeice and the Salvation of Ireland* (2012) and *Descendancy: Irish Protestant Histories since 1795* (2014).

RICHARD S. GRAYSON is Professor of Twentieth Century History at Goldsmiths, University of London. He is the author of *Belfast Boys: How Unionists and Nationalists Fought and Died Together in the First World War* (2009) and editor of *At War with the 16th Irish Division: The Staniforth Letters, 1914–18* (2012). He has engaged widely with community groups on First World War remembrance, especially the 6th Connaught Rangers Research Project. An associate member of the First World War Centenary Committee in Northern Ireland, he contributed to BBC NI's Ireland's Great War, co-edits www.irelandww1.org and chairs the Academic Advisory Group for the Digital Projects run by the Imperial War Museums.

ROISÍN HIGGINS is Senior Lecturer in History at Teesside University. She has published extensively on commemoration in Ireland, including *Transforming 1916: Meaning, Memory and the Fiftieth Anniversary of the Easter Rising* (2012), which won the ACIS James Donnelly Sr Prize for History and Social Science. She is also the editor, with Regina Uí Chollatáin, of *The Life and After-Life of P.H. Pearse/Pádraic Mac Piarais: Saol agus Oidhreacht* (2009). She has been the historical advisor on the commemoration zone of the permanent exhibition GPO Witness History in Dublin.

FEARGHAL MCGARRY is Reader in Irish History at Queen's University Belfast. His research focuses on modern Ireland. A new edition of his account of the rebellion, *The Rising. Ireland: Easter 1916*, has just been published. *Rebels: Voices from the Easter Rising* (2011), his edited collection of first-hand testimony by revolutionaries, has recently been adapted for the stage by Jimmy Murphy for the Abbey Theatre. His latest book is *The Abbey Rebels of 1916. A Lost Revolution* (2015). He is working on a number of projects related to the 1916 centenary, including the development of the permanent exhibition GPO Witness History in Dublin.

MARGARET O´CALLAGHAN is Senior Lecturer in Politics at Queen's University, Belfast. She has also taught at the Universities of Cambridge and Notre Dame. Her publications cover numerous aspects of British high politics and the state apparatus in Ireland from the late nineteenth century to the revolution, including the Royal Irish Constabulary; partition; the Boundary Commission of 1925; the fringe-fenian press; the careers of Richard Pigott, Roger Casement and Tom Kettle; Belfast in the 1960s and 1970s; Ian Paisley; and the Royal Ulster Constabulary. She co-edited with Mary E. Daly *1916 in 1966: Commemorating the Easter Rising* (2007).

HEATHER L. ROBERTS is a PhD candidate in the Department of History and the Keough-Naughton Institute for Irish Studies at the University of Notre Dame, where she works on the intersection of violence, memory and commemoration in modern Ireland. She is a recipient of the Murphy Irish Exchange Fellowship and is currently a Visiting Researcher in the College of Arts, Celtic Studies and Social Sciences at University College Cork.

Introduction

Richard S. Grayson and Fearghal McGarry

I

The year 1916 witnessed two events that would profoundly shape both politics and commemoration in Ireland over the course of the following century. Although the Easter Rising and the Battle of the Somme were important historical events in their own right, their significance also lay in how they came to be retrospectively understood as iconic moments in the emergence of Northern Ireland and the Irish Republic. The historical memory of both events shaped not only the identities of the two states but the political communities within them, so much so that a necessary starting point for understanding their commemoration over the past century is to distinguish between the historical events themselves and the subsequent ways their significance has been constructed, mythologised and revised.

The Easter Rising provided a source of legitimacy not only for the independent Irish state that emerged out of the Irish revolution but for subsequent republican movements, whether seeking to acquire political power or to justify the use of violence for political ends. From the 1960s, the Rising's contested legacy also became increasingly central to acrimonious debates about the writing of Irish history which, unusually for a historiographical dispute, were given wide public purchase by the outbreak of the Troubles. Despite the success of the peace process over the past two decades, commemoration of the Rising continues to provoke as much division as unity, both North and South.

In Ulster, a different form of blood sacrifice, the fatalities endured by the 36th Division on the Western Front, especially on 1 July 1916 on the Somme, provided the central foundation myth for the Northern Irish state. As with the legacy of the Rising for republicans, the Somme

These essays result from a Wiles colloquium, 'Remembering 1916', hosted by Queen's University Belfast on 27 March 2015. We would like to acknowledge the generosity of the Wiles Trust in funding this event, along with the support of the School of History and Anthropology at Queen's and the Department of History at Goldsmiths. We are grateful to all the participants, particularly Conor Campbell and Matthew Jackson.

represented a potent source of both political capital and intra-communal tension within unionist and loyalist political culture. Although long identified with one political tradition in the Irish commemorative landscape, as witnessed by the ubiquity of Somme imagery in loyalist murals, the aftermath of the Belfast/Good Friday Agreement has also witnessed the appropriation of the memory of the First World War to fashion a more conciliatory narrative of shared Catholic and Protestant experiences, a development bringing its own tensions in the North.

II

That the significance of '1916' for both political traditions in Ireland rests on such radically different events illustrates the extent of the island's divisions, as do the communal tensions that arise from their major anniversaries, such as occurred in Belfast in 1966.[1] Until recently, this divide existed not only in popular memory but much of the scholarship. While many academics have produced narratives that encompass both the Easter Rising and the Battle of the Somme, studies of the politics of memory have tended to focus on one or the other.[2]

The first aim of this volume is to explore the memory of the two events together, both to identify commonalities and differences and to consider how each commemorative tradition has shaped the other. A second is to widen the focus from 'official' commemoration, often narrowly conceived of in terms of the agency of the state or its political parties, to a broader framework loosely termed 'historical memory'. This reflects a growing understanding of the extent to which communities, families and even individuals make sense of their lives through ideas about the past, as well as an increasing awareness of the extent to which the meanings attached to the past are contested from below as much as imposed from above. Third, this volume aims to draw on the perspectives offered by a variety of disciplines such as history, political science, anthropology, cultural studies and museology. In doing so, we hope not merely to better understand how and why the events of 1916 came to assume such iconic importance but to provide a case study for exploring wider questions about the relationship between scholarly history, political identity,

[1] Mary E. Daly and Margaret O'Callaghan (eds.), *1916 in 1966: Commemorating the Easter Rising* (Dublin: Royal Irish Academy, 2007).
[2] An important exception and a key starting point for scholarly understanding of commemoration in Ireland is Ian McBride (ed.), *History and Memory in Modern Ireland* (Cambridge: Cambridge University Press, 2001). A concise but valuable recent publication which considers the memory of this period within the context of the Decade of Centenaries is John Horne and Edward Madigan (eds.), *Towards Commemoration: Ireland in War and Revolution 1912–1923* (Dublin: Royal Irish Academy, 2013).

communal memory and commemoration that will interest scholars of historical memory elsewhere.

Our project is timely considering how the commemoration of both events has become increasingly entwined as a result of the adoption of a shared commemorative framework by both Irish states and the UK government, a process which itself reflects a broader understanding of the interconnected nature of these events, along with more pragmatic political considerations. Previously in the South, major anniversaries of 1916 focused narrowly on the Easter Rising rather than the surrounding events of a decade of war and revolution. Official commemoration was shaped by the prevailing interests of the Southern state, as is clear from the now familiar commemorative narrative: the 25th anniversary was framed by 'the Emergency' (as the Second World War was known in Éire); the elaborate golden jubilee in 1966 reflected the efforts of the Taoiseach Seán Lemass to fashion a more constructive patriotism for a modernising state; while the muted 75th anniversary in 1991 was shaped by the sectarian violence of the Troubles. Following in the wake of the peace process and rise of the Celtic Tiger, the 90th anniversary was characterised by a more confident and celebratory approach.[3]

In the North, commemoration of the Rising has always conformed to a different pattern, one framed by the political context within that divided society. There was, for example, little danger of a triumphalist remembrance of the Rising in 1966 when loyalists demanded a ban on Easter commemorations. Widely ignored in the South until recent decades, commemoration of the Somme in Ulster fulfilled many of the same functions for the Northern state as the Rising in the South. As with the latter, the memory of the Somme also reflected political tensions within the majority community. In particular, the Troubles saw commemoration of the 36th (Ulster) Division – which has gradually come to displace King William and the battle of the Boyne as the pre-eminent focus of unionist historical memory – increasingly linked to paramilitarism and loyalist political identity.

More recently, the adoption of the Decade of Centenaries commemorative programme has resulted in both change and continuity. Encompassing the Home Rule crisis (1912–1914), the First World War (1914–1918), partition (1920), the War of Independence (1919–1921) and the Civil War (1922–1923), this approach is better placed to enhance public understanding of the broader historical context, particularly the

---

[3] For shifting historiographical and commemorative perspectives over the past century, see Diarmaid Ferriter, *A Nation and Not a Rabble. The Irish Revolution 1913–1923* (London: Profile, 2015), pp. 17–96, 319–408.

interdependent nature of the often instinctie unionist and nationalist political traditions. It also encompasses a broader social context than previous anniversaries, with events such as the 1913 Lockout and the role of women receiving greater recognition.

Another departure is the extent of co-ordination between Dublin, Belfast and London, with expert advisory groups and planning bodies established at different levels. The most obvious consequence of this is the emphasis on the need for a more pluralistic remembrance, in terms of both the range of issues, events and participants considered and the tone in which such commemoration is conducted. The Irish government's Decade of Centenaries website, for example, discusses the need to promote 'constructive dialogue' and 'deeper mutual understanding among people from different traditions on the island of Ireland'.[4] A joint statement along similar lines was issued in March 2012 by the British Prime Minster David Cameron and Irish Taoiseach Enda Kenny although, inevitably, this spirit has been much less in evidence in Northern Ireland where exclusivist commemorative impulses remain dominant, particularly in the political rather than civic sphere where more positive grassroots initiatives have emerged.[5]

Despite the radically different political context and much improved relations across the two islands, the current anniversaries are also characterised by considerable continuity. Notwithstanding the success of the peace process, squaring the need to remember with historical integrity the Easter Rising with the aim of enhancing relations between opposing political traditions remains a challenge. This difficulty lay at the heart of public disquiet at the Irish government's initial attempts to frame 1916 as an uncontentious celebration of Irish heritage, shorn of its associations with revolutionary violence.[6] Different commemorative tensions apply across the border. Although nationalists are increasingly willing to reclaim the memory of Catholic service in the First World War, commemoration of the Somme remains firmly embedded in unionist political culture, despite the role of the nationalist 16th (Irish) Division in the battle in early September 1916.

Another continuity is the extent to which commemoration of the iconic events of 1916 remains characterised by conflicts over ownership

---

[4] See: www.decadeofcentenaries.com/about/.
[5] See, for example, the initiatives of the Community Relations Council (www.community-relations.org.uk/programmes/marking-anniversaries/; the East Belfast and the Great War project (www.eastbelfastww1.com/); and The 6th Connaught Rangers, *Belfast Nationalists and the Great War* (Belfast: 6th Connaught Rangers Research Project, 2011).
[6] See, for example, Éanna Ó Caollaí, 'Don't Mention the War', *Irish Times*, 3 December 2014: www.irishtimes.com/culture/heritage/don-t-mention-the-war-1916-video-fails-to-mention-rising-1.1999460.

which owe more to opportunistic present-day politics than differing interpretations of history. In proposing an alternative to the Southern state's commemorative programme, Gerry Adams explained that Sinn Féin sought to allow the Irish people to rededicate themselves to 'the politics of ... Pádraig Pearse, and James Connolly [and] ... Bobby Sands'.[7] Contemporary commemoration of the Somme in the North, meanwhile, remains similarly bound up with intra-unionist tensions, as is demonstrated by the ubiquity of murals linking the UVF of 1913–1914 and the battle of the Somme to Belfast's more recent loyalist violence.

III

This volume is divided into four parts. The first steps back from a close focus on commemoration of 1916 to consider broader theories and practices relating to historical memory. Guy Beiner (Chapter 1) offers a critical discussion of some of the key terms used to conceptualise remembrance of the past, including myth, collective memory, public memory, popular memory, cultural memory, social memory and postmemory. He proposes a new concept, 'prememory', which he argues can be paired with 'postmemory' to advance explorations of historical memory. Dominic Bryan (Chapter 2), in contrast, challenges how terms such as memory, remembering and collective memory are used as conceptual tools in historical study. Arguing that what historians often regard as forms of memory are, in fact, manifestations of present-day politics, he suggests that commemorative rituals act as a 'time machine', enabling political actors to exploit the past in order to legitimise contemporary political practice and identity. Bryan's thesis questions the privileged role occupied by historians in events which, he argues, are not primarily about the past. Roisín Higgins (Chapter 3) examines the politics of memory in Ireland, placing commemoration of the Easter Rising in a wider framework, by considering the extent to which its tropes – including redemption, deliverance, resilience, heroic sacrifice and heroic failure – conform to commemorative practices elsewhere. She explores what, if anything, is distinctive about the practice in Ireland by examining its relation to territory, the state and the economy.

Part II more directly addresses the memorialisation of the events of 1916 by examining how historical narratives of 1916 have been

[7] Ronan McGreevy, 'Government "Embarrassed" by 1916 Rising, Adams Says', *Irish Times*, 6 February 2015: www.irishtimes.com/news/ireland/irish-news/government-emb arrassed-by-1916-rising-adams-says-1.2094281.

constructed, and evolved, over time. David Fitzpatrick (Chapter 4) investigates the ways in which actors and observers experienced contemporary events as if they were living out history and in history. Analysing how participants expressed and enacted this sense of being history-makers, Fitzpatrick proposes a tentative taxonomy to enable a future study of Ireland's 'instant histories'. In Chapter 5, Fearghal McGarry examines the commemoration of the Abbey Theatre's Easter rebels as a case study to demonstrate the complex and contested dynamics that shape commemorative processes. He explores how the individuals commemorated exerted agency over 1916 remembrance by constructing their own narratives of rebellion, and traces how family networks and the changing political context mediated the dissemination and reception of these narratives.

Richard Grayson (Chapter 6) explores the popular narrative of what happened to those members of the pre-war Ulster Volunteer Force who served in the British forces during the First World War. Drawing on data for 138 identified members of the UVF who were resident in West Belfast, his chapter argues that, if one is interested in the history of the UVF, then a focus on 1 July 1916 neglects a significant part of its experiences. Moving across the Atlantic, David Brundage (Chapter 7) examines how the Easter Rising was remembered in the United States between 1919 and 1963. Although a once powerful Irish-American republican movement shrank dramatically, the Rising continued to be remembered in different ways by Catholic churchmen, Irish-American labour activists, other ethnic communities and Hollywood film-makers. Remembering 1916 in America, Brundage argues, involved a diverse array of people, practices and motives, and the rebellion's legacy there sheds light on wider subjects ranging from African-American nationalism to representations of Ireland and the Irish in American popular culture.

Part III explores the relationship between remembering and literary and material cultures. Heather Roberts (Chapter 8) explores commemorative links between 1798 and 1916. She shows how the flurry of excitement surrounding the centenary commemoration of the 1798 rebellion contributed to the politicisation of a revolutionary generation, some of whom would go on to participate in the Easter Rising. She examines how, as a result of the impact of the Rising, the memory of the 'Rising generation' mingled with, and ultimately displaced, that of '98 in the Irish Free State's commemorative landscape. Nicholas Allen (Chapter 9) analyses a variety of cultural representations of the Easter Rising. He situates canonical texts by Yeats and Joyce within a complex process of cultural exchange stretching from Dublin and Belfast through London to the Western and Mediterranean fronts.

Emphasising a diverse cultural background to the war and rebellion that places empire and its practices at the centre of Irish experience, Allen examines how literature and art have shaped our subsequent view of the Easter Rising and the Somme as formative of twentieth-century Irish culture. William Blair (Chapter 10) surveys the evolution of the Ulster Museum's approach to the challenges of interpreting the First World War. He demonstrates how new museological practices have recovered and revised the significance of the museum's artefacts within multiple contexts ranging from personal and family experiences to broader themes of technological, social, political and cultural change.

Since 1969, the memory of 1916 has become increasingly entangled with the impact and legacy of the Troubles, an historical era from which we are now emerging. Part IV explores how the memory of 1916 has been refracted through the prism of the Troubles and its immediate aftermath. Margaret O'Callaghan (Chapter 11) analyses commemoration as a site of contestation for the meaning and ownership of republicanism at the height of the Troubles. She explores how the Irish state altered its approach to commemorating 1916 in an effort to reshape public attitudes to physical-force republicanism and Irish history. Kevin Bean (Chapter 12) considers aspects of the public and political debates surrounding the commemoration of the Easter Rising since 1994. He demonstrates how the Rising remained a problematic site of memory, providing a battleground for debates about the legitimacy of contemporary political projects, as well as the extent to which 'the ideals of 1916' had been achieved. His chapter demonstrates how the peace process and consolidation of a new dispensation in Northern Ireland since 1998 has not lessened the impact of these questions of legitimacy and historical achievement in both Irish polities. Bean argues that current commemorative tensions are not simply revivals of old conflicts, but also attempts to resolve contemporary problems of political authority, ideological legitimacy and a popular disenchantment with mainstream politics evident beyond Ireland.

The final chapter in the volume (Chapter 13), by Jonathan Evershed, explores loyalist commemoration of the Somme. Drawing on ethnographic fieldwork conducted in Belfast, his chapter examines the subscripts of Loyalist resistance which underwrite the emerging norms of new 'official' commemorations and their emphasis on 'shared sacrifice'. He argues that the ghosts of the 36th (Ulster) Division continue to shape the politics of Ulster loyalism in an historical moment defined by a chronic sense of ontological insecurity. There is a need, Evershed suggests, to understand and engage with

Loyalist memory of the Somme in a way which sees it not – as prevailing discourses suggest – as chiefly concerned with the past, but rather with an uncertain future.

IV

The contributors to this volume present a range of new perspectives rather than an overarching set of arguments, exploratory approaches rather than a model for understanding commemoration. Differences between disciplinary perspectives can be discerned. The historians, often adopting a diachronic perspective, allow greater space for the role of ideas about history – whether credible or misinformed – in shaping Irish political debate than the anthropologists who, applying a synchronic approach, are more inclined to interpret commemorative practices as rituals that mask political negotiations about power. While contributors may not always agree on the factors that shape historical memory, some key themes recur. There is a shared scepticism about the relationship between history and commemoration, and the need for sophisticated theoretical approaches to mediate between both of these forms of representing the past. The boom in memory studies over the past two decades has also witnessed a shift, particularly among historians, from a felt requirement to debunk popular memory to taking it seriously as a subject worthy of study in its own right.

These chapters also reflect a growing awareness of the complexity of the variety of ways in which the past is recalled and the need to utilise insights from a range of disciplines to understand these processes. This requires a broadening out of the idea of commemoration as a top-down process determined by the state or other official bodies to conceiving of it as a more diffuse, contested and contingent process shaped by diverse competing influences. The importance of tracing how ideas about the past are generated, transmitted and received, and identifying why some of these – within specific contexts – engender sufficient emotional resonance to shape popular understanding of the past is stressed by several contributors.

Commemoration, it has long been acknowledged, tells us more about the present than the past; it is a process driven more by emotional and political imperatives – particularly the desire to 'imagine the past and remember the future' – than by dispassionate scholarship.[8] Several contributors, however, emphasise the need to consider historical memory

---

[8] Lewis Namier, quoted in R. F. Foster, *The Irish Story: Telling Tales and Making it Up in Ireland* (London: Allen Lane, 2001), p. 33.

within more open-ended temporal perspectives. Those who made history on Ulster Day or Easter Monday, for example, were shaped by their own consciousness of historical precedents, as well as their anticipation of how their actions would be understood in the futures they expected to create. Later representations of their actions were shaped by a variety of contexts, including disappointment at their failure to achieve these expectations, subsequent generational shifts and altered political contexts. Close attention to the unfolding narratives of 1916 suggest that they are not so much invented as recycled, with alternative meanings, rooted in discernible historical pasts, reviving as required.

It remains to be seen how the events of 1916 will be remembered in 2016, or the extent to which their popular memory will be informed by historical understanding. Whatever happens in 2016, our hope is that these chapters will provide a variety of ways to interpret the meaning and significance which will be attached by the public to the centenary of these two momentous events.

Part I

Memory and commemoration

1   Making sense of memory: coming to terms with conceptualisations of historical remembrance

Guy Beiner

In considering remembrance of historical events, thought must first be given to what we mean by 'memory'. Obsessive preoccupation with this theme over the past thirty years or so has been labelled a 'memory boom'.[1] Irish scholarship caught up with this intellectual development at a delay but produced nonetheless a number of noteworthy publications, ranging from the trailblazing collection of essays edited by Ian McBride on *History and Memory in Modern Ireland* (2001) to the theoretically sophisticated four volumes of *Memory Ireland* edited by Oona Frawley (2010–2014).[2] In much of the voluminous literature, memory remains an elusive notion. It is therefore worth clarifying some of the key conceptualisations of historical memory and, while taking note of the strengths and limitations of each concept, suggesting how these terms can be employed in an exploration of remembering 1916.

Although the study of memory is inherently interdisciplinary, historical discussions have seldom engaged with models developed by neuroscientists and are mostly unconcerned with the concepts of memory developed by cognitive psychologists.[3] In its most immediate sense, historical

---

This essay was written during a Marie Curie fellowship, sponsored by the Gerda Henkel Foundation.

[1] See Jay Winter, 'The Generation of Memory: Reflections on the Memory Boom in Contemporary Historical Studies', *Bulletin of the German Historical Institute* 27 (2000), 69–92; Jay Winter, 'Notes on the Memory Boom: War, Remembrance, and the Uses of the Past' in Duncan Bell (ed.), *Memory, Trauma and World Politics: Reflections on the Relationship between Past and Present* (Basingstoke and New York: Palgrave Macmillan, 2006), pp. 54–73; David W. Blight, 'The Memory Boom: Why and Why Now?' in Pascal Boyer and James V. Wertsch (eds.), *Memory in Mind and Culture* (New York: Cambridge University Press, 2009), pp. 238–251. The term was apparently first introduced by Andreas Huyssen in his book *Twilight Memories: Marking Time in a Culture of Amnesia* (New York: Routledge, 1995), pp. 1–9.

[2] Ian McBride (ed.), *History and Memory in Modern Ireland* (Cambridge and New York: Cambridge University Press, 2001); Oona Frawley (ed.), *Memory Ireland*, 4 vols. (Syracuse: Syracuse University Press, 2010–2014).

[3] Attempts to bridge the studies of memory in neuroscience and the humanities have met with limited success. See, for example, the incongruity of the chapter by Idan Landau on

remembrance is associated with the recollections of participants and eye-witnesses of historical events. These personal recollections are influenced by the contexts in which they were recorded, which is typically at a remove from the events. Although they are sometimes cited unproblematically as factual evidence, witness testimonies reflect how 1916 was remembered in the specific circumstances of their documentation, whether in support of an application for a military service pension, as a lasting statement for posterity given to the Bureau of Military History or in response to the inquiry of interested scholars. These memories were remoulded with the passing of time. For example, the Easter Rising is absent in the memoir of Ernie O'Malley, written during the events, but appears as a significant moment of political conversion in the stylish autobiography he published twenty years later.[4] Analysis of such sources requires proficiency in the methodologies of oral history, which can be applied to mine details that shed new light on the past, as well as to appreciate how the past was subjectively remembered in a changing present.[5]

In his pioneering work on collective memory, Maurice Halbwachs forcefully posited that remembrance is not an autonomous activity of an individual but is dependent on the social contexts in which it takes place.[6] Although this argument has been misunderstood by some critics as a dismissal of memory 'proper' in favour of a reified metaphorical construct, there is now a well-established corpus of texts that discusses collective memory in its own right.[7] Attempts have been made to work

'What Changes in the Brain When We Learn' in the collection Doron Mendels (ed.), *On Memory: An Interdisciplinary Approach* (Oxford and New York: Peter Lang, 2007); see also Suzanne Nalbantian, Paul M. Matthews and James L. McClelland (eds.), *The Memory Process: Neuroscientific and Humanistic Perspectives* (Cambridge, MA: MIT Press, 2011). For 'Concepts of Memory' in cognitive psychology, see Endel Tulving and Fergus I. M. Craik (eds.), *The Oxford Handbook of Memory* (Oxford and New York: Oxford University Press, 2000), pp. 33–43.

[4] Richard English, *Ernie O'Malley: IRA Intellectual* (Oxford and New York: Oxford University Press, 1998), pp. 6–7.

[5] See Eve Morrison, 'Identity, Allegiance, War and Remembrance: The Bureau of Military History and the Irish Revolution' (PhD: Department of History, Trinity College Dublin, 2012); presently being adapted into a book for Liverpool University Press. Morrison's current research in progress looks at remembrance in Ernie O'Malley's notebooks. For an introductory discussion on the relations between memory and oral history, see Donald A. Ritchie, *Doing Oral History*, 3rd edn (Oxford and New York: Oxford University Press, 2015), pp. 14–28.

[6] Maurice Halbwachs, *Les cadres sociaux de la mémoire* (Paris: F. Alcan, 1925); Maurice Halbwachs, *La mémoire mollective* (Paris: Presses universitaires de France, 1968; orig. edn, 1950). For English translations, see respectively Maurice Halbwachs, *On Collective Memory* (Chicago and London: University of Chicago Press, 1992); Maurice Halbwachs, *The Collective Memory* (New York: Harper & Row, 1980).

[7] For a representative sample, see Jeffrey K. Olick, Vered Vinitzky-Seroussi and Daniel Levy (eds.), *The Collective Memory Reader* (New York and Oxford: Oxford University Press, 2011).

out in greater detail the connections between psychological studies of individual memory and sociological studies of collective memory.[8] A provocative critique, however, argued that '"collective memory" is but a misleading new name for the old familiar "myth"'.[9]

Though no longer in vogue, myth is a concept which should not be too readily brushed aside when considering memory of iconic events. The Gaelic Revival of the fin de siècle reintroduced Celtic mythology to a modern readership through Standish James O'Grady's influential *History of Ireland: Heroic Period* (1878 and 1880) and in subsequent, more popular writings, such as T. W. Rolleston's *Myths and Legends of the Celtic Race* (1911).[10] The Fenians popularised a commemorative culture of nationalist martyrdom, and the annual commemorative parades of Orange Order gained respectability among unionists.[11] Consequently, the generation that came of age in 1916 was schooled on quasi-historical mythology. In turn, 1916 was subject to instant mythologising. Both nationalists and unionists reworked pre-existing historical traditions of 'deep memory' that pivoted on themes of trauma and triumph. The new narratives were rapidly embellished and endorsed as foundation myths by ascendant political cultures: the Easter Rising for nationalist Independent Ireland and the Battle of the Somme for unionist Northern Ireland.[12]

In a groundbreaking essay published in 1967, F. X. Martin made a case for critical demystification of 1916.[13] This approach was in line with the doctrines of the 'new Irish history', which advocated dispassionate

---

[8] See the special issue of the journal *Memory* on the theme 'From Individual to Collective Memory: Theoretical and Empirical Perspectives' edited by Amanda J. Barnier and John Sutton; *Memory* 16 (2008).

[9] Noa Gedi and Yigal Elam, 'Collective Memory – What Is It?', *History and Memory* 8 (1996), 30–50 (47).

[10] See Gregory Castle, 'Nobler Forms: Standish James O'Grady's *History of Ireland* and the Irish Literary Revival' and José Lanters, 'Reading the Irish Future in the Celtic Past: T.W. Rolleston and the Politics of Myth' in Lawrence L. McBride (ed.), *Reading Irish Histories: Texts, Contexts, and Memory in Modern Ireland* (Dublin: Four Courts Press, 2003), pp. 156–177 and 178–195.

[11] Guy Beiner, 'Fenianism and the Martyrdom-Terrorism Nexus in Ireland before Independence' in Dominic Janes and Alex Houen (eds.), *Martyrdom and Terrorism: Pre-Modern to Contemporary Perspectives* (Oxford and New York: Oxford University Press, 2014), pp. 199–220; Dominic Bryan, *Orange Parades: The Politics of Ritual, Tradition, and Control* (London and Sterling, VA: Pluto Press, 2000), pp. 44–59.

[12] Guy Beiner, 'Between Trauma and Triumphalism: The Easter Rising, the Somme, and the Crux of Deep Memory in Modern Ireland', *Journal of British Studies* 46 (2007), 366–389. Whereas the aggrandisement of the Easter Rising was at first stalled and was then kindled by the public reaction to the execution of the leaders, mythography of the Somme commenced in Ulster immediately with the arrival of news of the catastrophe from the front; see David Officer, '"For God and Ulster": The Ulsterman on the Somme' in McBride (ed.), *History and Memory in Modern Ireland*, pp. 160–183.

[13] F. X. Martin, '1916: Myth, Fact, and Mystery', *Studia Hibernica* 7 (1967), 7–126.

scrutiny of national history. The commitment of Irish historians to deconstruct myths increased after the outbreak of the Troubles, when republican and loyalist paramilitaries justified acts of violence by claiming to be the rightful heirs of the valorised heroes of 1916. Against this charged background, T. W. Moody's presidential address to the Dublin University History Society on 10 May 1977 famously depicted 'Irish mythology' (i.e., memory) as a negative other to Irish history.[14]

There has since been a noticeable change in historical attitudes to modern myths, which, through the influence of cultural anthropology, have been recognised as highly meaningful narratives that shape social behaviour. It is now less common to simply disregard popular beliefs about the past on the grounds of factual inaccuracy. Instead, myths are seen as articulations of attitudes and reflections of mindsets. This shift became apparent in English historiography from the early 1990s in such publications as *The Myths We Live By* (1990), edited by Raphael Samuel and Paul Thomson, and *Myths of the English* (1992), edited by Roy Porter.[15] The ethno-symbolist approach to the study of nationalism, championed by Anthony D. Smith, found in historical myths the building blocks of national identity.[16] Jonathan Githens-Mazer fruitfully applied this method to Ireland in his study of *Myths and Memories of the Easter Rising*.[17]

In place of the binary opposition between history and myth that was characteristic of Irish revisionism, popular historical consciousness can be regarded as a synthesis, or 'mythistory'.[18] Ultimately, the drawing of a rigid dichotomy separating history from memory, which is the axiomatic premise of many of the key writings in the field, does not hold water. Pierre Nora, who insisted on this differentiation, nonetheless located his seminal concept of *lieux de mémoire* 'between history and memory', acknowledging that 'the boundary between the two is blurring'.[19] Rather than imposing artificial distinctions, it is more beneficial to follow

[14] T. W. Moody, 'Irish History and Irish Mythology' in Ciaran Brady (ed.), *Interpreting Irish History: The Debate on Historical Revisionism, 1938–1994* (Blackrock, Co. Dublin and Portland, OR: Irish Academic Press, 1994), pp. 71–86.

[15] Raphael Samuel and Paul Thompson (eds.), *The Myths We Live By* (London and New York: Routledge, 1990); Roy Porter (ed.), *Myths of the English* (Cambridge: Polity Press, 1992).

[16] Anthony D. Smith, *Myths and Memories of the Nation* (Oxford: Oxford University Press, 1999).

[17] Jonathan Githens-Mazer, *Myths and Memories of the Easter Rising: Cultural and Political Nationalism in Ireland* (Dublin: Irish Academic Press, 2006).

[18] See Guy Beiner, *Remembering the Year of the French: Irish Folk History and Social Memory* (Madison: University of Wisconsin Press, 2006), p. 33.

[19] Pierre Nora, 'Between Memory and History: Les Lieux de Mémoire', *Representations* 26 (1989), 7–24.

the manifold symbiotic interactions between various forms of engagement with the past. In this sense, historians of 1916 have much to learn from studies of myths by folklorists and anthropologists and to rethink their appreciation of myths accordingly.[20]

In a treatise on 'how societies remember', Paul Connerton advocated the need to look beyond the symbolic texts of myths and explore the performative functions of rituals that re-enact the past.[21] The concept of 'collective memory', which is the most commonly used term for communal remembrance, has proved to be particularly useful in focussing attention on the rituals of official commemoration ceremonies and the erection of monuments. Countless studies, which dwell on the efficacy of collective memory, have uncritically bought into the thesis of 'invention of tradition' associated with Eric Hobsbawm.[22] However, further probing reveals the limitations of manipulation from above. The notion of 'collective' misleadingly suggests a homogeneity, which is rarely, if ever, the case in practise.

Although the memory of 1916 was central to the ethos of the two states founded after the partition of Ireland, the authorities in Dublin and Belfast both encountered difficulties in consolidating and imparting a cohesive collective memory. David Fitzpatrick has suggested that the divisive legacy of the Irish Revolution inhibited official commemorative initiatives in the Irish Free State and thwarted efforts to promote shared commemoration of 1916: 'both parties made some attempt to reconcile disaffected groups by involving the state in non-partisan commemoration of the 1916 Rising and the Great War. These somewhat ecumenical enterprises proved no less contentious, not least because of the resentment from those whose mourning was personal and specific.'[23] After rising to power, de Valera increasingly appealed to collective memory in an effort to capitalise on its political dividends, yet government commemoration of 1916 remained a sensitive and often controversial

---

[20] For a useful primer, see William G. Doty, *Mythography: The Study of Myths and Rituals*, 2nd edn (Tuscaloosa: University of Alabama Press, 2000). For an historian's attempt to accommodate discrepancies between factual history and mythic memory, see Fearghal McGarry, '1916 and Irish Republicanism: Between Myth and History' in John Horne and Edward Madigan (eds.), *Towards Commemoration: Ireland in War and Revolution, 1912–1923* (Dublin: Royal Irish Academy, 2013), pp. 46–53.

[21] Paul Connerton, *How Societies Remember* (Cambridge and New York: Cambridge University Press, 1989).

[22] Eric Hobsbawm and Terence Ranger (eds.), *The Invention of Tradition* (Cambridge: Cambridge University Press, 1983); in particular, see Hobsbawm's introduction (pp. 1–14) and his seminal essay on 'Mass-Producing Traditions: Europe, 1870–1914' (pp. 263–308).

[23] David Fitzpatrick, 'Commemoration in the Irish Free State: A Chronicle of Embarrassment' in McBride (ed.), *History and Memory in Modern Ireland*, p. 203.

subject.[24] Commemoration of the Easter Rising climaxed in the excessively lavish jubilee celebrations of 1966, but even then, as demonstrated by Roisín Higgins, there were plentiful grass roots alternative commemorations that openly contested official commemoration.[25] The government of Northern Ireland was fully committed to commemoration of the Somme, as shown, for example, in its involvement in the design and construction of the memorial tower for the 36th Ulster Division at Thiepval.[26] But this public culture of commemoration was challenged by the recalcitrance of northern nationalists, whose preference to commemorate the Easter Rising could not be extinguished by the official imposition of heavy-handed prohibitions, which were eventually relaxed from the 1940s.[27]

In place of a unified notion of collective memory, a more sophisticated concept of 'popular memory', initially developed at the Birmingham Centre for Contemporary Cultural Studies, focusses on confrontations with dominant memory.[28] In a masterful deployment of this approach, Alistair Thomson used oral history interviews to show how Australian veterans maintained different memories of their experiences in the First World War, some of which were readapted to comply, while others persisted in disagreeing, with the national collective memory of the 'Anzac legend'.[29] In other studies, a somewhat similar concept of 'public memory' has been used to tease out the 'intersection of official and vernacular cultural expressions'.[30] In his writings, Halbwachs coined the term 'collective memory', with which he is associated, but his emphasis on social frameworks ('les cadres sociaux de la mémoire') sits better with the term 'social memory', which has since emerged as a viable

---

[24] Diarmaid Ferriter, 'Commemorating the Rising, 1922–65: "A Figurative Scramble for the Bones of the Patriot Dead"' in Margaret O'Callaghan and Mary E. Daly (eds.), *1916 in 1966: Commemorating the Easter Rising* (Dublin: Royal Irish Academy, 2007), pp. 198–218.

[25] Roisín Higgins, *Transforming 1916: Meaning, Memory and the Fiftieth Anniversary of the Easter Rising* (Cork: Cork University Press, 2012), pp. 30–85.

[26] See Catherine Switzer and Brian Graham, '"Ulster's Love in Letter'd Gold": The Battle of the Somme and the Ulster Memorial Tower, 1918–1935', *Journal of Historical Geography* 36 (2010), 183–193.

[27] See Margaret O'Callaghan, '"From Casement Park to Toomebridge": The Commemoration of the Easter Rising in Northern Ireland in 1966' in O'Callaghan and Daly (eds.), *1916 in 1966*, pp. 86–147; Higgins, *Transforming 1916*, pp. 86–112.

[28] Popular Memory Group, Richard Johnson and Graham Dawson, 'Popular Memory: Theory, Politics, Method' in R. Johnson, G. McLennan, B. Schwartz and D. Sutton (eds.), *Making Histories: Studies in History-Writing and Politics* (Abingdon: Routledge, 2007; orig. edn, 1982), pp. 205–252.

[29] Alistair Thomson, *Anzac Memories: Living with the Legend* (Clayton, VIC: Monash University Press, 2013; orig. edn, 1994).

[30] John E. Bodnar, *Remaking America: Public Memory, Commemoration, and Patriotism in the Twentieth Century* (Princeton, NJ: Princeton University Press, 1992), p. 13.

alternative to collective memory.[31] This approach to memory has been applied in the doctoral research of Antoine Guillemette to reveal the complexity of commemorative practices of the Easter Rising from 1916 to 1966.[32] Catherine Switzer examined the first two decades of unionist commemoration of the Great War with regard to the agency of local communities.[33] The current surge in social memory of the Somme at a local community level, which has been stoked for political purposes by loyalist former paramilitaries in post-conflict Northern Ireland, has attracted critical attention.[34] Between the dates of these studies, significant gaps still remain in our knowledge of the history of social remembrance of 1916.

The cultural turn in the humanities and social sciences promoted the study of 'cultural memory'.[35] Although this term has been used interchangeably with collective and social memory, cultural memory signifies a reconceptualisation, 'following a shift in stress from the social group to its modes of production'.[36] A focus on the cultural representations of 1916 is a particularly fertile field. The early commentary of F. X. Martin, which was complemented by W. I. Thompson's *The Imagination of an Insurrection* (1967), called attention to literary remembrance of the Easter Rising.[37] Irish writers also partook in the forming of the British literary cannon of the Great War.[38] Cultural memory of 1916 is ubiquitous in Irish poetry from W. B. Yeats to Michael Longley, prose fiction from Pádraic Ó Conaire and Eimar O'Duffy to Roddy Doyle and Sebastian Barry, and drama from Sean O'Casey to Frank McGuiness. To this could

---

[31] For an early study, see James Fentress and Chris Wickham, *Social Memory* (Oxford and Cambridge, MA: Blackwell, 1992). For a study of social memory set in Ireland, see Beiner, *Remembering the Year of the French*.

[32] Antoine Guillemette, 'Coming Together at Easter: Commemorating the Easter Rising in Ireland, 1916–1966' (PhD: Department of History, Concordia University, 2013).

[33] Catherine Switzer, *Unionists and Great War Commemoration in the North of Ireland 1914–1939* (Dublin: Irish Academic Press, 2007).

[34] Dominic Bryan, 'Forget 1690, Remember the Somme: Ulster Loyalist Battles in the Twenty-First Century' in Oona Frawley (ed.), *Memory Ireland* (Syracuse, NY: Syracuse University Press, 2014), vol. 3: *The Famine and the Troubles*, pp. 293–309; see also B. Graham and P. Shirlow, 'The Battle of the Somme in Ulster Memory and Identity', *Political Geography* 7 (2002), 881–904.

[35] See Astrid Erll and Ansgar Nünning (eds.), *Cultural Memory Studies: An International and Interdisciplinary Handbook* (Berlin and New York: Walter de Gruyter, 2008).

[36] Liliane Weissberg, 'Introduction' in Dan Ben-Amos and Liliane Weissberg (eds.), *Cultural Memory and the Construction of Identity* (Detroit: Wayne State University Press, 1999), p. 15.

[37] Martin, '1916: Myth, Fact, and Mystery'; William Irwin Thompson, *The Imagination of an Insurrection: Dublin, Easter 1916; a Study of an Ideological Movement* (New York: Oxford University Press, 1967).

[38] For poetry, see Fran Brearton, *The Great War in Irish Poetry: W. B. Yeats to Michael Longley* (Oxford and New York: Oxford University Press, 2000).

be added painting, sculpture, as well as the more modern media of radio and film, including television documentaries, most notably Louis Lentin's *Insurrection* (1966). Moreover, the memorials of 1916 can be studied as cultural artefacts. The value of focussed examination of heritage sites has been demonstrated by Clair Wills in her study of the General Post Office (GPO), the iconic site of the Easter Rising in Dublin, and by Nuala C. Johnson in a broader cultural-geography of sites of Great War commemoration across Ireland.[39]

A characteristic flaw of many studies of cultural memory is apparent in the tendency to privilege artistic representations without paying sufficient attention to readership, audiences and popular reception. Monuments, artworks, literary texts and countless other productions of cultural memory function as *aides-mémoire* but objects do not in themselves remember. Comprehensive studies of remembrance therefore require the pairing of cultural memory with social memory. Aleida Assman, building on the earlier work of Jan Assman, developed a model to disentangle the different forms of memory and to follow the transitions between them: from fragmentary individual memories (which 'are dissolved with the death of the person who owned and inhabited them'), to fluid social memory (in which individual memories are communicated over three generations or so within familial networks to constitute 'a community of shared experience'), to a more stabilised collective political memory (evident in national commemoration) and ultimate preservation as cultural memory (embodied in memorial institutions and deposited in archives). Convenient as this may seem for organising the various concepts of memory along an evolutionary timeline 'from short-term to long-term durability', in which 'an embodied, implicit, heterogeneous, and fuzzy bottom-up memory is transformed into an explicit homogeneous, and institutionalized top-down memory', this overly schematic model is ultimately misguided.[40] Memory, which is routinely reconstructed through

---

[39] Clair Wills, *Dublin 1916: The Siege of the GPO* (London: Profile, 2009), pp. 133–171; Nuala C. Johnson, *Ireland, the Great War, and the Geography of Remembrance* (Cambridge and New York: Cambridge University Press, 2003), pp. 80–111. See also Mark McCarthy, *Ireland's 1916 Rising: Explorations of History-Making, Commemoration & Heritage in Modern Times* (Farnham and Burlington: Ashgate, 2012).

[40] Aleida Assmann, 'Memory, Individual and Collective' in Robert E. Goodin and Charles Tilly (eds.), *The Oxford Handbook of Contextual Political Analysis* (Oxford and New York: Oxford University Press, 2006), pp. 210–224. For the earlier theoretical work of Jan Assman on the transition from communicative (i.e., social) memory to cultural memory, see Jan Assman, 'Collective Memory and Cultural Identity', *New German Critique* 65 (1995), 125–133; Jan Assman, 'Communicative and Cultural Memory' in Peter Meusburger, Michael Heffernan and Edgar Wunder (eds.), *Cultural Memories: The Geographical Point of View* (Dordrecht, Heidelberg, London and New York: Springer, 2011), pp. 15–27.

social interactions, continuously regenerated through cultural mediations and constantly subject to political negotiations at different levels, defies neat compartmentalisation.

Remembrance of the Holocaust has acquired a central place in the literature on memory and history. With the passing away of the generation of survivors, the term 'postmemory' has been floated to capture 'the experience of those who grew up dominated by narratives that preceded their birth'.[41] This concept, which was initially embraced in studies of the Second World War, has since gained currency further afield and appears in studies of memory in Latin America, Eastern Europe and the Irish diaspora.[42] Ongoing research by Caoimhe Nic Dháibhéid on the children of the executed leaders of the Easter Rising sets out to explore such postmemory issues and their relation to official commemoration. This line of inquiry can be expanded to encompass not only a select group of individuals but to refer more broadly to the second and third generations of Irishmen and women who grew up on hearing memories of 1916. That said, when taking into account that continuous mediation and reception are integral to social and cultural memory both within and beyond the first generation of eyewitnesses, the validity of making an essential distinction between an immediate primary memory and a distanced subsidiary postmemory is questionable.

I have suggested elsewhere that the term 'postmemory' can be redefined and complemented with a concept of 'prememory'. This can be done in a number of ways, but is perhaps most effective when applied as an analytical tool to tease out the intense emotions invested in the construction of memory. Prememory, in this sense, refers to the anticipations and expectations of those who are committed to predetermine how history will be remembered.[43] A corresponding reconceptualisation of postmemory refers to the anxieties and angst of self-appointed custodians of

---

[41] Marianne Hirsch, *Family Frames: Photography, Narrative and Postmemory* (Cambridge, MA: Harvard University Press, 1997), p. 22; see also Marianne Hirsch, *The Generation of Postmemory: Writing and Visual Culture after the Holocaust* (New York and Chichester: Columbia University Press, 2012).

[42] For examples, see Alejandra Serpente, 'The Traces of "Postmemory" in Second-Generation Chilean and Argentinean Identities' in Francesca Lessa and Vincent Druliolle (eds.), *The Memory of State Terrorism in the Southern Cone: Argentina, Chile, and Uruguay* (New York: Palgrave Macmillan, 2011), pp. 133–156; Uilleam Blacker, 'Living among the Ghosts of Others: Urban Postmemory in Eastern Europe' in Uilleam Blacker, Aleksandr Etkind and Julie Fedor (eds.), *Memory and Theory in Eastern Europe* (New York, 2013), pp. 173–193; Aidan Arrowsmith, 'Imaginary Connections? Postmemory and Irish Diaspora Writing' in Oona Frawley (ed.), *Memory Ireland* (Syracuse: Syracuse University Press, 2012), vol. 2: *Diaspora and Memory Practices*, pp. 12–23.

[43] This concept of prememory is, to an extent, analogous to the notion of 'instant history' outlined by David Fitzpatrick in his contribution (Chapter 4) to this volume.

memory over the changing nature of memory, as the past is reinterpreted in ways that inevitably drift away from the memory that they had aspired to bequest to future generations.[44] This approach promises to be particularly useful for closely re-examining the construction and transformation of the myths of 1916. Prememory is apparent in the writings of Patrick Pearse and his adoration of the early republican martyr Robert Emmet, which suggest that he was preparing in advance for his own martyrdom. Postmemory is evident in the opposition of the widows and sisters of 1916 rebels to the state commemoration in 1966. In a letter to the Taoiseach Seán Lemass, Kathleen Clarke (widow of Tom Clarke) claimed to 'know more about the events both before and after the Rising than anyone now alive'.[45] The concepts of affective prememory and postmemory can also be applied to reveal 'latent memories' that didn't materialise as expected. It is possible to excavate the hopeful prememories (found in diaries and personal correspondence) and the bitter postmemories (found in memoirs and in the Bureau of Military History testimonies) of those who had a 'bad 1916' and were disillusioned by the outcome of the Irish Revolution.[46] A similar investigation could uncover the unfulfilled expectations and lasting frustrations of Catholic nationalist soldiers, who had reason to expect that their contribution to the war effort would be remembered but were eventually excluded from the dominant unionist and republican myths of 1916.

No study of memory can be complete without consideration of forgetting. F. X. Martin notably decried the 'Great Oblivion' in regard to southern Irish mass participation in the First World War, which he labelled 'an example of national amnesia'.[47] Since the unveiling of the Island of Ireland Peace Park memorial site at Messines on 11 November 1998, rediscovered Irish interest in remembrance of the First World War has been evident in a growing number of academic and popular publications.[48] Public recognition was boosted during the visit of Queen Elizabeth II to Dublin in 2011 at a ceremony at the Irish War Memorial Garden in Islandbridge, and has since been marked in a

---

[44] See Guy Beiner, 'Probing the Boundaries of Irish Memory: From Postmemory to Prememory and Back', *Irish Historical Studies* 39, 154 (2014), 296–307.

[45] Ferriter, 'Commemorating the Rising', pp. 214–215; see also Higgins, *Transforming 1916*, p. 83.

[46] See R. F. Foster, *Vivid Faces: The Revolutionary Generation in Ireland, 1890–1923* (London: Allen Lane, 2014), pp. 289–325.

[47] Martin, '1916: Myth, Fact, and Mystery', p. 68.

[48] For the transformative impact of this commemorative event, see Keith Jeffery, 'Irish Varieties of Great War Commemoration' in John Horne and Edward Madigan (eds.), *Towards Commemoration: Ireland in War and Revolution, 1912–1923* (Dublin: Royal Irish Academy, 2013), pp. 117–125.

number of official ceremonies, leading up to the dedication of the Cross of Sacrifice at Dublin's Glasnevin Cemetery on 31 July 2014. The tribute paid to the anniversary of the Battle of the Somme by the Sinn Féin lord mayor of Belfast, Alex Maskey, who laid a wreath at the cenotaph outside Belfast City Hall in 2002, encouraged northern republicans to engage with remembrance of the Great War.

There is a need for a detailed historical study of the alleged forgetting that preceded this new-found openness. In response to Myles Dungan's review of *Ireland's Great War* by Kevin Myers (2014), a member of the public took issue with the claim that 'Ireland, in particular official Ireland had largely forgotten about one of the most significant passages in our recent history' and stated that growing up in a working-class area of Dublin in the '60s and '70s, 'most of the people I knew had some relative or other who had taken part in the First World War', insisting that these thousands were 'remembered by the people who mattered to them'.[49] Rather than buying into a superficial notion of total collective amnesia, a concept of 'social forgetting' can be employed to probe the tensions between private remembrance and public silence.[50] Such a study would also re-examine iconoclastic acts of decommemorating, such as the 1987 Remembrance Day bombing in Enniskillen, which, by deliberately targeting sites of commemoration, paradoxically raise awareness to memory, instead of stamping it out.[51]

The concepts of myth, collective memory, popular/public memory, social memory, cultural memory, postmemory/prememory and social forgetting briefly outlined in this essay offer a range of possibilities for coming to terms with historical remembrance. This is a powerful toolbox and there is evidently considerable scope for adapting and critically applying these theoretical apparatus to advance new directions in the study of remembering 1916.

---

[49] Eoghan Ó hÁinle, 'Kevin Myers and Myles Dungan on WWI', *History Ireland*, 23, 3 (2015), 12–13; responding to Myles Dungan's review of *Ireland's Great War* (Dublin: Lilliput Press, 2014) in *History Ireland* 23, 2 (March/April 2015), 61. For a study of various forms of commemoration in Dublin, Cork, Derry and Belfast, see Jason R. Myers, *The Great War and Memory in Irish Culture 1918–2010* (Bethesda : Maunsel and Company, 2013).

[50] For a discussion of the concept of social forgetting, see Guy Beiner, 'Disremembering 1798? An Archaeology of Social Forgetting and Remembrance in Ulster', *History & Memory*, 25 (2013), 9–50.

[51] For remembrance at the site of the Enniskillen bombing, see Graham Graham Dawson, *Making Peace with the Past? Memory, Trauma and the Irish Troubles* (Manchester: Manchester University Press, 2007), pp. 288–305.

2 Ritual, identity and nation: when the historian becomes the high priest of commemoration

Dominic Bryan

This chapter is an exploration, and speculative discussion, of the relationship between ritual acts of commemoration, national and ethnic identities, the discipline of history and the professional historian. It is built around a number of observations and propositions that together raise questions about the engagement of historians with commemorations for 1916. In short, I want to argue that history has a relationship with ritual commemorative practice which, due to the ideological construction of ritual commemorations, is unlike that of other academic disciplines. Consequently, the professional historian plays a legitimising role in commemorative practice by endorsing what are acts of political identity. I will make this argument through the following four propositions.

First, whilst commemorative practices appear to be about the past, they are actually about the present and the future. Commemorations are a way of capturing the sacrifices of the past for the legitimation of the political present and the imagined political future. Consequently, the nature of contemporary acts of commemoration is better understood by exploring the relationship between identity and contemporary politics than by examining the event being 'remembered'.

Second, the discipline of history plays a role in modern Irish society that has a different status from related subjects in the humanities and the social sciences. Our identities, particularly as imagined communities such as nations, but also as ethnic groups,[1] are invariably built around a historical narrative. As an explanatory tool for understanding 'who we are', history is predominant. Thus, in popular culture, the examination of group identities is usually undertaken by narrative histories. Disciplines such as anthropology, sociology, social psychology, political science and social psychology are better at dealing with the identity questions, but in popular discourse, they are less often utilised. The status that history has, over and above allied disciplines, is most clearly operative in the school

---

[1] Benedict Anderson, *Imagined Communities Reflections on the Origins and Spread of Nationalism* (London: Verso, 1991).

curriculum but is also predominant in the popular media, particularly with regard to commemorative practice.

Third, commemorations are conducted by the utilisation of symbols endowed through acts of ritual. To understand how commemorations are controlled, we must understand the nature of ritual practice. Rituals appear to defy time by linking participants with the past.[2] Through culturally embedded practice, the rituals form part of a narrative that imbues groups with a past that suggests they are in communion with those that are being remembered. Indeed, as participants of these rituals are frequently told, 'they died for us'.[3]

Despite my first proposition concerning the contemporary nature of commemoration, because of my second and third arguments suggesting the cultural status of history in identity formation and the role of commemoration in defining contemporary identity, my fourth proposition is that the historian occupies a particularly privileged role in the arena of commemorative ritual practice. Historians, above all others, are invited onto the media and to the ritual events to comment on the commemorative practice, not because they are the most qualified to do so (if my second premise is right, they are not), but because as 'experts' they, above all others, can legitimise the importance of history in our identity. As such, I conclude that, however noble their role might be as educators about a complex past, they are effectively part of contemporary commemoration and could indeed be seen as the 'high priests' of commemorative practice.

I would like to sustain this argument in the following way. I want to briefly explore the struggle that historians and others have had in Ireland, connected to the Decade of Centenaries, examining the process of memory, remembering and commemorations. Key to this debate is the model of cultural transmission and the role played by commemoration. I will suggest that there are two approaches to the understanding of commemorations: diachronic, which explores the ritual through the examination of the past, or 'where it comes from'; and synchronic, which examines the present political conditions in which the ritual is constructed. This second approach is the one most favoured through the social sciences and indeed by many historians of commemoration. However, it is counter to the

[2] Elizabeth Tonkin and Dominic Bryan, 'Political Ritual: Temporality and Tradition' in Asa Boholm (ed.), *Political Ritual* (Gothenburg: Institute for Advanced Studies in Social Anthropology, 1996), pp. 14–36; David Kertzer, *Ritual, Politics and Power* (New Haven: Yale University Press, 1988), pp. 39–40; Maurice Bloch, *From Blessing to Violence: History and Ideology in the Circumcision Ritual of the Merina of Madagascar* (Cambridge: Cambridge University Press, 1986), p. 184.

[3] George Mosse, *Fallen Soldiers: Reshaping the Memory of the World Wars* (Oxford: Oxford University Press, 1991).

narrative of the commemoration itself and to a popular understanding of the role of history. I will argue that we commemorate because of the nature of group identities, not because of the past. We can clearly see this when we analyse how commemoration is constructed through symbols and rituals. I will particularly examine how rituals of all types defy time and thus give the impression of being in communion with the past. But having constructed a model for commemorative practice and cultural transmission, I will look at the role of the historian in the practice of commemoration and suggest that the professional historian should remain very self-aware of his or her role given the relationship posited through the commemoration of its communion with the past.

Irish history, remembering and commemoration

Irish history has a problem with remembering. The struggle to theorise and conceptualise an understanding of historical memory in the Irish context has been well rehearsed by Beiner (2007, 2014), Frawley (2011) and McBride (2001).[4] Their work examines a range of theoretical approaches that might, as McBride puts it, 'characterise the relationship between past and present antagonisms'.[5] McBride goes on to ask whether what we remember is not determined by the past but instead 'what we choose to remember is dictated by our contemporary concerns'.[6] This is at the core of my third premise. This possibility is, of course, well recognised and is at the centre of a Durkeimian approach to the topic proposed by Halbwachs' *On Collective Memory*.[7]

What makes recent memories hang together is not that they are contiguous in time: it is rather they are part of a totality of thoughts common to a group, the group of people we have a relationship with at this moment, or whom we have had a relation on the preceding day or days.[8]

Whilst, as McBride points out, we might worry a little about the emphasis on Durkheimian collective consciousness,[9] the orientation of this

---

[4] Ian McBride (ed.), *History and Memory in Modern Ireland* (Cambridge: Cambridge University Press, 2001); Guy Beiner, *Remembering the Year of the French: Irish Folk History and Social Memory* (Madison: The University of Wisconsin Press, 2007); Guy Beiner, 'Probing the Boundaries of Irish Memory: From Postmemory to Prememory and Back', *Irish Historical Studies* 39 (2014), 296–307; Oona Frawley, 'Towards a Theory of Cultural Memory in an Irish Postcolonial Context' in Oona Frawley (ed.), *Memory Ireland Volume 1: History and Modernity* (New York: Syracuse University Press, 2011), pp. 18–34.
[5] McBride, *History and Memory*, p. 5.   [6] Ibid., p. 6.
[7] Maurice Halbwachs, *On Collective Memory* (Chicago: The University of Chicago Press, 1992).
[8] Ibid., p. 52.   [9] McBride, *History and Memory*, p. 7.

approach is to suggest that the present is the construct in which remembering takes place. The question over why such memories are durable[10] is not answered by the nature of what is remembered but by the durability of social structures and, as I will discuss below, the mechanisms of transmission. McBride sums up this approach by suggesting that

remembering and forgetting are social activities, and our images of the past are therefore reliant upon particular vocabularies, values and ideas and representations shared with other members of the present group.[11]

Keep this idea of 'vocabularies, values and ideas' in mind because I want to argue that the discipline of history plays a key and exaggerated role in this process. For sure, as McBride further argues, the present is in 'complex interaction'[12] with available materials from the past, but I would argue that the construction of the past is present oriented.

So what of the conceptual framework of memory, remembering and commemoration in which much of the debate takes place? The arena of memory studies or social memory or collective memory, or, as Frawley and others have more usefully termed it, 'cultural memory',[13] has been a rapidly expanding field.[14] I do not intend to review it here because I want to concentrate on commemoration, which is a particular aspect of the field; but it is important to understand the difficulties in using various models of memory in relation to historical studies. In a series of exciting books and essays, Beiner experimented with models of memory transmission and their relationship with historical study. In a later essay, he identified processes of postmemory and prememory as part of a model of memory 'as an open-sided series of recycled representations'.[15] Originally suggested by Hirsch, postmemory is that which takes place in future generations and is thus delayed and indirect.[16] This is the arena for many of the studies on commemoration and tradition.[17] However, Beiner and others identify processes called prememory, referring to the ways in which an event, even as it takes place, is being 'understood and interpreted through reference to memories of previous events' and how 'traditions of prememory shape and influence the subsequent memory of the event'.[18] An example of this might be the reception of the Battle of

[10] Ibid., p. 8.   [11] Ibid., p. 12.   [12] Ibid., p. 13.
[13] Frawley, *Memory Ireland Volume 1*, pp. xiii–xxiv.
[14] Barbara Misztal, *Theories of Social Remembering* (Berkshire: Open University Press, 2003).
[15] Beiner, 'Probing the Boundaries of Irish Memory', 304.
[16] Marianne Hirsch, quoted in Beiner, 'Probing the Boundaries of Irish Memory', 298–299.
[17] Most obviously in Eric Hobsbawm and Terence Ranger, *The Invention of Tradition* (Cambridge: Cambridge University Press, 1983).
[18] Beiner, 'Probing the Boundaries of Irish Memory', p. 300.

the Somme amongst Protestants in the north of Ireland, construcing the memory of the event through a pre-existing set of events captured within Orangeism.[19]

One of the ongoing tensions in the sort of models discussed by Beiner and Frawley is the relationship between social memory and the biology of individual memory. Frawley tackles this head on by examining cognitive theories of memory utilising Whitehouse and suggesting that ideology and political organisation might be derived from the universal feature of human memory rather than the other way around.[20] Frawley goes on to discuss the impact this might have on narratives in the construction of cultural memory[21] but recognises 'the formidable power of cultural imperatives to persist and to be shaped by the circumstances of culture' and also that 'cultural memory is fluid and processual'.[22]

The attempt to provide conceptual frameworks for remembering has been considerably influenced in Ireland by what has been called the Decade of Centenaries. This period, running from around 2012 to 2022, covers what are understandably deemed to be vitally important events in contemporary Irish history. However, although important as they may be, they conveniently take the events just out of living memory and are no more or less important 100 years on, unless the commemorative practices make this so. Their importance only varies because we choose, in a rather arbitrary manner, to decide that the centenary of these events is somehow important. Quinault has identified the 'cult of the centenary, c.1784–1914' and suggested, much as Hobsbawm and Ranger examined the invention of tradition, that it is a period of centenary production.[23] We consider this to be true because there is a political context in the present which makes them important. In other words, they provide symbolic (or political) capital to a range of contemporary agents. Their influence is largely dictated by the power structures of the social field in the present, not the past.[24] As such, to understand memory, remembering and commemorative practice, we need to have a clearer model of cultural transmission. Central to that understanding must be a present day-oriented research model. In other

---

[19] Dominic Bryan, 'Forget 1690, Remember the Somme' in Oona Frawley (ed.), *Memory Ireland Volume 3: The Famine and the Troubles* (New York: Syracuse University Press, 2014), pp. 293–309.

[20] Frawley, *Memory Ireland Volume 1*, pp. 22–23, quoting Harvey Whitehouse, *Arguments and Icons: Divergent Modes of Religiosity* (Oxford: Oxford University Press, 2000), pp. 5–9.

[21] Ibid., pp. 24–26.   [22] Ibid., p. 34.

[23] R. Quinault, 'The Cult of the Centenary c.1784–1914', *Historical Research* 71 (1998), 303–323; Hobsbawm and Ranger, *The Invention of Tradition*.

[24] Pierre Bourdieu, *In Other Words: Essays Towards a Reflexive Sociology* (Stanford: Stanford University Press, 1990), p. 135.

words, what are the synchronic factors that influence the remembering and commemorative processes and how are they transmitted? Why and how are historic events reproduced in the present?

If we take this position, then the model of memory and remembering becomes secondary. Commemorations are not about the past but about the present, and they are not about memory, but about identity. I want to be clear that there is plenty of historical practice that critically understands this position. Take the corpus of research that has been undertaken on the fiftieth anniversary of the 1916 Rising.[25] In a telling couple of lines, Higgins identifies what dictates the commemorative in the Ireland of 1966.

The commemoration was driven by two forces which gained in significance as the commemoration approached: to demonstrate the success of the modern Republic and to sideline the republican movement (as the IRA and its environs were referred to in the late 1960s).[26]

Commemoration is driven not by memory but by the politics of the present.[27] Indeed, it is vital to the politics of ritual commemoration that the concepts of memory (and sometimes tradition) are used to disguise what is taking place because they give the impression that legitimacy is gained from the past. Historians, in their understandable enthusiasm to educate people about their history, provide ideological cover for politics and power. History, when reproduced within the ambit of commemorative ritual, risks not being revelatory or educational but a disguise for relationships of power.

Identity, ritual and ethno-nationalism: an alternative model for commemoration

There is an alternative model for examining the cultural processes in which 'memory' plays a more minor role. Commemoration frequently appears in ritual form, created in the present by actors as an expression of their identity. It is a reflection of a group identity that could be local, institutional, ethnic or national. The ability to apparently transmit the past into the present is part of the function of the ritual. In

---

[25] Mary Daly and Margaret O'Callaghan (eds.), *1916 in 1966: Commemorating the Easter Rising* (Dublin: Royal Irish Academy, 2007); Rosin Higgins, *Transforming 1916: Meaning Memory and the Fiftieth Anniversary of the Easter Rising* (Cork: Cork University Press, 2012).

[26] Higgins, *Transforming 1916*, p. 3.

[27] See D. Berliner, 'Social Thought and Commentary: The Abuses of Memory: Reflections on the Memory Boom in Anthropology', *Anthropology Quarterly*, 78, (2005) 197–211.

commemoration, the ritual is, almost by definition, endowed with symbols and a narrative that appear to create a communion with the past, and yet it is created in the present, is chiefly about identity and is a comment on the present and the future.

Let me return to the basic problem. In trying to analyse the impact the past has on the present, we are struggling with transmission or, more broadly still, change and continuity in society. This is a problem at the heart of sociology and anthropology. Indeed, interestingly, if we look at the intellectual history of the discipline of anthropology, it also resorts to evolutionary or what are effectively historical answers. In the nineteenth century, prior to the full impact of Durkheimian sociology, anthropologists attempted to understand social institutions by tracing their evolutionary routes. We attempted to examine cultural traits and social institutions by tracing some sort of origin, whereby they were brought into existence and then handed down. The key theoretical change that effectively solved this problem, or at least provided an alternative perspective, was the functionalist turn in the social sciences. This theoretical shift was chiefly introduced through Durkheimian sociology, which in British social anthropology became known as structural functionalism.[28] One of its key messages was that to understand the existence of various social institutions, you needed to analyse how they worked in the present (in other words, how they functioned) rather than concentrate on how they evolved out of the past. This created a synchronic turn in the anthropological analysis of society. Rather than trace the evolution of an institution through types of historical or archaeological constructions, you conducted fieldwork in the present to see how that institution played a part in present-day society. The assumption is that the reason why a social or cultural trait exists lies in the present and not in the past. This necessitates examining the social relationships, or social structure, that exist in society and suggests a quite different methodology. This is true of a commemorative ritual just as much as it is true of rites of passage or cultural artefacts. As I will make clear, we are not ignoring history, but we are suggesting that it has reduced importance as an explanatory tool for understanding commemoration.

If we return then to the problem of transmission of historical events, to the issue of how and why remembering takes places, then this synchronic rather than diachronic approach offers us another type of answer. Instead of looking for mechanisms that somehow push this past into the present, we examine why the social relationships of the present reproduce the past.

---

[28] Marvin Harris, *The Rise of Anthropological Theory: A History of Theories of Culture* (London: Routledge and Kegan Paul, 1969), pp. 514–519.

We end up examining what might be called pull factors for transmission, not push factors. What we need to examine, in many ways, holds little relation to what happened in the past but is explained by the social relationships of the present.

A key mechanism, although clearly not the only mechanism, through which this process is managed, is ritual. Theorised heavily in anthropology, ritual provides us with a clear mechanism of transmission that is not really about memory, or rather does not necessitate the mechanism of memory as central. There are, of course, lots of arguments about the nature of ritual and how it might be defined, but there exists a broad model around the type of social practice that is repetitive, rule-bound, existing as a discrete social activity and, importantly, laden with symbolic practice and great potential emotional power.[29] They are thus important as rites of group cohesion or, as Victor Turner would phrase it, *communitas*.[30] The ritual provides a potential moment of social cohesion, or, to return to Durkheim, ritual provides 'effervesence'. In *Elementary Forms of the Religious Life*, he argues:

There can be no society which does not feel the need of upholding and reaffirming at regular intervals the collective sentiments and collective ideas which makes its unity and its personality. Now this moral remaking cannot be achieved except by the means of reunions, assemblies and meetings where the individual, being closely united to one another, reaffirm in common their common sentiments; hence come ceremonies which do not differ from regular religious ceremonies, either in their object, the results they produce, or the processes employed to attain these results.[31]

But ritual does more than simply reflect some broad set of social values. It utilises, in part through the use of symbols, what that social group might have in common even if that group or society is riven with conflict and difference. As Victor Turner puts it, '[a] society continually threatened with disintegration is continually performing reintegrative ritual'.[32] As David Kertzer points out in *Ritual, Politics and Power*, effectively the manual for anthropological approaches to ritual, the beauty of this approach is that it captures the psychological needs of individuals and explains how individuals' actions are converted into the social.[33]

[29] Catherine Bell, *Ritual Theory, Ritual Practice* (Oxford: Oxford University Press, 1992); Ronald L. Grimes, *The Craft of Ritual Studies* (Oxford: Oxford University Press, 2013); Kertzer, *Ritual, Politics and Power*.

[30] Victor Turner, *The Ritual Process* (Chicago: Aldine, 1969).

[31] Emile Durkeim, *The Elementary Forms of the Religious Life* (London: George Allen and Unwin, 1915), p. 427; see also Kertzer, *Ritual Politics and Power*, p. 62.

[32] Victor Turner, *Schism and Continuity in an African Society* (Manchester: Manchester University Press, 1957), p. 303.

[33] Kertzer, *Ritual Politics and Power*, p. 63.

Ritual then can create solidarity without consensus.[34] It does this in a number of ways, but of particular interest to my argument is the way that symbols work within the ritual. Symbols, of course, provide resources for meaning but, and this is important, they cannot be read simply as a text. It is participants in the ritual that provide symbols with meaning, and whilst they may share allegiance with those symbols, they do not need to share the same meaning. Symbols are usefully ambiguous. Anthony Cohen argues that they allow for 'the symbolic construction of community'.[35] This, in turn, can be linked to the broad theory of nationalism proposed by Benedict Anderson that the modern nation is an imagined community.[36] In part, maybe in large part, this community is imagined through rituals and symbols.

There is, however, another aspect to this model that should be put in place before we examine the nation. The relationship that a person shares with the different social groups they participate in is governed by identity. Identity is important because it builds a sense of self, who we believe we are, but it does so in relation to other people, the social groups around us and the physical environment. Of significance is not only the groups that we believe we are part of, but also the groups that we are not in. The social psychologists refer to these groups as in-groups and out-groups. Tajfel argued that this was the basis of pride and esteem.[37] It is the basis of our relation with others, of the way we present ourselves and interact with others, and how we judge who we are as an individual against the groups we are part of. It is the link between the individual and the social. Most significantly for my purposes, 'the meanings associated with any social identity are products of our collective history and present'.[38] The power of such an event results from the link between that identity and participation in a generalised notion of commemoration. To honour the fallen heroes of the social group that we believe we are part of is a huge statement. It is one of pride but also of potential social distinction and provides a narrative for our social group. It is a powerful statement of legitimation of who we are. On top of all this, it is usually highly gendered, almost always making statements about maleness and femaleness, and identifies our relationship with out-groups, sometimes known as 'perpetrators' or 'enemies'. The individual acts of commemoration are also, of course, wrapped

---

[34] Ibid., p. 67.
[35] Anthony Cohen, *The Symbolic Construction of Community* (London: Tavistock, 1985), pp. 15–19.
[36] Anderson, *Imagined Communities*.
[37] Henri Tajfel (ed.), *Differentiation between Social Groups: Studies in the Social Psychology of Intergroup Relations* (London: Academic Press, 1978).
[38] Stephen Reicher, Russell Spears and S. Alexander Haslam, 'The Social Identity Approach in Social Psychology' in M. S. Wetherell and C. T. Mohanty (eds.), *The Sage Identities Handbook* (London: Sage, 2010), pp. 45–62.

up in memories and narratives connected to the self but, crucially, they potentially provide social, public recognition of those narratives.

In the contemporary world, we are members of a range of groups, and therefore our sense of self can shift across a range of identities depending upon context. However, of all our potential groups, perhaps the most powerful are the imagined communities of ethnicity and nationhood.[39] In creating these imagined communities of ethnic group and nation, it is crucial that a link is made with the past, that there is a historical narrative about who we are and why. Politically, to glue these social groups together, the most powerful claim is that our 'forefathers', and note here 'fore*fathers*', sacrificed themselves in the name of the group and that they need to be honoured and respected.

The events or figures marked in commemoration are inextricably symbolically linked to the 'history' of the state/nation/ethnic group as a 'myth of origin'. Thus *the politics of memory* is intimately bound to *the politics of identity*.[40]

Consequently, such an ideologically powerful claim is used by politicians all the time to engender group cohesion and potential social action. Thus, the sacrifice of the past should remind us how to behave in the present or the future. It invokes a debt to be paid. What could be more powerful than the debt to those that gave up their lives? As such, we are told that we must remember them. The 'them' is very often people of whom we have no memory and who, particularly after a generation, have no voice independent of the words and deeds they left us before they died, but which we, and particularly those with power, can reinterpret. By remembering them, we can appropriate their sacrifice into present-day politics. What better way to legitimise that claim than with the presence of a professional historian? But I am getting ahead of myself.

Social groups are, of course, complex. Not everyone feels the same way about their relationship with groups of which they may be a part. People have individual identities. As such, people do not all interact with commemoration in the same way. As discussed above, rituals allow people to participate in common events without necessarily sharing the same meaning or narrative. Nevertheless, they offer apparent common belonging. But even more powerfully, and by powerfully I, of course, mean politically, a claim can be made on outlying members of the group who may feel resistance to the activities of the national and/or ethnic group. As such,

---

[39] See Richard Jenkins, *Rethinking Ethnicity: Arguments and Explorations* (London: Sage, 1997); Thomas Hylland Eriksen, *Ethnicity and Nationalism: Anthropological Perspectives* (London: Pluto, 1993).

[40] Rebecca Graff-McRae, *Remembering and Forgetting 1916: Commemoration and Conflict in Post-Peace Process Ireland* (Dublin: Irish Academic Press, 2010), p. 7.

ritual and symbolic activities are constructed to make people, even force people to, either show respect to the past, and thus endorse a particular understanding of the present, or take the difficult step of dissenting, and thus risk the accusation of not respecting the dead. Consequently, commemorative practice is also a boundary marker in the sense that Fredrick Barth describes in his classic exposition of the nature of ethnic groups:[41] 'The critical focus of the investigation from this point of view becomes the ethnic *boundary* the defines the group, not the cultural stuff that it encloses.'[42] Thus, commemorative rituals of republican and loyalist in Northern Ireland share much in common in terms of cultural background and the organisation and ideology of practice. The lily and the poppy are boundary makers and therefore frequently part of dispute, debate and negotiation.

Whilst clearly commemorative practice exists across a range of different types of groups, of particular interest here are the boundaries of ethnic and national groups. The longevity of the social groups we called nations is still a matter of dispute. However, I am clearly taking the position of a large number of theorists that, despite nationalists arguing that their particular nation has historical roots that go back centuries, the form of the nation that is now globally dominant took shape in the eighteenth century, reaching some of it first full expression with the French and American Revolutions. Without now participating in the debates about how and why this happened, Anderson, Hobsbawm and Gellner, to name three key theorists, remain important in articulating this argument for the instrumental rather than primordial view of the nation.[43] It is interesting that in elucidating his argument for the nation as an imagined community, '*imagined* because members of even the smallest nation will never know most of their fellow members ... yet in the minds of each lives the image of their communion',[44] Anderson starts with the question of why those who are part of this fraternity of the nation, 'conceived as a deep, horizontal comradeship', over the past two centuries, are 'willing to die for such limited imaginings'.[45] His answer starts with the suggestion that there are 'no more arresting emblems of the modern culture of nationalism than cenotaphs and the tomb of the Unknown Soldier'.[46] He adds, 'Yet void as these tombs are of identifiable mortal remains or immortal

---

[41] Fredrick Barth, *Ethnic Groups and Boundaries: The Social Organisation of Cultural Difference* (Illinois: Waveland Press, 1969, reissued 1998).
[42] Ibid., p. 15.
[43] Anderson, *Imagined Communities*; Ernest Gellner, *Nations and Nationalism* (Oxford: Basil Blackwell, 1983); Eric Hobsbawm, *Nations and Nationalism since 1780: Programme, Myth, Reality* (Cambridge: Cambridge University Press, 1990).
[44] Anderson, *Imagined Communities*, p. 6.   [45] Ibid., p. 7.   [46] Ibid., p. 9.

souls, they are nonetheless saturates with ghostly *national* imaginings.'[47] Crucial to the idea of a nation is that it exists, as a community, over time. No more powerful element of that image exists than the idea that members of that community sacrificed themselves for the community.

On the construction of the nation, and returning to the differences between history and anthropology with which I started this section, Eriksen perceptively notes that 'While many historians tend to try to find out what *really* happened – some even distinguishing between "invented" traditions and "real" traditions – most anthropologists would rather concentrate on showing the ways in which particular historical accounts are used as tools in the *contemporary* creation of identities and in politics.'[48] Reicher and Hopkins point out that 'whether nations are recent or ancient is not the point, what counts is that they are always imagined as ancient'.[49] The key site for these 'historical imaginings' is rituals, and the most powerful of these are surely commemorative rituals. As is understood generally with the symbolic construction of community, ritual provides an opportunity for common involvement by potentially diverse groups which may not, indeed very likely will not, share the same understanding of participation. Thus, those involved may construct different narratives from the event yet still share participation. Those with power within the ritual, however, are better able to utilise the symbolic capital. These social institutions are thus particular sites for social relationships imbued with power.[50] Rituals are important in the creation, maintenance and negotiation of political legitimacy. Perhaps the most important way they do this is to offer a sense of continuity over time and therefore a powerful potential to create a *communitas* with the past.[51] They are frequently central to 'tradition' and also at the heart of commemorative practice. They are beloved research sites for anthropologists and political scientists, as they reveal both the nature of key social relationships in a society and also the narratives of legitimacy that accompany those social relationships.

Rituals are therefore the mechanism by which synchronic social relationships, the political relationships of the present, are converted, ideologically, into a communion with the past. These rituals take place in public spaces, with specific roles for people with power and a narrative which they will attempt to define.

---

[47] Ibid., p. 9.
[48] Thomas Hylland Eriksen, *Ethnicity and Nationalism* (London: Pluto, 1993, 2nd edition 2003), pp. 71–72.
[49] Stephen Reicher and Nick Hopkins, *Self and Nation* (London: Sage, 2001), p. 17.
[50] Kertzer, *Ritual Politics and Power*, pp. 174–185.
[51] Tonkin and Bryan, 'Political Ritual', pp. 14–36; Bloch, *From Blessing to Violence*, p. 184.

The ritual therefore acts as a form of cultural transmission capable of being taught and re-taught. Although it appears to give continuity over time, it is constructed and reconstructed in the present. Each rehearsal of the ritual is unique. Continuity is not provided by some memory over time but by the existence of a set of social relationships over time.

[R]ituals are recognised as such because they are recognisable as formalised events, and thus by inference they are repetitive. Yet they can also be recognised as events thus by inference they include actions. They are symbolic and at once both repetitive and unique.[52]

It is the social structure where continuity, discontinuity and contest are played out. Weakly propositional, but potentially highly emotional, commemoration rituals allow potential contestation, but political power also offers dominant political narratives an advantage. As such, the important public spaces and the key moments in time are held and controlled by those in power. Those contesting these narratives need to look for alternative spaces or times through which to utilise the potential symbolic capital available through commemorative union with the past.

I would go further and argue that even when events look like they have continuity, the rituals have not changed over time (although usually close examination reveals they have), and that it is likely that those using these legitimatising events have changed. In other words, the ritual and the symbols might remain fixed even though the social relationships have altered.[53] Crucial to the process is the contemporary relationship of politics and power. Or to put it another way, the key factors for remembering and commemoration are synchronic and not diachronic. Any analysis of transmission must start with the contemporary period. What is being remembered is relatively unimportant; it is the why and how that are crucial. As social relationships of power have continuity, transmission can be partially assured. The reasons for transmission lie not in the past but in the relationships of power in the present. Those relationships are negotiated with acts of resistance appearing through tension in those power relationships.[54] It is the job of the anthropologist and historian to map these relationships.

Commemorations given a synchronic rather than diachronic analysis are much more explicable. My suggestions is that if we take this approach, and let me be clear again that many historian effectively do, then our problems of transmission become easier to solve. Roisin Higgins, a

[52] Tonkin and Bryan, 'Political Ritual', pp. 14–15.
[53] Dominic Bryan, *Orange Parades: The Politics of Ritual, Tradition and Control* (London: Pluto Press, 2000), pp. 19–22.
[54] Ibid.

historian, does exactly this in her work on the commemoration of 1916 in 1966.[55] I also think that hazy mechanisms such as 'memory' and 'trauma' can be analysed in a quite different way, as part of the narrative, and do not need to bare the explanatory weight that makes them look so problematic. Activities such as commemoration given a synchronic rather than diachronic analysis are much more explicable.

Ritual is, of course, not the only form of transmission. There are many other mechanisms ranging from formal history through to oral histories, via varieties of archives – from sites of memory such as memorials through to individual memories. It is important that the historian's relationship to these other forms, such as museums and archives, is potentially different to that of ritual. But regardless of the mechanism, all of these forms of transmission rely on construction and interpretation in the present. The past may be transmitted through a variety of mechanisms, but the important aspect of the interpretation of that past is the social relationships of the present. Out of these arise dominant narratives, dominant ideologies, and whilst we can find alternatives fostered in parts of society, and whilst contestation might be taking place, they will only prosper if social relationships are changing.

What is the relationship between historian and commemoration?

Commemoration, therefore, is not determined by the calendar. It is a matter of choice. It is not essentially about history – it is about culture. It is about ideas of the 'historic' that are always shaped by the present-day concerns and power structures.[56]

If the model I have described (which, despite a few key debates, I think would be broadly accepted across the political and social sciences) is valid, then it raises the issue of the role of historians. As Fintan O'Toole asks, 'What should historians have to do with any of this?'[57] Well, judging by their involvement on committees and also on sorts of media that connected the Irish Decade of Centenaries, the answer seems to be: quite a lot. For major events, the attempt to provide a narrative will be done using the mass media. As such, TV, radio, the press and online media will be searching for historians of the historical moment to be remembered in order to discuss what is taking place. Local councils, government

[55] Higgins, *Transforming 1916*.
[56] Fintan O'Toole, 'Beyond Amnesia and Piety' in John Horne and Edward Madigan (eds.), *Towards Commemoration: Ireland in War and Revolution 1912–1923* (Dublin: Royal Irish Academy).
[57] Ibid., p. 155.

agencies, community groups and documentary-makers search for the historian that might tell us why the commemoration is taking place and why it is important. In contrast, the social and political scientists are much more rarely seen. Yet, if I am right, they are the people who can better explain commemoration.

Let me make some observations about the discipline of history, then look at the relationship of the historian to commemoration, before, some might be relieved to hear, discussing why history is important. Without judging the value of different disciplines, there seems to be a hierarchy within our society, particularly pertinent at schools. History has a place in our society that is unlike other disciplines in the social and political sciences because it has a role in nationalism unlike other disciplines. It has a place in our schools unlike the other social and political sciences. It has a place on the TV channels unlike those other disciplines. It has a place in popular Irish culture unlike any of those other disciplines, except, maybe, a popular version of psychology. In terms of understanding 'who we are', history, apparently, provides the answer. There is an obvious reason for this. As already discussed, we live as part of nations and states that legitimise themselves through historical narrative. Jenkins suggests that a key component of nationalism is the 'appeal to the past – an ethnic-national history embodied in such things as myths of origin, royal genealogies or cultural romanticism – in a construction of a collective project for the future'.[58] Jenkins and Benedict Anderson are attracted to the powerful imagery of Walter Benjamin's 'angel of history', as Jenkins puts it 'looking back, in nostalgia and anger, but irresistibly propelled forward at the mercy of progress'.[59] This rather dark view of nationalism might be countered with examples of civic nationalism, and a more nuanced view would be necessary in a longer argument. Nevertheless, the role of history as a discipline for nationalism is very specific and, of course, historians have played, and continue to play, a full part in the creation of the national story. Whilst this is sometimes to present complexity and take part in myth busting, as well as, in the case of historians such as Hobsbawm,[60] developing the critical ideas to examine the inventing of nationalist traditions, popular history lies at the core of nationalist ideological constructions. History has a relationship to nationalism that is not dissimilar to the relationship biology has to 'race'. As I have described elsewhere, I have always been struck by the claim, particularly amongst people in working-class Protestant groups in

[58] Jenkins, *Rethinking Ethnicity*, p. 162.
[59] Jenkins, *Rethinking Ethnicity*, p. 162; Anderson, *Imagined Communities*, p. 147.
[60] Hobsbawm and Ranger, *Invention of Tradition*.

Northern Ireland, that young people need to learn their history so that they can know their identity.[61]

The position that the discipline of history has within our society, and particularly in our education system, is important because, whilst history is good at teaching about the nation, it is less good at theorising about nationalism. Those disciplines that might offer such critical tools – sociology, anthropology, political science – are much less frequently taught, certainly to children under the age of 16. Subjects such as social psychology and anthropology that might develop critical tools around identity are virtually absent from the school curriculum.

In addition, the idea that our identity, who we are, can be defined through what we are told is 'our history' is a powerful idea on the media. We are told where we have come from and who we are through a historical narrative. Whilst I am absolutely not denying the importance of understanding a history from many perspectives, and as a vital part of learning what it is to be human, the discipline of history has an elevated status next to those other disciplines. In popular culture, regardless of the more nuanced world of academic history, when the people want to know what their identity is, they turn to historians.

Unsurprisingly then, but I would also suggest problematically, when the Decade of Centenaries approaches, to understand why they might be commemorated and what is being commemorated, the media and policy-makers turn to the historian. Thus, we are left with the strange contradiction. Whilst the critical tools for understanding the processes of commemoration are provided by the political and social scientists, it is the historians that are invited to mould and comment on the events. Of course, they would be, because the whole rational of the commemoration is that history is important, that the past legitimises who we are, that we are in communion with the people that went before us. As such, the very presence of the historian, even the historian out to myth bust and critically analyse what is taking place, actually legitimises the practice. Historians are the high priests of the commemorative rituals. As commentators and advisors, they are also participants. With notable exceptions, the historian is unlikely to suggest that today's commemoration has little to do with the events of the past and everything to do with political identity.

I want to be clear about a couple of aspects of this process lest my analysis is mistaken simply as an attack on the discipline and on historians. First, I fully appreciate that the periods of commemoration provide historians with spaces of potential public education and they

[61] Dominic Bryan, 'The Politics of Community', *Critical Review of International Social and Political Philosophy* 9 (2006), 603–617.

understandably jump at this opportunity. It is an arena for public history. My issue is not with good education through history teaching from good, critically-engaged, historians. Indeed, it is vital. However, I am suggesting that a period of commemoration is problematic for that process precisely because the commemorative practice is first and foremost an exposition of public identity. The apparent educational opportunity is also a reaffirmation of a particular political identity to which the historian, of all 'experts', is likely to provide legitimacy. Second, there is a role for the historian to present more complex pictures of our past and that this does make the commemorative space a potentially critical and negotiated space. Indeed, there is an argument that it would be worse for historians not to get involved. In other words, I can see the potential for change through engagement. However, I think change is far more likely to be driven by alterations in the fundamental social and power relationship in society than through some realisation or consciousness raising about the nature of the past. The historian does provide legitimacy to the ritual just by their presence. Third, and most importantly, there are historians of commemoration who are not only vital in understanding these processes but have been, and are, critical in understanding the reproduction of the past in the present. Central to the argument I am making is the need for historical analysis of commemorative practice.[62] However, I am suggesting that the role of the discipline of history in both the practices of commemoration and in the understanding of memory and remembering is problematic as it lacks the conceptual tools for the task. It therefore profiles particular types of transmission over others, thereby frequently disguising the extent to which commemoration is necessarily and, fundamentally, a synchronic process.

Conclusion

History and commemoration are not incompatible, but the proper relationship between these two pursuits is contested and uneasy.[63]

Let me finish with 1916 and the dramatic events at Easter in Dublin and later on the fields of Flanders. Both made a massive and traumatic impression upon those who survived. In both cases, practices of commemoration began almost immediately, driven in part by the psychological needs of survivors and people in the society into which they reentered. But, from those moments on, commemorative practice was

---

[62] Daly and O'Callaghan, *1916 in 1966*; Higgins, *Transforming 1916*.
[63] David Fitzpatrick, 'Historian and the Commemoration of Irish Conflicts, 1912–23' in John Horne and Edward Madigan (eds.), *Towards Commemoration: Ireland in War and Revolution 1912–1923* (Dublin: Royal Irish Academy, 2013), p. 126.

defined not by what took place but by the social and political relationships that then existed. The relatively small military excursion in Dublin and the executions that followed were to be constructed through social relationships that turned a handful of Irish rebels into martyrs and founders of a new country. The Irishmen who died in the battles of the First World War, such as those at Suvla Bay during the Dardanelles Campaign, were destined for a much lower profile until political relationships in the next century were to determine that their symbolic capital would rise again.[64] That occurred just as the Australians who died at Gallipoli in that same Dardanelles campaign were coming to be seen as the founders of a proper independent nation at the southern end of the Pacific Ocean.[65]

These historical events are areas for negotiation and dispute amongst historians and others. But we must distinguish different types of contestation. There may well be a variety of interpretations of the past events. However, the most significant forms of contestation, although less often discussed, are the political relationships of the present, the synchronic social relationships, within which the construction of the commemoration is taking place.[66] For these commemorations are not first and foremost about the past, they are about the present and the future. They are a function of contemporary political relationships as well as a potential mechanism to create change in the social relationships. It is precisely these relationships that reproduce historical events into the present, legitimised as acts of 'remembering' and of memory. The danger of using commemoration as a moment for historical engagement is that you collude with a statement of political identity, legitimising and possibly disguising the politics of the present with the cloak of the past. Whilst it is understandable that historians feel it is important to use the commemorative space to complicate our understanding of the past, or to myth bust, they are dealing with powerful, possibly the most powerful, types of claims that nationalism makes. Rather than myth bust, they might simply be legitimising the political claims by appearing as the 'high priest' of the past.

I have suggested that the discipline of history has a problematic role in analysing this process because it provides much of the material for a more diachronic understanding of practice. It does this by continually

[64] Dominic Bryan and Stuart Ward, '"The Deficit of Remembrance": The Great War Revival in Australia and Ireland' in Katie Holmes and Stuart Ward (eds.), *Exhuming Passions: The Pressure of the Past in Ireland and Australia* (Dublin: Irish Academic Press, 2011), pp. 163–186.

[65] Ibid.

[66] See, in particular, Graff-McCrae, *Remembering and Forgetting 1916*; Elisabetta Viggiani, *Talking Stones: The Politics of Memorialisation in Post-Conflict Northern Ireland* (Oxford: Berghahn Books, 2014).

highlighting the importance of the historical events themselves, thus disguising the contemporary political context. In other words, it tends to suggest that we remember 1916 because of 1916 and not because of 2016. The historian, often through a claim to 'bust myths', thus becomes part of the disguise process giving legitimacy to contemporary political actors. Second, an analysis of the mechanisms of transmission reveals how the contemporary actors control the narratives largely dictated by the use of commemorative rituals. Rituals become the mechanism with which synchronic political factors are 'converted' into diachronic claims of legitimacy. The provision of an expert historian in the popular, media-driven, production of commemorative practice, and the use of historians where acts of remembering are understood through the concept of memory, give symbolic capital to the acts of political practice. At every commemorative occasion, the newspapers, TV and radio studios are populated by historians who, with some exceptions, are usually historians of the period(s) being commemorated. It may be that historians are attractive to the media because, unlike many other disciplines, theirs is a language relatively free of complex and uncommon terminology and 'isms', precisely because they tend not to theorise. The historians may be there for very noble reasons. However, if my argument about the synchronic nature of remembrance practices is correct, what they are doing is embellishing the symbolic capital, the legitimacy, of the rituals. It is a complex form of legitimacy, as historians are undoubtedly engaged in critical debate over the historical events being commemorated; nevertheless, it still serves to provide a diachronic form of legitimacy to an essentially synchronic political practice.

3 'The Irish Republic was proclaimed by poster': the politics of commemorating the Easter Rising

Roisín Higgins

In a city beset by rumours, the leaders of the Easter Rising quickly began to consolidate their message. On the second day of the insurrection, they issued *War News*, a four-page news sheet priced at a penny: '"War News" is published today because a momentous thing has happened . . . The Irish Republic was proclaimed by poster, which was prominently displayed in Dublin.' *War News* also carried a report of the statement made by Patrick Pearse that morning which said:

The Irish Republic was proclaimed in Dublin on Easter Monday, 24th April, at 12 noon. Simultaneously with the issue of the proclamation of the Provisional Government the Dublin Division of the Army of the Republic, including the Irish Volunteers, Citizen Army, Hibernian Rifles, and other bodies, occupied dominating points in the city. The G.P.O was seized at 12 noon, the Castle was attacked at the same moment, and shortly afterwards the Four Courts were occupied.[1]

Two things are striking about this account of the events of Easter Monday. Firstly, there is a very clear attempt to specify the exact moment of origin – to convey a sense of absolute alignment – and, secondly, there is no reference to the Proclamation having been read aloud. The Irish Republic was proclaimed not by Pearse but by poster. Therefore, even though a considerable amount of attention was being paid to how the Easter Rising should be recorded and remembered, the most powerful feature of its subsequent commemorative ritual was overlooked. The true significance of the Easter Rising would only be understood in retrospect and, indeed, its complex meaning in Irish society owed as much to how it was commemorated as to the original event.

Also on 25 April, James Stephens wrote: 'On this day the rumours began, and I think it will be many a year before the rumours cease.'[2]

---

[1] *War News*, 25 April 1916.
[2] J. Stephens, *The Insurrection in Dublin*, 3rd edn (Dublin: Maunsel & Company, 1965), p. 7.

Stephens's contemporaneous account of his experiences during Easter week is suffused with the impossibility of discovering anything truthful about the events unfolding in front of him. He met a man who 'spat rumour as though his mouth were a machine gun or linotype machine'. This 'wild individual' believed everything he heard and transformed it 'as by magic favourable to his hopes'.[3] Stephens anticipated that the Rising would be an unknowable event and this facilitated the myth-making which permeated the ways it was narrated, remembered and commemorated. The importance of the Rising in Irish life transcends the events of one week in April. Easter 1916 came to represent a moment of possibility against which all subsequent realities could be measured or on which they could be blamed. It has become a conduit for expressions of Irishness and for explorations of the nature of Irish society; a discursive space as well as a historical event.

'Seething with rumour'

The *Irish Times* was the only newspaper published in Dublin throughout Easter week 1916. Once martial law was introduced, censorship increased and facts became scarce. Railway travel and the post office service were suspended and local newspapers, being weekly, did not provide day-to-day coverage of events in Dublin. Many press reports characterised the rebellion as pro-German, Larkinite or anti-Home Rule, explaining, to some extent, the population's initial antipathy towards the rebels. The *Wicklow People* reported that the Dublin outbreak was almost entirely the work of Larkin's Citizen Army and Sinn Féin volunteers: 'With the Larkin Citizen Army, the spirit of syndicalism is abroad, hence Dublin suffered so severely by the destruction of our public and commercial buildings and the looting of shops.'[4] A sense of chaos was evident in other reports. By 6 May, the *Leitrim Observer* stated that 'within a mile radius of the city centre there is scarcely a house which cannot show its bullet-hole, its splintered chimney or its cracked slates as a memento of the rebels' relentless guerrilla warfare'. Adding to this horror, it reported, was the fact that Dublin was beset with the imminence of famine.[5]

In more muted tones, the *Irish Times* conceded never having been published in stranger circumstances but welcomed the fact that the Royal Dublin Society's Spring Show would open as planned.[6] Throughout the week, it continued to print gardening tips, features on fashion and answers to readers' queries regarding questions of morality,

---

[3] Stephens, *Insurrection*, p. 32.   [4] *Wicklow People*, 29 April 1916.
[5] *Leitrim Observer*, 6 May 1916.   [6] *Irish Times*, 25 April 1916.

legality and etiquette, reinforcing the sense that the Rising was an event that was happening parallel to real life. Onlookers remembered that in the immediate vicinity of the General Post Office (GPO) there was a lively atmosphere underlined by the fact that the first victim of looters was Noblett's sweetshop. Fr Michael Curran, Secretary to the Archbishop of Dublin (who left an extensive record of his memories of that week), noted, 'I am sure that eye-witnesses that late afternoon and next day would say that what most impressed them, and impressed them most unfavourably, was the frivolity of the crowd, most of all women and children.'[7] John Ervine, who was manager of the Abbey Theatre, recalled the atmosphere on Sackville Street: 'We were all extraordinarily lacking in prescience. We thought of this thing as a kid's rebellion, a school-boys' escapade. "Silly young asses!" people were saying, "they'll only get into trouble".'[8] Even for those participating in the Rising, there were discordant moments. One man remembered that George Plunkett, who led a band of sixty insurrectionists from Kimmage, on boarding a tram, 'insisted on paying the conductor for tickets'.[9] On Wednesday 26 April, the *Irish Times* reported that peace briefly reigned in the country. James Stephens wondered: 'Is the country so extraordinarily peaceful that it can be dismissed in three lines? There is either too much peace or too much reticence ...'[10] It all added to the sense of other-worldliness: the Rising, even in Dublin, was an elsewhere event.

In the House of Commons, Prime Minister Asquith conceded that the breakdown in the postal service and telecommunications was a cause of 'anxiety and embarrassment' as MPs struggled to debate an event about which so little was known.[11] The *Mirror* described Dublin as 'seething with rumours', while the *Times* noted that 'Those who are in a position to know the facts keep their secrets, while those who perhaps are not so reliably informed, being Irishmen, are not wanting in communicativeness.'[12] It carried early reports that James Connolly had been shot dead and Patrick Pearse shot in the leg.[13] The *Washington Post* reported that a force of at least 10,000 rebels was involved in Dublin and neighbouring Irish counties and that 'John (or Eoin) MacNeill, leader of the Irish Volunteers ..., has been shot, but whether in the fighting with the British troops or after arrest is not known here.'[14] Communication

---

[7] Bureau of Military History, Witness Statement (hereafter BMH WS) 687, Michael Curran, Secretary to the Archbishop of Dublin in 1916, p. 47.

[8] K. Jeffery, *The GPO and the Easter Rising* (Dublin: Irish Academic Press, 2006), pp. 171–172.

[9] F. McGarry, *The Rising: Ireland Easter 1916* (Oxford: Oxford University Press, 2010), p. 131.

[10] Stephens, *Insurrection*, p. 37.   [11] *Times*, 27 April 1916.

[12] *Mirror*, 12 May 1916; *Times*, 2 May 1916.   [13] *Times*, 1 May 1916.

[14] *Washington Post*, 27 April 1916.

among the rebels was also difficult. The countermanding order led to confusion across the country and reduced the number who turned out on Easter Monday. Information was conveyed inconsistently among the members of the Volunteers, Citizen Army and Cumann na mBan. One man recalled that 'quite a number of Volunteers who paraded had no idea where they were going or what was to take place'.[15]

Clair Wills has noted the way in which the sense of time was very imprecise for those who participated in the Rising. As a result, signature moments such as the hoisting of the flags (a tricolour and a green flag bearing the words 'Irish Republic' were raised above the GPO on Easter Monday), the reading of the Proclamation and Pearse's table-top speech in the GPO on 25 April provided temporal bearings within narrative accounts of the week.[16] However, this was truer for those who heard of events rather than those who bore witness. A visual representation of Pearse's speech was recreated in a sketch by Charles Saurin while he was in Frongoch prison camp. The drawing represents an imagined moment, as Saurin had not been in the GPO at the time of the speech.[17] Significantly, also, the most famous poetic rendering of the Rising, Yeats's *Easter 1916*, was the creation of someone who was not there. In Lady Gregory's autobiography, she remembers Yeats's comments on her chapter on the Rising, 'You have given us the most important part of history – its lies . . . I don't believe that events have been shaped so much by the facts as by the lies that people believed about them.'[18]

Of the flags above the GPO, Fr Michael Curran recorded: 'It was either during my absence in the Pro-Cathedral or while I was at lunch in the Gresham (I think it was the latter) that the flags were hoisted on the G.P.O. As far as I remember there were only two.'[19] When the Republic was being proclaimed, many Dubliners were thinking about lunch. James Stephens wrote of Easter Monday afternoon: 'I went to my office at the usual hour . . . Peace was in the building, and if attendants had any knowledge of rumours of war they did not mention it to me. At one o'clock I went to lunch.'[20] The hour, which in retrospect would seem so pivotal, was, for Stephens, entirely unremarkable. Mary Louisa Norway, wife of Arthur, Secretary of the Irish Post Office, remembered of that

---

[15] McGarry, *The Rising*, p. 130.
[16] C. Wills, *Dublin 1916: The Siege of the GPO* (London: Profile Books, 2009), p. 44.
[17] Wills, *Dublin 1916*, p. 53.
[18] Lady A. Gregory, *Seventy Years: 1852–1922*, ed. Colin Smythe (Gerrard's Cross: Colin Smythe), p. 549, quoted in G. Higgins, *Heroic Revivals from Carlyle to Yeats* (New York: Palgrave Macmillan, 2012), p. 134.
[19] BMH WS 687 (Michael Curran).   [20] Stephens, *Insurrection*, p. 15.

morning, 'I did some sewing and wrote letters etc., and when [my son Nevil] came in about 12.30 I said I wanted a walk before lunch.'[21]

Even those who witnessed it did not appreciate the significance of the moment when Pearse read the Proclamation. The writer Stephen McKenna would later record that he felt sad for Pearse because the response from the crowd was chilling. There were no wild hurrahs, no scenes reminiscent of the excitement which had gripped the French mob before they stormed the Bastille. The Irish simply listened and shrugged their shoulders, or sniggered a little and then glanced round to see if the police were coming.[22] Other accounts in the following decades confirmed the muted atmosphere on Sackville Street. William Fallon remembered:

There was very little noise in the street – practically silent. The crowd numbered about 200 and I'm sure that many of them didn't recognise the significance of what Pearse was saying. His voice didn't carry too well and it was difficult to hear him.

He had the document of the Proclamation in his hand, standing between the columns of the G. P. O., in the middle, on what I judged to be a chair.

But there was no reaction ... when he had finished the crowd melted ...'[23]

Geraldine Plunkett, who had just married Thomas Dillon, recalled watching the scene from the Imperial Hotel on Sackville Street. A sudden hush fell over the street as Pearse began to read the Proclamation of the Republic: 'Slowly the crowd broke up. Some strolled across to the Pillar, where they idly read the Proclamation; others just stood and stared up at the unfamiliar flags. Quite a few, bored with the whole affair, simply turned and wandered away.'[24] However, as early as 1 May 1916, the event had been transformed, by the *Chicago Tribune*, to one in which huge crowds of civilians thronged the streets while Pearse read the Proclamation, 'attired in some sort of fantastic uniform, with golden tassels and a sword'. When he had finished, the *Tribune* reported, 'thundering shouts rent the air, lasting for many minutes. The cries were taken up all along Sackville Street and the adjoining thoroughfares.'[25]

In fact, most newspapers reporting in the immediate aftermath carried no reference to the reading of the Proclamation. The *Daily Express* was typical in noting simply that copies of the 'Rebel Proclamation' were handed at the GPO to passers-by.[26] One thousand copies had been printed in Liberty Hall on Easter Monday morning by Christopher Brady, Michael Molloy and Liam O Briain. These were posted on walls across the city and

[21] Jeffery, *The GPO*, p. 66.
[22] M. Caufield, *The Easter Rebellion* (London: Four Square, 1965), p. 100.
[23] *Sunday Press*, 14 April 1963.   [24] *Evening Herald*, 6 May 1964.
[25] *Chicago Tribune*, 1 May 1916.   [26] *Daily Express*, 6 May 1916.

given out to newsboys for distribution, at least one of whom sold his copies and returned to the GPO 'holding his cap by the peak and the back, full of silver coins, mostly 2/- and 2/6d pieces'.[27] It was the physicality of the Proclamation rather than its performance which mattered most on Easter Monday. Yet even the physical document proved somewhat elusive. Seán T O'Kelly, who was staff captain to Pearse, attempted to save the Proclamation for posterity and posted three copies in British Government official envelopes obtained from the GPO. He sent a copy to Curran, the Archbishop's Secretary; one to Philis Ryan, his fiancée; and the third copy to his mother. The envelopes were not posted at the GPO, yet only one (to his mother) was delivered successfully.[28]

Dick Humphreys, a former pupil at St Enda's who was a 20-year-old rebel in 1916, wrote later that Pearse's eyes lit up with intense joy when told that the posters were attracting attention and excitement. However, Oscar Traynor spent the best part of Easter week as a Volunteer in the GPO without, he said, ever seeing the Proclamation.[29] In contrast, Kathleen Murphy, a member of Cumann na mBan, along with six other young women from Belfast, was one of the first people to see a copy having been shown it by James Connolly in Liberty Hall. The intention was to send a copy north, and Murphy remembered that, as she was the tallest of the girls, Connolly had suggested that she should be the person to carry it concealed under her blouse: 'I folded the Proclamation and fitted it under my blouse. I can't now recollect what happened to [it]. I was speaking to Mr. Connolly again before we left Liberty Hall. Perhaps Mr. Connolly may have taken the Proclamation from me as the carrying of it would mean so much danger. My mind is blank on what happened to the Proclamation.'[30] For the printing of the original document, the signatures of the leaders were appended on a separate piece of paper. The compositor Michael Molloy recalled:

> I took this with me and put it in my pocket and had it on my person when I was later a prisoner in Richmond barracks. Realising how dangerous it would be if the document containing actual signatures of the Proclamation was found, I destroyed it by chewing it up into small pieces and spitting it out on the floor. Actually the suggestion came from a fellow-prisoner. When he saw that I was beginning to tear this document he advised me that the best thing to do was to chew it up into small bits.[31]

[27] BMH WS 824 (Charles Donnelly). Donnelly was a member of E Company, 4th Battalion, of the Irish Volunteers in 1916.
[28] J. O'Connor, *The 1916 Proclamation* (Dublin: Anvil Books, 1986), pp. 31–32.
[29] BMH WS 824 (Charles Donnelly).
[30] BMH WS 180 (Kathleen Murphy). Murphy was a member of Cumann na mBan.
[31] BMH WS 716 (Michael Molloy). Molloy, one of the printers of the Proclamation, was a compositor in the office of *The Irish Republic* and a member of E Company 2nd Battalion.

Therefore, for some of those intimately involved in the Rising, the Proclamation was, by turns absent, lost, chewed up and spat on the floor. Nonetheless, it acted, as intended, as notice that something significant had changed. Its reproduction would be central to the structure and symbolism of all subsequent commemorations.

In the memory, too, the hour at which the Republic had been proclaimed became almost immediately a point of synchronicity. The *Times* repeated the version of events promoted in *War News* and reported: 'At the stroke of 12 separate bodies of rebels seized three important points in the heart of the city.'[32] Dick Humphreys, who recorded his account on toilet paper while in Wakefield Prison in May 1916, remembered that at noon on Easter Monday:

> Suddenly through the lovely summer-like air of that fatal bank holiday two shots ring out reverberatingly. Then follows a machine-gun-like succession of reports, and finally an immense explosion. People stop on the footpaths and look questionably at one another. A very few straightaway realise what has happened, and become the centres of chattering crowds. All at once one notices that a great silence, terrible in its unnaturalness, has fallen on the city.[33]

Solemnity was written into the event which, for Stephen McKenna, had unfolded amid shrugs and sniggers. A moment of origin had been agreed, although, unlike Bastille Day, the date of Easter Monday was ever-changing. Fittingly, therefore, like most commemorations, that of the Easter Rising has always been, to some degree, a collision between that which is fixed and that which is fluid. As early as May 1916, the ritualistic markers of future commemorations were already being established. However, twelve months later, there was no certainty the Easter Rising would be commemorated at all.

'The copy is more valuable than the original'

Helena Molony, a member of the Citizen Army, was released from Aylesbury Jail on Christmas Eve 1916. With Jinny Shanahan and Winnie Carney, she decided to 'have a demonstration to commemorate the rebellion' on its first anniversary. They agreed that the central features would be to 'beflag all the positions that had been occupied in the 1916 Rising . . . and to get out the proclamation, and to proclaim it again, and to try to establish the position that the fight was not over and that the Republic still lives'.[34] Making three flags, and with the assistance of a

---

[32] *Times*, 1 May 1916.   [33] Jeffery, *The GPO*, p. 141.
[34] BMH WS 391 (Helena Molony). Molony was Secretary of Inghinidhe na hÉireann, 1907–1914, and a member of Cumann na mBan.

Glaswegian sailor called Moran and 'Baby' Murray, a Fianna boy, they managed to raise the tricolor onto a large flagstaff at the GPO. Their efforts were so successful that it took the authorities until 6 pm to take it down, by which point a large crowd had gathered. The *Irish Times* reported that the anniversary was marked in Dublin by a good deal of excitement and gatherings, which together made up 'a very considerable aggregation of persons'. The considerable excitement had been generated simply by Molony's plan surreptitiously to hoist the flag over the GPO:

The crowd in Sackville Street grew in numbers during the morning, and at noon another incident attracted wide notice. A man walked along the parapet and raised the flag once more on the staff. This was the signal for an outburst of cheering, and various other demonstrations of approval on a wide scale ... When excitement had somewhat subsided a police constable, by use of a ladder, climbed on to the parapet, and after a good deal of work removed the staff from its position ... The crowd afterwards made their way by Lower Abbey Street to Liberty Hall, with a good deal of cheering and waving of small *Sinn Fein* flags. A number of persons in the crowds which gathered in Sackville street during the day wore black bands, surmounted with ribbons of the *Sinn Féin* colours on their arms, while groups of girls, with paper flags and coloured papers in their hair, paraded Sackville street ... As usual a good deal of disturbances, and some damage to windows in Middle Abbey street, was caused by youths, who rushed about shouting, while the newsboys added to the commotion constantly by the combined, raucous and senseless clamour.[35]

The *Irish Times* deftly undermined the legitimacy of the event for its readers with reference to rowdy youths and news-boys. It instantly read a pattern into this first anniversary with the dismissive, weary 'as usual'. However, the demonstration had the benefit of being both a re-enactment and heavy with symbolism. The crowd mimicked the flag hoisting with their personal emblems, which continued the traditions of earlier nationalists and prefigured the importance of flags and emblems in future commemorations of the Rising.

Molony and her fellow-organisers also ordered facsimiles of the Proclamation using some of the type-setting from the original, which was retrieved from Liberty Hall. The plan to distribute them was abandoned because an order came, it was assumed from the IRB, that there was to be no demonstration and that flags were not to be flown.[36] Molony and Shanahan succeeded nevertheless in creating their own demonstration without the sanction of the Trade Union men whom she said 'did not want the Citizen Army men there at all'. They displayed a calico scroll outside Liberty Hall that said, 'James Connolly Murdered – May 12th, 1916'.[37]

---

[35] *Irish Times*, 10 April 1917.   [36] BMH WS 391 (Helena Molony).   [37] Ibid.

Helena Molony told the Bureau of Military History, not without good reason, that this first celebration 'established the 1916 Commemoration'.[38] The central features had been identified: the Proclamation, flags and emblems would become part of the battle for legitimacy not just between Republicans and the State, but among Republicans themselves; and women would adopt the mantle of guardians of the ideals of the Rising. Moreover, on the first anniversary, the elements of the original Proclamation had been combined with new typeset to create a replica document. Molony recalled being told by a representative of the National Library that there were more extant copies of the 1916 Proclamation than of the 1917 one. He told her: 'The copy is more valuable than the original. We have three copies of the 1917 proclamation and fifteen of the original.'[39] Only an expert eye could see the difference. Claims of authenticity would be central to the politics of all subsequent commemorations of the Rising.

'In the Easter Lily it is raised again'

The Easter Rising was itself a commemorative event. In his writings, Patrick Pearse had located himself within Ireland's mythical, nationalist and religious traditions, and the Proclamation explicitly set the Rising within a longer sequence of rebellions. Moreover, each commemoration of Easter 1916 carries echoes of previous demonstrations and anniversaries so that they can be understood better as palimpsest than replica. This is why the Irish public's relationship with the Easter Rising can be so vivid; it is part of an ongoing, multi-layered negotiation with the present through the past. The significance of the Rising lies more in its symbolic capital than in the literal interpretation of events. Therefore, it is appropriate that it has been most effectively remembered through metaphorical representations and these have proved themselves to be very resilient.

Ribbons and colours had been effectively employed by nineteenth-century Irish nationalists to circumvent the fact that the flying of flags and banners was illegal. The Rising too was remembered in furtive as well as formal ways through the distribution of Mass cards, the singing of songs and the wearing of certain colours. It was, indeed, in a symbolic representation that memory of the Rising would find its most resilient form: the Easter lily. The lily was adopted as a badge of the Rising by Cumann na mBan in the 1920s. It was regarded as a less compromised symbol than the tricolour, which had been debased by its association with the partitioned state.[40] Cumann na mBan publicity material explained

[38] Ibid. [39] Ibid.
[40] S. Swan, *Official Irish Republicanism, 1962–1972* (N.P.: Lulu, 2007), p. 122.

that the men of 1916 had 'raised the banner of complete separation from England, and the wisdom of their demand united all the people of Ireland. That banner has been basely lowered. In the Easter Lily it is raised again.'[41]

Therefore, the lily was worn in opposition to the State and as an alternative to its flag. Moreover, the sale of the lily represented an important source of income for republicans, which (despite attempts by several governments) was not significantly curtailed until 1962 when the Street and House to House Collections Act was passed south of the border. It required that vendors obtain a permit from the Chief Superintendent of the locality, and the refusal of republicans to apply for permits (from a state they did not recognise) meant that the government could have those who sold the Easter lily arrested without having banned the sale of the lily itself.[42] There was, however, little public sympathy for this policy as Proinsias MacAonghusa explained in March 1964: 'The public does not support the physical force movement: it gives less support to efforts to harass Republicans on minor matters.'[43]

The Irish government attempted to supplant the lily in 1966 by devising a new logo for the fiftieth anniversary of the Easter Rising and ran a public competition for the design of a commemorative badge. The winning motif, 'An Claidheamh Soluis' (the Sword of Light), was chosen because it symbolised 'intuitive knowledge, education and progress' and, in fact, bore a marked resemblance to a stylised lily.[44] However, the Easter lily was not so easily expunged. The sisters and niece of Seán Mac Diarmada, in refusing to attend the official commemoration for their brother to be held in his home town of Kiltyclogher, explained in a letter to the Minister of Defence:

We believe that it is hypocritical for that Government to attempt to do honour to Sean Mac Diarmada while at the same time announcing a ban on the historic Easter Lily, the emblem of Easter week 1916. Sean died for a 32 – County republic which has yet to be achieved.[45]

---

[41] *Honesty*, 19 April 1930 in E. Morris, *Our Own Devices: National Symbols and Political Conflict in Twentieth-Century Ireland* (Dublin: Irish Academic Press, 2005), p. 46.

[42] 'Review of Unlawful and Allied Organisations: December 1, 1964, to November 21, 1966', Report from the Commissioner, An Garda Síochána, November 1966, Department of the Taoiseach (hereafter DT) 98/6/495, National Archives of Ireland (hereafter NAI).

[43] *Sunday Independent*, 29 March 1964.

[44] Department of External Affairs, *Cuimhneachán 1916–1966* (Dublin: Department of External Affairs, 1966), p. 93.

[45] Margaret McDermott, Rose McDermott and K. B. Keany to Minster of Defence, 2 April 1966, Department of Defence 48151/3 (118), (Irish) Military Archives.

In Northern Ireland, the Prime Minister's Secretary made enquiries regarding reports that the Easter lily had been banned south of the border. The Minister of Home Affairs, Brian McConnell clarified the position and reported that

the Easter Lily is really the symbol of the Easter Week Rebellion and is usually worn by people attending a commemoration service such as those held every year at Milltown Cemetery and at other towns in the North. Under our law if they wish to take up street collections they would require a permit under the Street Collection Regulations (Northern Ireland) 1927 and the Police of course would refuse such permits. However, the house-to-house collections only refer in Northern Ireland to house-to-house charitable collections and if the organizers here wish to hold house-to-house collections they would not be committing any offence.[46]

The idea of banning the lily as an emblem of republicanism had been considered by the Northern Ireland government in 1928 but a draft order was abandoned due to the difficulty in defining the emblem the government intended to prohibit.[47] Nevertheless, it was made clear that the public sale, distribution or wearing of the lily was prejudicial to the preservation of the peace and the police had the authority to remove offending items.[48] Both jurisdictions had attempted to limit the visibility and use of the Easter lily and, as a result, both had enhanced its symbolic power. It continued to represent the importance of unofficial commemorative practices in sustaining the memory of the Easter Rising.

The hoisting of flags above the GPO on Easter Monday 1916 had provided concrete evidence to those in Dublin that rebels had taken over the city centre and that their intentions were serious. The tricolour had also been central to commemoration of the Rising on its first anniversary. Fr Michael Curran recorded of April 1917 that numerous Requiem Masses were held nationwide and that 'Republican flags were hoisted at different places throughout the country and hauled down by the military. In one case, the flag was fired on.'[49]

In Northern Ireland, the tricolour continued to function as a potent and defiant symbol of nationalist memory and identity, particularly when connected to commemorations of the Rising. It was not within the power of the devolved government in Northern Ireland to ban a foreign flag outright but its display was heavily policed.[50] The Flags and Emblems

---

[46] Ministry of Home Affairs to the Prime Minister's Office, 31 March 1966, HA/32/2/19 (24), Public Records of Northern Ireland (hereafter PRONI).
[47] L. K. Donohue, 'Regulating Northern Ireland: The Special Powers Acts, 1922-1972', *Historical Journal* 41 (1998), p. 1096.
[48] Ibid., p. 1096.   [49] BMH WS 687 (Michael Curran).
[50] Donohue, 'Regulating Northern Ireland', p. 1108.

(Display) Act (Northern Ireland) of 1954 had been designed to protect the Union flag by making it an offence to interfere with its display and gave the police the power to remove any non-Union flag judged to threaten the maintenance of peace. Objection to the appearance of a tricolour in the Sinn Féin offices on Divis Street in 1964 became the spark for serious clashes between the Royal Ulster Constabulary (RUC) and Republicans. In 1966, the flying of the Irish flag was one of the most contentious aspects of the jubilee commemorations in Northern Ireland. The Loyal Orange Lodge in Magherafelt was representative of other Lodges in passing a resolution stating that, while they had no desire to oppose peaceful and limited celebrations in the district, they did wish 'to place on record our determination to oppose the flying of the Tricolour or provocative parades headed by the Tricolour, during the Easter Rising (1916) celebrations'.[51]

The Irish Republican Army (IRA) in Belfast saw the commemoration as 'a golden opportunity to drive a coach and four' through the Flags and Emblems Act and from January until April had devoted all their energies to preparing for the commemorations.[52] Liam McMillen, organising secretary on the commemoration committee, recalled that the services of every member of Cumann na mBan and dozens of other women were enlisted to make thousands of tricolour flags and bunting, which were distributed throughout all the nationalist areas of Belfast.[53] As a result, these areas were festooned in green, white and orange, and the Flags and Emblems Act was virtually unenforceable. The commemoration in Belfast in 1966 showed just how effective a flag could be in signalling opposition to the power of the State. Material symbols elicited a strong emotional response both from those who identified with them and from those who saw them as a direct challenge to their own identity. Where there were incidents of unrest during the Easter commemorations in Belfast in 1966, they were often linked to the public display of lilies and other emblems. Three young girls wearing tricolour emblems were chased by a crowd attending a march organised by Ian Paisley, and the windows were stoned and shattered in the house in which one girl sought refuge.[54] One young man had to be rescued by police when he was attacked by crowds waiting for the parade to pass. He was reported to have been wearing a tricolour ribbon and an Easter lily on his coat. He was

---

[51] Magherafelt District Loyal Orange Lodge No 3 to Brian McConnell, 21 February 1966, HA/32/2/8 (16), PRONI.
[52] Liam McMillen, 'The Role of the IRA' in D. Ó h-Agáin (ed.), *Liam McMillen: Separatist Socialist Republican* (Dublin: REPSOL Pamphlet no. 21, 1976), p. 6.
[53] McMillen, 'The Role of the IRA', p. 6.   [54] *Irish Times*, 18 April 1966.

set upon by a crowd of women who battered him with their umbrellas and several men tried to pull him to the ground. The police officer pulled him free and ran with him up Howard street. When the officer realised he was being followed by a large section of the crowd some of whom were crying 'Kill him, kill him' he turned and ran back through the crowd dragging the young man with him into the safe neutrality of a Chinese restaurant.[55]

Nationalist identity did not find easy accommodation within Northern Ireland and, in 1966, the tricolour and lily were interpreted as a rejection of the State and a threat to Unionist hegemony. The Easter Rising preceded partition and northern nationalists were ever alert to any attempt to exclude them from this history and resolute in their remembrance.

Challenging authority

Commemorations are part of the process of stabilising historical events that represent moments of rupture. They take an event which may have been violent or catastrophic and ritualise it into a force for social cohesion. However, the instability of the original event can reverberate (often inaudibly) in each act of remembrance. Large-scale commemorations do not entirely neutralise all other renditions of an event: covert, illicit, defiant memories continue to exist and to offer receptacles of resistance to formalised social memory. Commemorations of significant historical events retain the potential to challenge authority; as a result, no political party could afford to ignore the Easter Rising.

In the Irish Free State, Easter commemorations offered an opportunity for the government to assert its legitimacy and for Republican groups to register their opposition to the partitioned settlement. Civil war politics were as important as the original event in shaping subsequent commemorations of Easter 1916. The first formal military commemoration of the Rising took place in 1924 under the Cumann na nGaedheal government but, although invitations were issued to all the relatives of the executed leaders, due to the divisive politics of the civil war, only Michael Mallin's widow attended.[56] On the tenth anniversary, Eamon de Valera and Seán Lemass participated in an unofficial commemoration which was organised by anti-treaty republicans in Glasnevin cemetery. When de Valera, as Taoiseach, unveiled the statue of Cúchulainn in the GPO in 1935, members of the Cumann na nGaedheal opposition party were not invited to the event. The same year, an estimated one thousand people marched

[55] Ibid.
[56] D. Fitzpatrick, 'Commemoration in the Irish Free State: A Chronicle of Embarrassment' in I. McBride (ed.), *History and Memory in Modern Ireland* (Cambridge: Cambridge University Press, 2001), p. 196.

to Glasnevin cemetery for an alternative commemoration that was addressed by the Chief of Staff of the IRA, Maurice Twomey.[57] However, by the twenty-fifth anniversary of the Rising in 1941, the southern State was strong enough to chart its own foreign policy during the Second World War. The 1916 commemoration was used to demonstrate the strength of this assertion of independence with a display in Dublin that included 20,000 members of the Defence Forces, aeroplanes, the nursing service and fire-fighters. In 1966, the official commemoration was deployed to lend legitimacy to the economic policy of modernisation and to celebrate the successes of the independent State. In contrast to the Rising itself, its fiftieth anniversary, viewed as a success as it unfolded, was reread in increasingly critical terms in the light of subsequent events.[58]

In Northern Ireland, Easter 1916 represented a different form of threat to those in authority and was seen as alien to the State. Commemorations of the Rising consistently attracted more legal controls than any other event or assembly. Individual Easter commemorations were banned under Section 4 of the Special Powers Act from 1926, with the number of events prohibited increasing until an outright ban was imposed on all commemorations across Northern Ireland during Easter week in 1936.[59] This ban was renewed annually until 1949, when commemorations were assessed on an individual basis. Parades attracted groups from across the nationalist spectrum such as the Irish National Foresters, the Gaelic Athletic Association (GAA) and certain trade unionists.[60] However, events in the late 1960s transformed the context for commemorations of the Rising and they became overwhelmingly Republican events.

The fiftieth anniversary of the Easter Rising has been given a pivotal place in the history of the Troubles in Northern Ireland. The future Ulster Unionist leader, David Trimble credited it with starting 'the destabilisation of Ulster'.[61] However, instability did not begin or end with nationalist plans to commemorate the Easter Rising. Economic and social change in Northern Ireland, and moderate attempts at political reform,

---

[57] Y. Whelan, *Reinventing Modern Dublin: Streetscape, Iconography and the Politics of Identity* (Dublin: University College Dublin Press, 2003), pp. 166–167.

[58] For a discussion of the fiftieth anniversary of the Easter Rising, see R. Higgins, *Transforming 1916: Meaning, Memory and the Fiftieth Anniversary of the Easter Rising* (Cork: Cork University Press, 2012).

[59] Donohue, 'Regulating Northern Ireland', p. 1096.

[60] N. Jarman, 'Commemorating 1916, Celebrating Difference: Parading and Painting in Belfast' in A. Forty and S. Küchler (eds.), *The Art of Forgetting* (Oxford: Berg, 2001), p. 188.

[61] D. Trimble, *The Easter Rebellion of 1916* (Lurgan: Ulster Society Publications, 1992), p. 33.

led to a certain volatility within the society. Tensions were high in anticipation of the anniversary and an upcoming general election was moved
forward, Prime Minister O'Neill stated, in order to avoid clashing with
the commemoration.[62] A special security committee had been set up in
Stormont at the beginning of April 1966, all police leave was cancelled
over the Easter period with the RUC and the British Army was described
as being in a state of 'instant readiness'.[63] Security sources suggested that
the IRA was planning a new campaign in 1966, and Loyalist agitation had
reached such a level that by the summer of that year intelligence reports
assessed the threat from 'extremist Protestant groups' to be greater than
that of Republicans.[64] The anniversary of the Rising, however, passed off
with little disruption. Only one parade was banned (in the Loup, Co
Derry).The main trouble occurred as a result of clashes between nationalists and those taking part in a counter-march through Belfast city centre
organised by Rev Ian Paisley; it began with a service in the Ulster Hall
offered in thanksgiving for the defeat of the 1916 Rising. A large police
presence kept the marchers apart but there were several skirmishes and six
people were detained by the RUC.[65]

Terence O'Neill described 1966 as 'not a very easy year'.[66] He
expressed his frustration at Catholics in Belfast who had 'insist[ed] on
celebrating the Dublin rebellion' and recorded, 'It was 1966 which made
1968 inevitable and was bound to put the whole future of Northern
Ireland in the melting pot.'[67] This statement gave too much power to
the anniversary of the Rising. In a healthy society, commemorations offer
a safe space for public debate, but in an already fractured society, the past
has the capacity to explode into the present. Nevertheless, the proximity
of the jubilee of the Rising to the outbreak of Troubles compounded the
sense that commemorations of 1916 were potentially dangerous events.
Between 1972 and 2006, the military parade in Dublin, which had been
central to commemorations of the Rising, was suspended and until the
ninetieth anniversary the Irish government staged low-key official

[62] See C. O'Donnell, 'Pragmatism versus Unity: The Stormont Government and the 1966
    Easter Commemoration' in M. Daly and M. O'Callaghan (eds.), *1916 in 1966:
    Commemorating the Easter Rising* (Dublin: Royal Irish Academy), pp. 241–242.
[63] *Irish Times*, 8 April 1966.
[64] RUC Inspector General to J. E. Greeves at Home Affairs, 22 June 1966, CAB9B/300/1,
    PRONI, quoted in M. O'Callaghan and C. O'Donnell, 'The Northern Ireland
    Government, the "Paisleyite Movement" and Ulster Unionism in 1966', *Irish Political
    Studies* 21 (2006), 210.
[65] *Irish Times*, 18 April 1966.
[66] *Times*, 28 April 1967 in T. O'Neill, *Ulster at the Crossroads* (London: Faber and Faber,
    1969), p. 125.
[67] T. O'Neill, *The Autobiography of Terence O'Neill* (London: Rupert Hart-Davis, 1972),
    pp. 78, 87.

ceremonies. Republicans across Ireland continued to hold annual com memorative events and, as with the earliest anniversaries, legitimacy was claimed through Easter ancestry.

'If the men they killed in '16 were alive today they'd be up here with us'

The flag bearing the words 'Irish Republic', which had been hoisted over the GPO on Easter Monday 1916, was handed back to the Irish people by the British Ambassador in a private ceremony in April 1966. Taoiseach Seán Lemass said, on its arrival in the National Museum, 'I hope [this flag] will be preserved as one of the most important relics of that important event in Irish history and as a source of inspiration for all who come to this museum.'[68] There had been some concern over whether or not the correct flag had been nominated for return, as the British Museum had been displaying a tricolour which had, in fact, originated in Limerick. However, the flag was verified as genuine and it took its place among the original artifacts of the Easter week 1916.[69]

More problematic was determining the authentic legacy of the Rising. The Republic had been declared but not achieved on Easter Monday and, as a result of this ambiguity and unfulfilled aspiration, a great deal of tension was generated. Commemorations became contests over who qualified as the Rising's rightful heirs. Frank Robbins, who had been a sergeant in the Citizen Army during Easter week, believed that as early as 1918 'the majority of the men . . . in no way resembled or held the outlook which was dominant up to 1916 and which was responsible for the great deeds performed during Easter Week by the Irish Citizen Army'. He recalled that it was to demonstrate this that the Socialist Party of Ireland in 1919 decided to have a Connolly commemoration in the Mansion House on the anniversary of his birth, 5th June.[70] Across the political spectrum, anniversaries were represented as opportunities to recommit to the ideals of the Easter leaders. These could be understood in terms of revival, reinterpretation or as purely rhetorical gestures.

Burial places were also used to assert an unbroken line between the actions of the living and the aspirations of the dead, with graves playing a central part in commemorations of the Easter Rising. Patrick Pearse had a very clear understanding of the power of the graveside oration, and it was through similar rituals that others would avow themselves his successors.

---

[68] *Irish Press*, 13 April 1966.   [69] DT 97/6/532, NAI. *Irish Press*, 13 April 1966.
[70] BMH WS 586 (Frank Robbins). Robbins was a sergeant in the Irish Citizen Army in 1916.

Historically, funerals had provided a legal way of holding mass political gatherings and graveyards continued to serve a similar function. In Northern Ireland, when parades were banned in either Belfast or Derry, large numbers of people gathered instead in Milltown and Brandywell cemeteries.[71] Graveyards were vital to the claims of those who rejected official state commemorations and operated as spaces in which the dead were used to bestow legitimacy to whichever version of Republicanism was assembled.

The group most consistent in its observations was the National Graves Association (NGA), which was founded in 1926 with the aim of recording, renovating and preserving patriot graves. It provided an umbrella structure for Republicans, many of whom were former and serving members of the IRA. The primary work of the NGA concerned the Republican plot in Glasnevin, a cemetery which had long operated as a commemorative site of opposition to State nationalism.[72] The plot in Glasnevin held the bodies of the 'unknown soldiers' of the Rising, who had been buried before their relatives could be found to claim them. It contained sixteen of the sixty-four rebels killed in action during Easter Week. The plot was refurbished for the fiftieth anniversary of the Rising and the unveiling ceremony was attended by 2,500 people.[73] The memorial asserts an unbroken line of Republicanism and contains the dates 1798, 1803, 1848, 1867, 1882 and 1916, with the inscription 'We know their dreams. They dreamed and are dead.' Joseph Clarke, who had fought during the Rising at Mount Street Bridge and was one of the founding members of the NGA, was at the commemoration in Glasnevin cemetery on Easter Sunday 1966, having turned down invitations to the official ceremony at the GPO, and was certain, 'If the men they killed in '16 were alive today they'd be up here with us. Our parade is much closer to what they fought for than the [official] one in O'Connell street.'[74]

The authority to interpret the wishes of the Easter rebels was also asserted by their relatives. The blood or marriage line held a potentially powerful challenge to the politicians who claimed to act in the name of the men and women of 1916. Women were particularly vocal as keepers of the true legacy of the dead and saw themselves as unwavering and unchanging in this service. The obituary notice for Margaret Pearse,

[71] N. Jarman and D. Bryan, 'Green Parades in an Orange State: Nationalist and Republican Commemorations and Demonstrations from Partition to the Troubles, 1920-70' in T. G. Fraser (ed.), *The Irish Parading Tradition: Following the Drum*, (Basingstoke: Macmillan, 2000), p. 98.

[72] N. Johnson, *Ireland, the Great War and the Geography of Remembrance* (Cambridge: Cambridge University Press, 2003), pp. 153–161.

[73] 'Review of Unlawful and Allied Organisations', DT 98/6/495, NAI.

[74] *Irish Times*, 11 April 1966.

mother of Patrick and Willie, who died in 1932, observed that 'in one sense it was always Nineteen Sixteen with her'.[75] Kathleen Clarke was a particularly formidable advocate on behalf of the legacy of her husband Tom, having been a founding member of the NGA and a trustee of the Wolfe Tone Memorial Fund. She thought Patrick Pearse beneath contempt for signing himself President of the Republic when the honour clearly belonged to her husband: 'Surely Pearse should have been satisfied with the honour of Commander-in-Chief when he knew as much about commanding as my dog.'[76] Clarke's offer to serve on the commemoration committee for the fiftieth anniversary of the Rising was declined by Seán Lemass, who said the inclusion of close relatives might detract from the tribute being prepared for the 1916 leaders.[77] The sisters of Seán Mac Diarmada made clear their disdain for the State and refused to participate in the official commemoration, attending instead that organised by the NGA. Nevertheless, relatives of the leaders of the Rising were invited each year to official commemorations and, on guest lists, formed something of an aristocracy for the new State, embodying the living link with the Easter martyrs. Yeats anticipated something of the conflicted position they would hold within Irish society when he said of his fellow Free State Senators: 'hot and vague, always disturbed, always hating something or other ... [they] had ... signed the death-warrant[s] of their dearest friend[s] ... Yet their descendants, if they grow rich enough for the travel and leisure that make a finished man, will constitute our ruling class, and date their origin from the Post Office as American families date theirs from the Mayflower.'[78]

Conclusion

When Tom Clarke was asked, 'Why a Republic?' he is reported to have replied, 'You must have something striking in order to appeal to the imagination of the world.'[79] It was clearly understood by those who organised it that the Easter Rising would be most effective as an idea rather than reality. Its success, although not initially apparent, would be evident not in its certainties but in its adaptability in the nation's memory. Some of the structures of commemoration were established early: the use of flags and emblems as a way of both asserting and challenging authority;

[75] M. McCarthy, *Ireland's 1916 Rising: Explorations of History-Making, Commemoration & Heritage in Modern Times* (Farnham: Ashgate Publishing, 2012), p. 142.
[76] Kathleen Clarke to Éamon Martin, 29 March 1965, DT 97/6/469, NAI.
[77] Seán Lemass to Kathleen Clarke, 14 May 1965, DT 97/6/469, NAI.
[78] W. B. Yeats, *On the Boiler* (Dublin: The Cuala Press, 1938), p. 12.
[79] Quoted in McGarry, *The Rising*, p. 154.

factions arguing over the true legacy of the event and the oppositional voices of relatives. These have become part of the choreography of remembrance. Launching a programme of events for the centenary, the Taoiseach, Enda Kenny, described Easter 1916 as 'one of those seminal weeks when the fault lines of history shifted'.[80] This too has echoes of the early propaganda of the rebels, which declared that a break with the past had occurred at exactly 12 noon on 24 April 1916. This sense of rupture in the imaginative horizon has become an accepted part of the narrative of the Easter Rising. The moment when Pearse read the Proclamation aloud has been imbued, in retrospect, with the power to change what was thought possible. The Easter Rising in Irish life, therefore, carries the weight of great hope and extreme disillusionment. Its commemorations have, at times, been exceedingly contentious and, by the ninetieth anniversary, heavily commodified. The anticipation surrounding the centenary suggests that a great deal is expected still, emotionally and politically, of the Easter Rising. The danger, however, with an event into which so much has been read is that by 2016 it will have almost no meaning at all.

[80] 2016 Commemoration Launch, speech by Taoiseach Enda Kenny, TD. Published on 13 November 2014.

Part II

Narratives

4   Instant history: 1912, 1916, 1918

David Fitzpatrick

I

What historian of revolutionary Ireland can claim to have remained utterly impervious to seduction during the current orgy of centennial commemoration? The study of how distant events have been remembered is suddenly both popular and profitable, offering almost irresistible attractions. The core documentation for public commemorative practices is typically compact and easily accessible: downloadable press reports of anniversary or jubilee events, perhaps a few boxes of official files. The focus of interest in commemorative studies has long since shifted from the original episodes and participants to politicised constructions of the past and the political functions of current ceremonies. Though of some intrinsic interest as well as 'relevance' in the eyes of funders, this genre tends to produce soft, easily digestible history. The hard questions of history (what actually happened and who thought what, why, and with what consequences) are neatly avoided. Released from tiresome delving into the distant past, historians easily mutate into columnists and pundits, accorded spurious authority because of their past credentials as scholars. Most of us will probably emerge only slightly scathed, to document another day when public interest wanes and the orgy fizzles out. However, the most prudent strategy for scrupulous historians is to avoid binge-commemorating and limit self-indulgence to the occasional review, hedge-school, or Friday colloquium.

In this chapter, I shall chart an intermediate course between the study of events and that of their commemoration, by scrutinising 'instant history'. By this I mean the ways in which actors and observers experienced contemporary events as if they were living out history and in history. Ulster Day (28 September 1912), Easter Week (24–29 April 1916), and Anti-Conscription Day (21 April 1918) were all 'historic' moments for contemporaries as well as for later generations. Each whipped up a widespread sense of excitement, even awe, social solidarity, and confidence that Irish politics and life could be transformed through mass participation in a novel and dangerous experiment. The meanings attributed by contemporaries to these episodes were not mere products of political manipulation, but shaped by personal observation and experience. To make sense of 'instant history', one must rehearse all those hard questions. How did both organisers and observers express and enact their sense of being history-makers? How important were embedded beliefs about past history in gathering communities into these collective performances? How did the experience of optimism and solidarity, however evanescent, mould Ireland's subsequent political development? My purpose here is not to answer these questions, but to propose and illustrate a tentative taxonomy for some future study of Ireland's instant histories. The final section will discuss the applicability of this model to Ulster's sacrifice on the Somme (1–2 July 1916).

Each of the episodes under discussion was theatrical, in several senses. First came the script, minutely revised and choreographed to engage and engross as many contemporaries as possible. Second came the performance, in which participants performed their assigned parts in public, often improvising additional dramatic touches. Performance generated interaction with the audience, whether positive or negative, so drawing the wider public into the experience of living out history. Very soon after the curtain fell, the sense of history-making was reinforced by the production of historical and biographical studies by journalists and polemicists, feeding the public appetite for information and explanation. Popular consumption of history was not restricted to reading books and articles, but took more intimate forms (medals, souvenirs, postcard portraits, parchments, poems, personal relics, and tokens). Finally came the inevitable anniversary and jubilee commemorations, gradually losing their personal significance and changing their meaning as instant history became formulaic observance.

II

The most methodical Irish example of meticulously-prepared theatre is surely Ulster Day, designed to cajole the masses into a common act of defiance through administration of pledges, revealed long after the script had been drafted and the arrangements for collecting signatures had been perfected. By keeping the ambiguous wording of Ulster's Solemn League and Covenant and the Women's Declaration secret until nine days beforehand, the organisers managed to enrol many agents and clergy who might have been unhappy with the political implications of the texts if circulated earlier. Belated publication also created a sense of mystery and anticipation prior to the performance. The text was a much simplified adaptation of 'the Solemn League and Covenant' of 1643, 'for reformation and defence of religion, the honour and happiness of the King, and the peace and safety of the three kingdoms'. Despite frequent suggestions otherwise, neither document remotely resembled 'the National Covenant; or, the Confession of Faith', another fundamental text of Presbyterianism adopted by parliament in 1638. For Presbyterians, though not for other Ulster reformed churches, the Solemn League and Covenant of 1643 was still celebrated as a Scottish-sponsored assertion of civil and religious liberty, forced upon a reluctant English church and parliament and eventually upon an even more reluctant Charles II as a price for his coronation in Scotland. Elsewhere, I have discussed in detail the techniques by which Ulster's protest against Home Rule was dramatised, through church services of intercession and preparation endorsed by all major Protestant denominations (except the Old Covenanters), regimented processions from church to hall, the display of texts as wall posters, the distribution of pretty vellum souvenirs, and the accompanying barrage of propaganda through newspapers and pamphlets.[1]

So effective was the Ulster prototype that it was minutely imitated by the Sinn Féin-dominated Mansion House committee in April 1918, which closely echoed the wording of the Ulster Covenant when devising 'Ireland's Solemn League and Covenant: a National Pledge'. Once again, arrangements were made for uniform administration of the pledge, this time at Catholic Church gates, following nationwide Masses of Intercession, reinforced by nightly recitations of the Rosary in Catholic homes and a National Novena. Once again, the profoundly ambiguous wording of the pledge was unveiled only a few days before its application. Once again, signatories were given certificates with decorative borders and faintly Celtic type-face, adorned by photographs of the Mansion House, Maynooth College, and members of the anti-Conscription Conference.[2] The shameless appropriation of Ulster's marketing tricks, characteristic of the mutually mimetic history of Irish political propaganda, was a resounding tribute to the theatrical success of Ulster Day.

Though the performance at Easter 1916 took a different form, it too was carefully rehearsed and scripted, as many scholars have pointed out.[3]

---

[1] David Fitzpatrick, *Descendancy: Irish Protestant Histories since 1795* (Cambridge: Cambridge University Press, 2014), ch. 6 (esp. p. 111).

[2] In Castleblayney, Co. Monaghan (Catholic parish of Muckno), where all 411 signatories were men, the signature sheet itself was an illuminated 'Solemn Covenant' with green and gold ornaments, a harp, and the nationalist motto 'Dhia Saor Éire' or 'God Save Ireland': MS 3110, National Library of Ireland [NLI]. By contrast, the signature sheets for the Ulster Covenant and Women's Declaration were functional and unadorned.

[3] For discussion of 1916 as theatre, see William Irwin Thompson, *The Imagination of an Insurrection, Dublin, Easter 1916: A Study of an Ideological Movement* (New York: Oxford University Press, 1967); Seán Farrell Moran, *Patrick Pearse and the Politics of Redemption: The Mind of the Easter Rising, 1916* (Washington, DC: Catholic University of America,

In this case, popular participation was initially minimal, and the rebels were not given little decorated 'proclamations' to take home to their little Irish mothers. But care was taken to display symbols of the republic, especially the two flags flown from the General Post Office (GPO), and to post copies of the so-called proclamation of 'the Irish Republic as a Sovereign Independent State' in various public places.[4] Both the tricolour and the proclamation asserted continuity with earlier failed rebellions, especially the Fenian fiasco of 1867. Yet, the most resonant script of the rebellion, only faintly exhibited in flags or proclamations, was the remarkably powerful sacrifice motif, whereby Pearse, Plunkett, and MacDonagh had self-consciously sought martyrdom through a secular re-enactment of Christ's crucifixion and resurrection. Opportunities for martyrdom were maximised by the decisions to occupy various public buildings, passively invite attack, surrender without significant rebel losses in action, and await execution. In most practical respects, prior arrangements were slipshod by comparison with 1912 or 1918. Yet, the planners of 1916 had one great practical and theatrical advantage, that of unpredictability: the very existence of a rebellion script was known only to a small circle, and the curiosity engendered by the undisclosed wording of the covenants paled by comparison with the general incredulity that greeted the Dublin bloodbath. This was truly a *coup de théâtre*.

The actual performance of each episode varied somewhat from the script, as the actors improvised additional dramatic flourishes or dealt with unexpected glitches. The performance on Ulster Day was enhanced by reports that leaders such as Major Fred Crawford, chemical manufacturer and gun-runner, had signed it in his own blood as he claimed an ancestor had done in '1638'.[5] Otherwise, the religious and secular ceremonies of signature varied little between localities, with remarkable harmonisation of procedure and rhetoric and very few expressions of dissent by either clergy or Protestant laity. The mobilisation of over 400,000 Ulster men and women was rightly regarded as an astonishing exhibition of communal solidarity, bringing together religious and political factions which had often been bitterly divided. Even dissentients were impressed

---

1994); Declan Kiberd, *Inventing Ireland: The Literature of the Modern Nation* (London: Jonathan Cape, 1995), pp. 196–217.

[4] The noun 'proclamation' was first used in Pearse's address on behalf of 'The Provisional Government to the Citizens of Dublin', not in the Easter Monday address by the seven members of 'The Provisional Government of the Irish Republic to the People of Ireland'. The entity so proclaimed was not the Republic (already proclaimed in 1867) but the 'State' that now embodied it.

[5] A. T. Q. Stewart, *The Ulster Crisis: Resistance to Home Rule, 1912–1914* (London: Faber, 1967), p. 91.

by the spirit of Ulster Day and its progeny, the Ulster Volunteer Force. Like his poet-son, the Revd Frederick MacNeice was adept in irony:

In Ulster it was indeed a wonderful time. Every county had its organisation: every town and district had its own corps. The young manhood of Ulster enlisted and went into training. Men of all ranks and occupations met together, in the evenings, for drill. There resulted a great comradeship. Barriers of class were broken down or forgotten. Protestant Ulster became a fellowship.[6]

Nationwide administration of the anti-Conscription pledge in 1918 was helped by the fact that the organisers had to mobilise only one clerical army rather than half a dozen as on Ulster Day. Admittedly, the organisers were less slickly methodical than their Ulster precursors, squandering the opportunity to count and publicise the number of signatories in order to underline the breadth of opposition to compulsory service in nationalist Ireland. Such exercises were impeded by increasing violence and unrest, and the arrest of most Republican leaders only a month after Anti-Conscription Day. Yet, the pledge proved highly effective in bringing Labour and all nationalist factions into a single campaign and stimulating rapid growth of the Irish Volunteers throughout Catholic Ireland. This too, for a short period, became a fellowship.

Easter Week departed significantly from the script, partly as a result of MacNeill's cancellation of the 'manoeuvres' scheduled for Easter Sunday. This led not only to the non-participation of most potential rebels but also to postponement of the mock crucifixion–resurrection until Monday, a day without symbolic significance in the Paschal calendar. The determination of the leaders to stage a rebellion marked by honour and chivalry, if not to follow Christ's example by succumbing without a fight, was inevitably sullied by cases of brutal or cowardly conduct, callousness towards civilians, and looting. Even so, the rebels emerged after the surrender with impressive dignity to meet their fate, often expecting and even hoping for execution, only to be embarrassed by moderate prison sentences or mere internment for their pains.

All three performances resembled street theatre, in which actors and spectators mingle and interact. This element in the creation of instant history is best documented for Easter Week, during which numerous observers witnessed the unexpected eruption at close quarters as they walked to and from work or school. Unlike the Great War, which had to be visualised through the distorting lens of official reports, approved

---

[6] John Frederick MacNeice, *Carrickfergus and Its Contacts: Some Chapters in the History of Ulster* (London: Simpkin, Mashall and Belfast: W. Erskine Mayne, 1928), p. 76; David Fitzpatrick, *'Solitary and Wild': Frederick MacNeice and the Salvation of Ireland* (Dublin: Lilliput Press, 2012), ch. 7.

photographs, and censored correspondence, the Dublin rebellion was extraordinarily immediate, accessible, and visible. The sense of witnessing a performance is clearly conveyed in contemporary diaries and letters, expressing the phlegmatic response of Dubliners to the disruption and destruction of so much of their city. Despite the undeniable antipathy of most nationalists as well as unionists to the Republican demand and the resort to force without prospect of success, the convulsion aroused feelings of excitement, even perverse pride, among those who should have deplored it most.[7]

Not all interaction was benign, as attested by salvoes of abuse, refuse, and vegetables flung at the surrendered rebels by alleged 'separation women' (apparently uninhibited by wartime food shortage exacerbated by the rebellion). Even abuse, however, belonged firmly to the Dublin theatrical tradition so vividly expressed nine years earlier, in the riots and rowdy debates that greeted Synge's *Playboy of the Western World* in the Abbey Theatre. The protesters against the *Playboy* had created an informal drama that engulfed and transcended the intended performance, their gestures and actions being reported with gusto in the press along with equally stagey responses by W. B. Yeats and his volatile father, both zestful in cultivating unpopularity. Likewise, the self-righteousness of the rebels was sanctified by their public humiliation, just as Christ had been tested by the taunts of the Jews, spears of the centurions, and crown of thorns. Their vilification by dependents of servicemen, derided by republicans as traitors to the nation, was quickly integrated into Republican narratives of the rebellion as a proof of virtue.

III

Each performance was quickly followed by a deluge of explanatory articles and pamphlets, as writers and journalists competed for attention while public interest lasted. The Dublin rebellion also prompted half a dozen books and booklets published in 1916 alone. Apart from two works published in London and New York, these commentaries catered primarily for Irish audiences ill prepared for the transformative events they had just experienced. Most of these works used the term 'rebellion', but 'insurrection', 'rising', and 'revolt' also featured in titles.[8] Newspapers provided

---

[7] See, for example, Adrian and Sally Warwick-Haller (eds.), *Letters from Dublin, Easter 1916: Alfred Fannin's Diary of the Rising* (Dublin: Irish Academic Press, 1995).

[8] The following 1916 imprints appear in the catalogues of the British Library or NLI: James Stephens, *Insurrection in Dublin* (Dublin: Maunsel); Warre B. Wells and N. Marlowe, *A History of the Irish Rebellion* (Dublin: Maunsel); J. W. Boyle, *The Irish Rebellion of 1916* (London: Constable); F. A. Mackenzie, *The Irish Rebellion: What Happened and Why*

retrospective documentation through records such as the still useful *Sinn Féin Rebellion Handbook*.[9] Newsreels brought images of the rebellion into cinemas and halls throughout the country. Photographic firms flooded the market with pictorial souvenirs portraying the devastation of Dublin as if it were a wrecked city in Belgium, often reproducing portraits of the leaders and facsimiles of the proclamation and other documents.[10] Catholic magazines published sentimental poems and pen-portraits of the rebels, most famously in the *Catholic Bulletin*'s 'Events of Easter Week', a lavishly illustrated serial initiated in July 1916 and still running in spring 1919. Later instalments seamlessly incorporated post-1916 heroes without any change of title, illustrating the ease with which subsequent 'events' were woven into ever-changing political narratives.[11]

There were more imaginative ways of affirming one's connection with 'historic' events than reading potted histories and photo-essays. Within three months of the rebellion, 'Editor's Gossip' in the *Irish Book Lover* reported great popular demand for Sinn Féin pamphlets (stocks having been depleted by the burning of Maunsel's stock in Easter Week). Thomas MacDonagh's *Poems*, available for 2/– before the rebellion, were now fetching 25/–.[12] A few months later, *Irish Opinion* advertised 'SINN FEIN STAMPS (Orange and Green) and 2 Year Books for Sale. What offers?'[13] There was much demand for tokens of the rebels in the form of postcard portraits, illuminated posters modelled on military rolls of honour, Mass cards, and medals.

Military mementoes were equally appealing: one album of photographs featured a montage of 'Volunteer Relics Arms & Accoutrements', including a belt plate, two French bayonets, and a cartridge.[14] A postcard

---

(London: C. Arthur Pearson); Maurice Joy (ed.), *The Irish Rebellion and Its Martyrs* (New York: Devin Adair); Frederic William Pim, *The Sinn Fein Rising: A Narrative and Some Reflections* (Dublin: Hodges Figgis).

[9] Weekly Irish Times, *Sinn Fein Rebellion Handbook: Easter, 1916* (Dublin: *Irish Times*, Ltd., 1916).

[10] Library holdings include *Dublin after the six Days' Insurrection: 35 Pictures from the Camera of T. W. Murphy* (Dublin: Mecredy, Percy); *A Record of the Irish Rebellion of 1916* (Dublin: *Irish Life*); *Dublin and the 'Sinn Féin Rising': Portraits Documents Pictures Volunteer Relics Arms & Accoutrements; Story of the Rising* (Dublin: Wilson Hartnell); *The Rebellion in Dublin, April, 1916* (Dublin: Eason); *Irish Rebellion, 1916* (postcards in book form: several sets in NLI); Thomas J. Westropp, *Photographs of the Ruins of Dublin after the Sinn Féin Rebellion, April 24th, 1916; Sinn Fein Revolt, 1916: 12 Interesting Views* (Dublin: T. J. Coleman); *The Sinn Fein Rebellion, 1916: Picture Souvenir* (Belfast: W. & G. Baird, 1917).

[11] *Catholic Bulletin*, vi, 7 (July 1916); ix, 3 (March 1919).

[12] *Irish Book Lover*, viii (July–August 1916).

[13] *Irish Opinion*, i, 24 (25 November 1916). Several such stamps are reproduced in the *Sinn Fein Rebellion Handbook*.

[14] *Dublin and the 'Sinn Féin Rising'*, (Dublin: Wilson Hartnell, 1916), p. 4.

entitled 'Scenes in Dublin after the Rebellion' displayed 'A Doctor's Collection of Trophies taken from Sinn Feiners, including German Swords, Belts, Cartridges, Trenching Tools, Haversacks, etc., photographed in Dublin Castle'.[15] The martial appeal of instant history was not confined to adults, as 'An Irishman' recalled in 1929:

One visible aftermath of the Rebellion was the new pastime of the children in the streets: they were 'sojers and Sinn Feiners', hunting or being hunted, leading or being led to jail with the proper solemnity; nor could I see that one rôle was more favoured than the other.[16]

A comprehensive inventory of the post-rebellion cult is provided by the catalogue of a three-day gift sale in support of Republican relief organisations, opened by the Lord Mayor on 20 April 1917.[17] All unlicensed public meetings and processions in the Dublin police district were prohibited by military proclamation on the following day, for fear of 'grave disorder' arising from the anniversary, and the sale was the only meeting permitted in the Mansion House for the remainder of the month.[18] The link with earlier rebellions was evoked by artefacts such as pikes, Volunteer uniforms, and a Fenian bond-certificate. Relics included the 'Block on which Robert Emmet was Beheaded' (sold for £5 10s., equivalent to £400 today) and his heavily ornamented wallet (10 guineas). One might also acquire 'Piece of outer Coffin which contained the Remains of Lord Edward Fitzgerald' (1 guinea), and the sword by which he was fatally wounded, wielded by Major Sirr but acquired by Patrick Pearse (£19). Widows and mothers of the 'martyrs' contributed Eamon Ceannt's 'Gold-mounted Fountain Pen' (5 guineas), his imitation ancient-Irish costume worn when playing the Irish war-pipes before Pope Pius X in 1908 (£6), and a pair of James Connolly's gloves (25s.). A memorial ring, inscribed with the initials of the brothers Pearse (£10), was gallantly returned by the priest-purchaser to the finger of Mrs Pearse, 'who was much affected by the kindly act'.[19] One survivor was also on the path to sainthood: in the absence of her husband in Lewes Prison, Mrs de

---

[15] Postcard (Dublin, Valentine), digitally accessible through NLI catalogue (EPH A139).

[16] An Irishman [F. C. Moore?], *My Countrymen* (Edinburgh: William Blackwood, 1929), pp. 286–287.

[17] *Irish National Aid and Volunteer Dependents' Fund: Catalogue of Gift Sale to be Held in Aid of above at the Mansion House, Dublin on Friday and Saturday, 20th and 21st April*: MS. 35,262/27(1), NLI. Sale prices are taken from reports in the *Irish Times*, *Irish Independent*, and *Freeman's Journal*, 21, 23 April 1917.

[18] Cancelled events included a concert organised by the O'Daly Literary Club with an address by Arthur Griffith, a discussion of the 'impending food scarcity', a concert for the Babies' Club, a drill display by Dublin Working Girls, and a meeting of the Protestant Girls' Brigade: *Irish Independent*, 23 April 1917.

[19] *Irish Independent*, 23 April 1917.

Valera donated 'Pocket Flask, the Property of Edward de Valera, with his initials on case' (2 guineas).

Purchasers could secure other tokens such as letters and books autographed by rebels, copies of their own poetry and publications, and portrait sketches (5 guineas for Patrick Pearse by Lily Williams). Plunkett's copy of the first collected edition of Yeats's *Poems* (1895, 'very scarce') was sold for £15, whereas Michael Mallin's collection of Indian lepidoptera and two of his autographed music books fetched only £1 10s. Other tempting lots included 'Cumann-na-mBan Brooch (Auxiliary of the Irish Volunteers), and Volunteer Button', and a potpourri comprising 'Volunteer Marching Song, two pages; Volunteer Christmas Card; two Flag Badges; five Sinn Féin Stamps, blue, and Badge; Water-colour Sketch, with S.F. stamp attached'. 'An anonymous donor' contributed a full set of the *Catholic Bulletin* bound in half calf, the vehicle for 'Events of Easter Week' having itself become a collector's item. A copy of *Irish War News* circulated during Easter Week fetched no less than £2, outdoing 'a handbill of the Proclamation of the "Irish Republic"'(18s.). Centennial connoisseurs and collectors can only dream of what they might have snapped up at the Mansion House in 1917. Far larger sums were paid for items with no iconographic value – blank canvases presented by Lavery and Orpen, on which well-heeled self-determinators could have their portraits painted.[20]

The importance of tokens and souvenirs was equally evident immediately after Ulster Day. Two days later, the Ulster Day Committee appointed a sub-committee to edit 'a Souvenir for Ulster Week', of which 5,000 copies were ordered a month later: 'It was decided not to bind up the Certificate Covenants in the Souvenir.'[21] The vellum certificates themselves instantly became historic artefacts, a marketing opportunity exploited by Henry Savage, a painter and decorator with a shop in High Street, Newtownards. As Savage declared a week after Ulster Day:

You have signed the Covenant ... Your next duty is to have it neatly framed; as this Solemn Document is of permanent historic interest, and should be preserved as an inspiration to future generations. I have prepared a series of Attractive Frames, samples of which may be seen in my window. Those living at a distance have only to post their Certificates to the undermentioned address, and they will receive the Covenant handsomely framed and securely packed, from 6d to 3/6. DON'T DELAY, POST TO-DAY.

[20] Canvases by John Lavery (6' × 3', framed) and William Orpen (only 25" × 30") sold for 600 and 210 guineas, respectively.
[21] Ulster Day Committee, Minutes (30 September, 30 October 1912), D1327/2/7, Public Record Office of Northern Ireland.

This appeal was reinforced by a reporter for the *Newtownards Chronicle and County Down Observer*: 'You will want to preserve the copy of the Covenant you signed so that it can be handed down for years to come untarnished. The best way to do so is to get it neatly framed, as all loyal Covenanters are doing.'[22] Having helped to make history, participants became its guardians.

Another enduring memento was the 'Covenant button', still a subject of banter in Cavan in September 1916. During a petty-sessions hearing arising from a fight in the town on Lady Day (15 August), one of the protagonists was asked: 'Are you another of the button men?' Since Lady Day (along with St Patrick's Day) was the major festival of the Ancient Order of Hibernians, the 'button men' may have been followers of Joseph Devlin. When the servant-boy Michael Tierney denied wearing a button, his solicitor declared: 'It is no disgrace to wear a button. The Ulster Covenanters wear a button.' This observation from the nationalist member for West Cavan (Vincent Kennedy) drew a sarcastic response from his legal adversary: 'It is a glorious thing to wear a Covenant button.'[23]

'Ireland's Solemn League and Covenant' was one of several decorative keepsakes of the campaign against Conscription in 1918. The verso image, incorporating an ingeniously worded endorsement by the united Catholic hierarchy, was headed by the four provincial coats of arms, the names and titles of each prelate being preceded by a cross conferring, extra-sacred authority.[24] A Cork printer issued the pledge, under a mitre, as 'The Bishops' Pledge against Conscription', with spaces for signatures under the heading 'Family Record' and a menacing motto ('Amach leis an sasanach' or 'let the English get out'). When the example of the Ulster 'Women's Declaration' was belatedly imitated on St Colmcille's Day (9 June 1918), it too generated an ornamental certificate with the provincial arms and images associated with the patron saint of Derry and Raphoe. The title was 'Lá na mBan: A Solemn Pledge for the Women of Ireland'.[25] In Ballyhaunis, County Mayo, contributors to the National Defence Fund (aimed at 'resisting the Tyranny of Conscription, and saving the Irish Race and Nation from Slavery, Disaster and Destruction') likewise received a certificate. This featured a gold harp

---

[22] *Newtownards Chronicle*, 5 October 1912.   [23] *Anglo-Celt*, 2 September 1916.
[24] The souvenir was drawn by J. J. O'Reilly and printed by Wilson, Hartnell & Co. (Dublin), with photographs by Keogh Brothers, Lafayette, and Cashman.
[25] Along with Patrick, St Columba (otherwise Colmcille) was designated a Patron of Ireland, whose death on Iona in 597 was celebrated on 9 June: *The Irish Catholic Directory and Almanac for 1920* (Dublin: James Duffy, 1920), p. xiv. For an account of '"Woman's Day" in Dublin', stating that 'handbills were freely circulated' containing the pledge and other declarations as Cumann na mBan and other bodies marched to City Hall for the main ceremony, see *Weekly Irish Times*, 15 June 1918.

on a green background – the design used for one of the flags raised on the GPO in 1916, hitherto an emblem of constitutional nationalism.[26] This resonance was amplified by the motto 'God Save Ireland'. By the end of the campaign in November 1918, nationalist mantelpieces must have been ablaze with green, white, gold, and Celtic characters.

IV

Through long practice of annual commemorative ceremonies, advocates of Ulster's cause or the 'ideals' of Easter Week effortlessly inserted these episodes into the Irish commemorative calendar. Ulster Day was widely celebrated in anniversary services between 1913 and 1915, even by clergymen such as Frederick MacNeice, who had declined to sign the Covenant or endorse its content despite his involvement as a chaplain in the Loyal Orange Institution. In Carrickfergus, MacNeice used the first anniversary to counteract sectarianism, ordaining 'a day of prayer for Ireland' with a 'devotional' service of almost 'penitential character', inviting participation 'by men and women of goodwill no matter what their political opinions'.[27] In his morning sermon on the Lord's Prayer, MacNeice declared that 'a great worry has been done on our side' through 'appeals ... to race hatred, and to religious, or rather irreligious bigotry'. He went on to deplore the implications of Home Rule and to warn that 'its passing will be, as we fear, the signal for strife and war – civil war – in which the treasure will be squandered and lives lost'. But he warned the congregation that, if Home Rule were to secure a popular mandate in the United Kingdom, 'we shall have to consider afresh our responsibilities' and, as always, seek guidance from God.[28]

Most of his fellow clergymen, however, devoted their anniversary sermons to reiterating Ulster's case against Home Rule and the need for continued vigilance and solidarity as Home Rule shuffled towards the Statute Book. In Newtownards, the recently ordained Church of Ireland curate attracted striking subheadings in bold type in the *Newtownards Chronicle*: 'We simply want to do our work and to play our part ... A Government whose policy would be dictated by the Church of Rome ... It may come to pass that we shall have to fight for our liberty.' Momentarily reverting to more pious sentiments, he continued:

[26] Images of these certificates are accessible through the NLI catalogue (EPH D44, D21, D108). For discussion of flags flown in 1916, see G. A. Hayes-McCoy, *A History of Irish Flags from Earliest Times* (Dublin: Academy Press, 1979), pp. 206–220; Charles Townshend, *Easter 1916: The Irish Rebellion* (London: Allen Lane, 2005), pp. 159–160.

[27] *Carrickfergus Advertiser*, 26 September 1913.

[28] *Carrickfergus Advertiser*, 3 October 1913.

Let us pray for deliverance from such a horror. Nevertheless we must face the fact that our forefathers did not shirk the battlefield to defend their country from Roman Catholic interference. If fighting is again necessary, let there be no faltering when the great decision is made. We are prepared to lay down our lives before we allow the domination of the Church of Rome to make this country into a hell.[29]

The speaker, L. V. Uprichard, became a prominent Orangeman, not merely as a chaplain but as a county Grand Master.[30] The fact that the anniversary was immediately preceded by a meeting of the Ulster Unionist Council at the Ulster Hall which approved plans for a provisional government, and a general review of the Ulster Volunteer Force at Balmoral, highlighted the grim implications of the moral commitment sealed in September 1912.[31]

The next anniversary service in Carrickfergus, in the second month of war, cemented the continuity between the Covenant, the Ulster Volunteers, and the new 36th (Ulster) Division. MacNeice faced a crowded congregation, following 'a church parade of the Ulster Volunteers of Carrickfergus and district', in which company commanders marched their men to service 'equipped with caps, belts, and armlets'. 'The Clandeboye contingent' was absent, being already in training for overseas service with the Ulster Division. MacNeice reminded the congregation that 'many of them recently were nobly ready to sacrifice much for their country. Let them, face to face with possibly the greatest struggle of the nations in history, learn to sacrifice something for internal peace . . . They would show their fellow-countrymen . . . that they might be of different religious faith and politics and yet be at one in their love of the Empire, their loyalty to the King.'[32] Already, two years after the original Ulster Day, the meaning of the event had been transformed from a veiled threat of rebellion to an affirmation of shared imperial loyalty.

Even so, it proved difficult to avoid partisan declarations out of keeping with the hastily agreed 'party truce'. Less than a fortnight before the third Ulster Day, the unionist party had walked out of the House of Commons in protest at the government's decision, approved by Redmond's nationalists, to simultaneously enact and suspend Home Rule. In Bangor, Canon Peacocke's Ulster Day congregation included half a battalion of Ulster Volunteers who had paraded through large crowds to the parish

[29] *Newtownards Chronicle*, 4 October 1913.
[30] Leonard Victor Uprichard (1888–1959), later rector of Coleraine (1930–1959) and canon of St Anne's cathedral, Belfast (1945–1959); Grand Master, Co. Londonderry (1933–1959).
[31] The Provisional Government was publicly announced on the preceding Wednesday, 24 September, and the review was held on the Saturday: *Newtownards Chronicle*, 27 September, 4 October 1913.
[32] *Carrickfergus Advertiser*, 2 October 1914.

church. Peacocke, a future bishop who spent the last sixty-six years of his life as an Orange Grand Chaplain of Ireland,[33] assured them that 'we Ulster Covenanters have not moved a foot from the position which we had taken up ... But for the present – while the war lasts and the Empire's very existence is at stake – the question of Home Rule stands to one side.' The war was paramount:

It is the war news for which we rush to the papers: it is the war news we discuss with one another: the one question which absorbs the thought of every loyal man and woman all over the Empire, is the question, How can I help against Germany?[34]

Yet the decision by King George V to enact the hated Government of Ireland Bill still rankled among some unionists, as evident from an address given by an Ulster Volunteer commander in Newtownards before leading his men to the First Presbyterian Church for the anniversary service. The rather condescending speaker was Montserrat Henry Walker, a wealthy linen miller and magistrate:

The first duty of the Volunteers was loyalty to the King – even although he had signed the Home Rule Bill. The King, now, had not the power many people imagined, and he had to sign the Bills presented to him ... He knew that many people were saying now that the Bill was on the Statute Book they need not be loyal ... it would never be the law of the land in Ulster. Therefore he would impress on them that no matter what any person said, their duty was to be loyal to the King.

This message was reinforced by Dr William Wright, another prominent Orange chaplain,[35] who rejoiced in his sermon that 'the Loyalists of Ulster were proving day by day that they were willing to give everything – even the best of their men – in this great crisis that meant life and death to them all'. Three hundred men had already joined up from Newtownards, 'but he would like to see many others going'.[36]

As the third anniversary approached, the need to uphold the 'Party Truce' prompted a directive from the standing committee of the Ulster Unionist Council, supported by leaders of the three major Protestant churches, to avoid 'any meetings or observances of a political kind in connection with the anniversary of "Ulster Day"'. Instead, the anniversary would be observed 'as a day of humiliation and intercession with the

[33] Joseph Irvine Peacocke (1866–1962), Rector of Bangor (1903–1916), Bishop of Derry and Raphoe (1916–1944); Grand Chaplain of Ireland (1896–1962).
[34] *County Down Spectator*, 2 October 1914.
[35] William Wright (1856–1919), Presbyterian minister, 1st Newtownards (1879–1919), Deputy Grand Chaplain of Ireland (1901–1919).
[36] *Newtownards Chronicle*, 3 October 1914.

Lord of Hosts to preserve our King and Empire, safeguard our gallant
soldiers and sailors and crown our arms with victory'. As in 1912, 'where
it is deemed advisable local committees should be appointed to arrange
such Services in conjunction with the clergy': in Belfast, a 'special united
Service' was arranged in the Ulster Hall.[37] The address was given by Dr
Henry Montgomery, the former Presbyterian moderator who had helped
draft the Covenant: 'Whilst their Service that day was to be purely
religious, they did not forget, nor did they regret, what had been done
in that city and province three years ago. They commended their cause,
then, to God in prayer, and where they stood then they stood now, by the
help of the Almighty.'[38]

In Bangor, Canon Peacocke bemoaned the tortuous pace of the war:

Our Ulster lads who had joined the regiments of the Ulster Division ... had no
idea that 12 months would still see them in England ... After all that has been
sacrificed and spent, we seem to have advanced so little – the projects of the Allies
seem to have made so little headway towards their accomplishment, and the calls
upon us are greater than ever.

He warned of the moral perils associated with war, wearily admitting that
'it would have been easier metaphorically to have waved the Union Jack
and to have denounced our country's foes'.[39] By the following anniversary, the Ulster Division had finally reached the front, and the battle of the
Somme had become the focus of instant history in Protestant Ulster. No
further Ulster Day services have been traced.

In the case of the anti-Conscription pledge, the armistice had resolved
the ostensible issue even before the first anniversary in April 1919, while
the subsequent eruption of violence made protestations of communal
solidarity based on passive resistance seem outmoded and irrelevant.
The fact that the pledge was taken within a few days of the anniversary
of the rebellion also discouraged separate commemoration, as
Republicans drew no distinction between the aspirations that inspired
the proclamation of a Republican state and the repudiation of 'the right of
the British Government to enforce compulsory service in this country'.

Even Easter Week was unmarked by systematic anniversary celebrations in the early years. The Catholic Hierarchy never endorsed the
strategy of violent rebellion and would not have countenanced celebratory services, and secular celebrations were curtailed by Defence of the
Realm regulations. Public observance of the first anniversary in 1917 was
particularly restricted by the temporary prohibition of assemblies in
Dublin, and in Cork by Bishop Cohalan's instruction through his clergy

---

[37] *Irish Times*, 16 September 1915.   [38] *Irish Times*, 27 September 1915.
[39] *County Down Spectator*, 1 October 1915.

'that there shall be no processions or demonstrations in the streets on the occasion of memorial Masses for those who fell in Dublin during the rebellion, as they would only lead to conflict and disorder'.[40] Nevertheless, informal celebrations were reported on Easter Monday (9 April) as well as 24 April, with the display of Sinn Féin bunting, surreptitious hoisting of flags, stone-throwing, and vandalism. The Easter Monday crowds included people wearing 'black bands, surmounted with ribbons of the *Sinn Fein* colours on their arms, while groups of girls, with paper flags and coloured papers in their hair, paraded Sackville street'. On 22 April, flags were waved from Dublin tramcars and 'small shop-keepers did a brisk trade in photographs of rebel leaders'. Two days later, police in Carrickmore, Co Tyrone, were temporarily confounded by flags on treetops, which were secured by cutting down the offending trees.[41]

In 1918, memorial Masses were held in Cork on Easter Monday (1 April), but Sinn Féin organisers abandoned a procession to the Catholic cathedral when prohibited by the police.[42] Decorating the GPO had already become a Republican counterpart to the Orangemen's former custom of 'dressing the statue' of William III in College Green on 12 July. But the new custom was already in decline by Easter Monday 1919:

The gaunt walls of the burned-out General Post Office in Sackville street were yesterday kept under pretty close observation by both uniformed and plain clothes police officers. There was apparently an idea that the Sinn Feiners might again scale the broken heights of the roofless building, and 'decorate' the statues with republican tri-coloured flags, as on former anniversaries of the Easter Monday Rebellion of 1916. No one essayed the climb on Monday, however.[43]

Official commemoration of Easter Week did not get underway until the first ceremony at Arbour Hill on 3 May 1924, the eighth anniversary of the first batch of executions.[44] Tidy commemoration continued to be hampered by the absence of a clear calendar focus: should it mark Easter Monday, or the actual anniversary of the outbreak, or that of the executions? Unofficial functions were often marred by rival ceremonies staged by hostile political and military factions, each claiming its legacy.[45] As with Ulster Day after the outbreak of war, the meaning of Easter Week was fundamentally changed by what followed, drawing a sharp division

[40] *Irish Independent*, 23 April 1917.
[41] *Irish Times*, 10 April 1917; *Irish Independent*, 23 April; *Ulster Herald*, 28 April.
[42] *Weekly Irish Times*, 6 April 1918.   [43] *Weekly Irish Times*, 26 April 1919.
[44] *Irish Times*, 5 April 1924.
[45] David Fitzpatrick, 'Commemoration in the Irish Free State: A Chronicle of Embarrassment' in Ian McBride (ed.), *History and Memory in Modern Ireland* (Cambridge: Cambridge University Press, 2001), pp. 184–203 (esp. 196–198).

between the vivid experiences of contemporaries and the bizarre historical constructions of the event forged during and after the subsequent revolution.

V

The street theatre of 1912, 1916, and 1918 would have fallen flat, had it failed to embody the passions, hopes, and resentments associated with past history. The Covenanters of 1912 imagined that they were impersonating those of 1643, while those of 1918 were using the tools and texts of their Ulster predecessors to bully the government into abandonment of an obnoxious policy. By proclaiming their affinity to those who had risen 'six times during the past three hundred years', the rebels of 1916 were invoking not just the manly tradition of physical force but also the quixotic doctrine that heroic failure in battle only strengthened the case for renewed war. The solidarity mustered in 1912 and 1918 was immediate and obvious, whereas that generated by 1916 was retrospective, just as the military failures of 1798, 1848, and 1867 had perversely provided moral underpinning for subsequent non-violent nationalist campaigns. The Dublin performance in 1916, superficially an arrogant assertion of ideological superiority by an unpopular élite, also conveyed the prospect of a future change of outlook on the part of the hostile or indifferent spectators. Dubliners were given a glimpse of what they too might be saying, and perhaps doing, in the future.

All three performances of instant history had a genuinely transformative impact on Ireland's future political trajectory, though not as intended by the script-writers. The only campaign to achieve its ostensible aim was the protest against Conscription, yet no subsequent phase of the Irish revolution achieved comparable levels of political consensus and popular mobilisation among non-unionists. Home Rule in six counties of Ulster, and dominion status for the remainder of Ireland, was scarcely a triumphant outcome for Ulster's campaign against Home Rule in 'Ulster, as well as . . . the whole of Ireland'. The defensive urban insurrection of 1916 provided a powerful negative example for the military campaigns of 1917–1923, which relied initially on mass mobilisation of Volunteers in open defiance of the government, followed by guerrilla attacks designed to maximise enemy losses rather than Republican martyrdom. The ideals proclaimed in 1916 were progressively modified or abandoned by most of those claiming to venerate them, whether followers of Collins, de Valera or Adams. Yet, the fact that the objectives of 1912 and 1916 were never attained only intensified their retrospective appeal. Later generations, tarnished and troubled by subsequent compromises, looked back to a golden age of honest, hot-blooded assertion of belief. In this delusion, they were assisted by the relentless propaganda of politicians claiming the legacy of the 'founding fathers', especially by the surviving activists of 1912 and 1916 who for so long dominated politics in the two Irish states.

Thus the events of 1912, 1916, and 1918 were not merely performances of 'instant history', but re-enactments of past episodes and inspirations for the future. Each episode was performed and commemorated in the manner of a religious rite, in which biblical precedents (Abraham's covenant with God, Christ's crucifixion) gave additional force to the notion that the actors were trustees of a sacred legacy and obligation. The historical chain was tenuous, in the sense that past events were wilfully manipulated and misinterpreted by rebel re-enactors, while the aspirations of 1912 and 1916 were ruthlessly abused by those who claimed their legacy. Yet, the fact that rebels and commemorators alike practised bad history does not invalidate the actual historical continuities outlined in this paper. Ideas about history, whether credible or misinformed, continue to colour Irish political debate to a degree remarkable in the formerly 'British Isles', at least. Their power in the revolutionary era was to become still greater, helping to persuade myriad Irish men and women that they were not merely spectators of events, but history-makers.

VI

To what extent is my categorisation of 'instant history' applicable to Irish involvement in the Great War, most dramatically exhibited on the Somme in July 1916? In several respects, the performance of war differed radically from home protests and rebellions. First, the basic plot was determined not by Irishmen but by the politicians, strategists, and commanders whose decisions embroiled millions in the attritional trench warfare epitomised by the first battle of the Somme. Second, the Irish element was only part of a multi-ethnic drama in which it was difficult to distinguish the relative intensity of suffering, heroism, and bravura displayed by Irish and non-Irish participants. Third, the Irish audience neither witnessed the performance nor interacted with the performers, being reliant on censored and highly coloured retrospective reports.

Despite these impediments, the advocates of Ulster's mobilisation in the Great War did their best to convert the First Day of the Somme into almost instant history, in the hope of bolstering home support for the war effort. Since the attack failed, at appalling human cost, to achieve any significant military gain, the Somme advance (like the Dublin rebellion) was best imagined as a glorious defeat. Germans continued to control Thiepval, British politicians and generals continued to recriminate, but Ireland's military reputation prospered. Stories of personal heroism and *esprit de corps* in the Ulster Division seemed all the more impressive in the context of reckless planning, poor intelligence, and other command failures that were gradually revealed after an initial surge of optimism. As in the case of the Anzacs, whose first blooding at Gallipoli was promptly perceived as a national *rite de passage* in Australia and (to some extent) New Zealand, national pride and loyalty to imperial ideals proved compatible with resentment at the arrogance and incompetence of the British government and high command. Whether in Australasia or Ulster, such strategic failures demonstrated that the British Empire was too valuable to be left under solely British control. If Australasia and Ulster needed the empire, the empire needed their full involvement if it were truly to become a commonwealth.

The heroic if futile endeavours of the 36th (Ulster) Division provided an irresistible loyalist narrative, with Thiepval as the latest instalment in Ulster's age-old struggle for civil and religious liberty. Despite Ulster's relatively weak tradition of service in the pre-war British army, and the fact that Ulster unionism was dominated by merchant and manufacturing families with typically shallow military roots, propagandists were able to sacralise the Somme by joining it with the Boyne. Incorporation of the Somme into the Orange litany of commemoration was eased by the accident that the Somme offensive of 1 July, having been postponed for two days because of rain, coincided with the 226th anniversary of the battle of the Boyne (old-style).

The assimilation of the 'charge of the Ulster division' into the serial narrative of Protestant loyalism was easily accomplished. After all, most members of the division in July 1916 were indeed veterans of the UVF and therefore signatories of the Ulster Covenant.[46] Throughout almost two years of training, the activities and spirit of the Ulster Division had been minutely chronicled by every unionist newspaper in Ulster: they had become heroes long before facing the enemy. Many belonged to the Loyal Orange Institution, often joining military lodges formed during training in Ireland or England. For such men, their first (and often last) taste of combat at the Somme was an opportunity to demonstrate Ulster's once

---

[46] Non-Orangemen enlisting in the newly formed UVF were required to present a witnessed declaration on a printed form that they had signed the 'Ulster Covenant', giving the place of signature (Orangemen were to enlist through their lodges). A specimen form used in Cookstown, Co Tyrone, was submitted by District Inspector S. R. Kingston to his County Inspector on 28 December 1912, five days before the first public enrolment: CO 904/27/2, National Archives, London.

questionable loyalty, unsapped by the poor leadership offered by English commanders and the inadequacy of supporting units and artillery. The fact that many members carried Bibles distributed in camp by the English Orange institution, while some allegedly sported orange handkerchiefs or favours, gave dramatic form to the equation of their battle of the Somme with Ulster's unending struggle for liberty.

This equation was promptly and widely asserted in the unionist press, providing a powerful narrative of instant history and the framework for commemoration over the next century. Unlike the landings at Helles and Suvla in April and August 1915, the long-awaited attempt to break through the German lines on the Somme was almost immediately the subject of detailed press despatches and personal accounts.[47] Within a week of the Thiepval advance, provincial newspapers carried an anonymous tribute written on the second day, evidently by an officer of the 36th Division: 'How Ulster Troops Led the Attack. An Eye-Witness's Stirring Story.' This became a foundation text for commemoration: 'I am not an Ulsterman, but yesterday, the 1st July, as I followed their amazing attack I felt that I would rather be an Ulsterman than anything else in this world.'[48]

The Ulstermen had been 'suddenly let loose as they charged over the two front lines of enemy trenches, shouting "No Surrender, boys" ... battalion after battalion came out of the awful wood as steadily as I have seen them at Ballykinlar, Clandeboye, or Shane's Castle.' Having cleared the fourth line without sufficient support from the flanks, they had gone ahead regardless of an order to halt:

The order arrived too late, or perhaps the Ulstermen, mindful that it was the anniversary of the Boyne, would not be denied, but pressed on. I could see only a small portion of this advance, but could watch our men go forward, seem to escape the shell fire by miracle, and now, much reduced indeed, enter the fifth line of the enemy trenches, our final objective. It could not be held, however, as the Division had advanced into a narrow salient.

All key elements of the Somme story were already present: echoes of the siege of Derry and battle of the Boyne, reckless courage, and astonishing feats undermined by inadequate planning. The tragic narrative was sustained, week after week, by publication of shocking local casualty lists, elegiac verses, official despatches honouring the Ulstermen, and letters

---

[47] Philip Orr, *The Road to the Somme: Men of the Ulster Division Tell Their Story* (Belfast: Blackstaff Press, 1987), pp. 194–197.

[48] *County Down Spectator*, 7 July 1916. Similar but variant accounts appeared in the first detailed account of the Ulstermen in the *Belfast News-Letter* of the same date: Orr, *Road to the Somme*, p. 194.

from the front showing little sign of censorship beyond absence of place names. Such was the torrent of information that those at home could visualise the battle more colourfully, if less accurately, than the participants themselves.

By comparison with the rapid proliferation of works purporting to explain the Dublin rebellion, detailed chronicles of the Ulster Division on the Somme were slow to appear. The first sustained treatment was three chapters in Michael MacDonagh's *The Irish on the Somme*, introduced by John Redmond and published in 1917. Though devoting twice as much space and vastly more enthusiasm to the daredevil feats and genial characteristics of the 16th Division, MacDonagh's book made a point of being inclusive. This was in keeping with Redmond's view of the war as a path towards reconciliation in Ireland: 'I am as proud of the Ulster regiments as I am of the Nationalist regiments.'[49] The next sustained narrative was a surprisingly balanced 'souvenir of Peace Day' on 6 August 1919, 'presented on behalf of the Citizens of Belfast by the Citizens' Committee to the Ulster Service Men'.[50] Though this emphatically unionist publication gave what might be deemed 'undue prominence' to the Ulster Division, the space allotted to the two Irish divisions and the 'Old Contemptibles' was actually greater.[51] Echoing Redmond's sentiments, the preface declared that 'no distinction is made in the measure of praise that is due to Irishmen of all creeds and classes who joined His Majesty's Forces in a period of great national emergency'.[52]

A divisional history by Captain Cyril Falls appeared three years later, 'under the patronage' of Lord Carson, Sir James Craig, and the divisional commander Sir Oliver Nugent. In his introduction, Field-Marshal Lord Plumer drily noted the focus on 'glorious failures', and the lack of 'reference to any great strategical movements or brilliant tactical operations, because there were none such to describe'.[53] Though Falls devoted only one of his sixteen chapters to 'The Battle of the Somme', it was that catastrophic initiation which most captured public imagination and shaped all subsequent remembrance of the Ulster Division.

The religious thrust of Ulster's sacrifice was immediately expressed in the Orange anniversary services that replaced the cancelled Twelfth

---

[49] Michael MacDonagh, *The Irish on the Somme: Being the Second Series of 'The Irish at the Front'* (London: Hodder & Stoughton, 1917), p. 5.
[50] *The Great War, 1914–1918: Ulster Greets Her Brave and Faithful Sons and Remembers Her Glorious Dead* (Belfast: W. & G. Baird, 1919).
[51] 34 pages were directly devoted to 'The 36th (Ulster) Division', 14 to 'The 10th Division at Gallipoli', 9 to 'Ulster in the 16th division', and 27 to 'The Old Contemptibles'.
[52] *The Great War*, p. [5].
[53] Cyril Falls, *The History of the 36th (Ulster) Division* (London: Constable, 1922), esp. pp. ix–xiii.

processions in 1916. In Ballycarry Presbyterian Church, Co Antrim, on the preceding Sunday, the anniversary service was 'both commemorative and intercessional'. An additional memorial service for 'Carrick's dead heroes' was held at St Nicholas's parish church on 13 August, the 'musical part of the service' being supplied by the band of the 4th battalion, Royal Irish Rifles, while the offertory was devoted to the UVF Patriotic Fund. Having declared that 'the choice was between war and dishonour', Frederick MacNeice spoke of the 'price paid' for the safety of those at home: 'the price is the blood of our townsmen. Their sacrifice on the fields of France should be followed by our conservation here in Ireland . . . Henceforth let life be fuller of love and sympathy, let your aims be higher, your interests wider.'[54] By July 1917, commemoration of the Somme was embedded in Orange services and platform resolutions as well as anniversary services of intercession, and a year later, Beadle's painting of the charge of the Ulster Division was first reproduced on a lodge banner.[55] And so Ulster's Somme story was projected forwards as a renewed inspiration for Orangemen and unionists, incorporated into a growing portfolio of commemorative events. Though the cult of 1 July 1916 has never faltered, its political meaning (like that of all the episodes discussed in this paper) was to be bitterly contested as paramilitary groups and their apologists claimed the Somme heritage.

By contrast, the heroism and suffering of the Irish at Gallipoli never became the stuff of national legend, despite the strenuous efforts of Redmond, the early historians of the 10th Division, and survivors of the campaign. This reminds us that Irish history is littered with instant histories which misfired, as well as those which periodically revitalised familiar historical narratives and, in some cases, transformed Ireland's political history. Is Ireland exceptional in the extent to which politics has been performed through historical re-enactment? Is the current commemorative obsession proof of Irish exceptionalism in this respect, or merely the outcome of a political calculation, designed to improve Anglo-Irish and North–South relations by identifying common ground in a neutralised past? And, finally, when and where will it all end?

[54] *Carrickfergus Advertiser*, 14 July, 18 August 1916.
[55] See David Hume (ed.), *Battles beyond the Boyne* (Belfast: GOL of Ireland, 2005), p. 40; Jane Leonard, 'Memorials of the Great War in County Down, 1914–1939' in Mike King (ed.), *County Down at War, 1850–1945* (Downpatrick: Down County Museum, 2004), pp. 51–63 (at 55).

Hard service: remembering the Abbey
     Theatre's rebels

Fearghal McGarry

> You have given us the most important part of history – its lies . . . I don't
> believe that events have been shaped so much by the facts as by the lies
> that people believed about them.
>
> W. B. Yeats to Lady Gregory, on reading her autobiographical account
> of the Easter Rising.[1]

I

On 23 July 1966, the Taoiseach Seán Lemass addressed an audience at
the Abbey Theatre to pay tribute to seven rebels who had fought in the
Easter Rising. They included the actor Sean Connolly, who led the opening attack against Dublin Castle; Máire Nic Shiubhlaigh, the Abbey's first
leading lady who had served at Jacob's factory; and Helena Molony, who
fought with the Citizen Army. The best known were the Abbey Theatre's
former prop-man, Peadar Kearney, author of the Irish national anthem,
and the Hollywood actor Arthur Shields. Largely forgotten by then were
the theatre's long-serving usher, Nellie Bushell, and Barney Murphy, a
former stage-hand who had fought at the Four Courts but was remembered at the Abbey as the prompter with no respect for dramatic pauses.

Only two remained alive. Molony, frail and wheelchair-bound,
attended the ceremony. She died several months later. Unable to travel
from California due to ill-health, Arthur Shields was represented by his
daughter Christine. Relatives of the deceased rebels attended the 'brief,
dignified, ceremony'.[2] The presence of Máire Nic Shiubhlaigh's sister,
Gypsy, her brother Frank, and the 86-year-old carpenter, Sean Barlow,
represented the Abbey's last living links to the turn-of-the-century cultural revival. The quote inscribed on the cheap plaque – 'It is hard service
they take that help me' – came from *Cathleen ni Houlihan*, the 1902 play

---

[1] Lady Isabella Augusta Gregory, *Seventy Years: 1852–1922*, ed. Colin Smythe (Gerrard's
Cross: Colin Smythe, 1974), p. 549.
[2] *Irish Times*, 25 July 1966.

which, more than any other work in the Abbey's repertoire, symbolised the link between the revival and the Irish revolution. Set in 1798, the Year of the French, Yeats's and Lady Gregory's powerful evocation of the willingness of young men to sacrifice their lives had been widely credited with popularising insurrectionary ideals among the younger generation which brought about the rebellion of 1916.

Yeats, admittedly, had a hand in promoting this notion. When he accepted his Nobel Prize in 1923, he insisted that the political revolution had been a product of the literary revival in which he and the Abbey's founders had played such a central role. He continued to promote this idea, most notably in lines learned by later generations of schoolchildren: 'Did that play of mine send out/Certain men the English shot?'[3] But he was not the first to suggest the connection. Before the Rising, the Irish Party politician Stephen Gwynn had famously asked whether 'such plays should be produced unless one was prepared for people to go out to shoot and be shot'.[4] The journalist P. J. Little, who met Yeats on the street shortly after the rebellion, recalled that 'by way of a joke, I said to him that I would tell the British authorities that he, with his *Kathleen ni Houlihan*, was responsible for the Rising'.[5]

There were also intriguing connections between the event and the play. The role of Cathleen on the Abbey's opening night had been played by Máire Nic Shiubhlaigh, who went on to perform in what she described as 'the greatest drama of all' in 1916.[6] Among the 'certain men' whom Yeats fretted that he had sent out was the first rebel fatality, Sean Connolly, whose final performance at the Abbey was in its March 1916 production of *Cathleen ni Houlihan*. After the revolution, the Abbey became the first theatre in the English-speaking world to receive a state subsidy, a tacit acknowledgement of its political significance. The Irish National Theatre's advocates – including its long-serving managing director, Ernest Blythe – were rarely slow thereafter to draw attention to the Abbey's role in raising 'the fighting spirit of the people . . . making possible the hard military and political effort which secured the establishment of a sovereign Irish state'.[7]

---

[3] W. B. Yeats, 'The Man and the Echo', in *Last Poems and Two Plays* (Dublin: The Cuala Press, 1939), pp. 27–29.

[4] Colin Reid, *The Lost Ireland of Stephen Gwynn. Irish Constitutional Nationalism and Cultural Politics, 1864–1950* (Manchester: Manchester University Press, 2011), pp. 52–53.

[5] Bureau of Military History (BMH) witness statement (WS) 1769 (P. J. Little), (Irish) Military Archives.

[6] Maire Nic Shiubhlaigh, *The Splendid Years. Recollections of Maire Nic Shiubhlaigh; as told to Edward Kenny* (Dublin: Duffy, 1955).

[7] Ernest Blythe, *The Abbey Theatre* (Dublin: National Theatre Society, 1963).

The historical reality was, inevitably, more complex than the myth.[8] Most of those honoured in 1966 had actually broken with the Abbey prior to the Rising as a result of their political commitment, and only one attributed their politicisation to Yeats's influence. In contrast to the theatre's 'elitist, reformist, Ascendancy' founders,[9] its players and staff were mainly working-class Catholics. Many were committed to radical impulses such as feminism and socialism. By 1966, however, these ideals were largely obscured from popular memory, as was the role played in the Abbey's founding by Inghinidhe na hÉireann (the militant women's organisation with which several of the rebels were associated). The popular identification of Yeats with the Easter Rising, an event in which he played no part, was reflected by both the ubiquity of references to the rebellion as 'a terrible beauty' and the *Sunday Independent*'s observation that the purpose of the commemoration was to honour the seven men and women who took 'part in the fighting for which the tone of so many Abbey plays had conditioned the nation'.[10]

In 'official' commemoration, the dead often appear to be little more than props, trapped in myths of other's making. But to what extent did these individuals exert agency over how their lives would be remembered by recording their own narratives of 1916? Analysing the wide variety of recorded memories the Abbey rebels left behind, this chapter considers how and why these narratives were constructed and transmitted, and the extent to which the reception of their stories was shaped by subsequent social and political shifts.

II

Products of pre-war Dublin's tiny revolutionary subculture, the Abbey's rebels were (with the exception of the more youthful Shields) politicised during the turn-of-the-century revival. Most progressed from the Gaelic League to more militant republican organisations. Kearney swore an oath to the Irish Republican Brotherhood (IRB) in 1904. Nic Shiubhlaigh and Molony joined Inghinidhe na hÉireann, while Connolly belonged to its dramatic company. Ellen Bushell, a silk weaver, made kilts for Na Fianna Éireann, a republican scout movement with which Barney Murphy and

---

[8] For further biographical details, see Fearghal McGarry, *The Abbey Rebels of 1916. A Lost Revolution* (Dublin: Gill & Macmillan, 2015).

[9] Lauren Arrington, *W. B. Yeats, the Abbey Theatre, Censorship, and the Irish State* (Oxford: Oxford University Press, 2010), p. 2.

[10] Roisín Higgins, *Transforming 1916. Meaning, Memory and the Fiftieth Anniversary of the Easter Rising* (Cork: Cork University Press, 2012), pp. 162–164; *Sunday Independent*, 24 July 1966.

Molony were also associated. All were subsequently swept up in the militarisation of politics triggered by the Ulster crisis and Lockout. Kearney, Murphy and Shields joined the Irish Volunteers; Connolly and Molony enlisted in the Irish Citizen Army, while Nic Shiubhlaigh was a member of Cumann na mBan, the female counterpart to the Irish Volunteers.

Connolly and Molony, who participated in the attack on Dublin Castle, saw the most fighting in 1916, but Arthur Shields fought bravely at the General Post Office. Máire Nic Shiubhlaigh and Peadar Kearney spent a frustrating week confined to Jacob's factory. Although not a combatant, Nellie Bushell was kept busy delivering despatches and scouting for the rebels as they moved between vulnerable outposts in the Liberties. All except Connolly – shot on the roof of City Hall – survived. Molony, captured when City Hall fell to British soldiers, and Shields (who was present at the last stand at Moore Street) were interned in Britain after the rebellion, but the others escaped into the crowds that turned out to observe the spectacle.

They were generally less prominent in the military campaign that followed. Released from Frongoch in August 1916, Arthur Shields heeded Justice Pim's suggestion that he 'go home, stick to the theatre and forget about all this revolutionary nonsense'.[11] Murphy's post-1916 service was 'mostly unofficial'.[12] Bushell played an auxiliary (if dangerous) role for the Volunteers for whom she spied and stored weapons at the Abbey. Nic Shiubhlaigh performed similarly gendered roles: fund-raising, caring for prisoners' dependents, performing at concerts, canvassing and assisting at public rallies and funerals. Having moved to Drogheda to work in a cinema, she was largely out of the revolutionary picture by 1918. Molony returned to the Abbey but, unlike Shields, remained politically active. She served briefly on Sinn Féin's executive in 1917, and later as a Dáil court judge. Due to her high profile as a public speaker, she was kept under observation and raided by the British (and, later, the Irish Free State) authorities.[13] During the War of Independence, Kearney formed part of an informal network of 'unknown soldiers' at Phil Shanahan's Foley Street pub, a haunt for chancers, prostitutes and gunmen up from the country. A fixer, he was responsible for 'procuring and distributing arms, collecting intelligence reports' and other jobs requiring discretion and contacts. Arrested in November 1920, he saw out the war at

[11] *Irish Times*, 28 September 1964.
[12] Bernard Murphy, Military Service Pensions Collection (MSPC), (Irish) Military Archives.
[13] BMH WS 391 (Helena Molony).

Ballykinlar internment camp. A supporter of the Treaty, he worked as a censor in various prisons during the Civil War.[14]

III

How did the Abbey rebels remember their involvement in 1916? How conscious were they that the event in which they had participated was being reshaped in collective memory? To what extent were their own narratives constructed to shape the popular memory of 1916? How did these narratives, and their reception, change over time? There now exists a vast body of sources to allow us to analyse such questions.

The most important 'official' repository of revolutionary 'memory' is the Military Service Pensions (MSP) collection. Its vast archive of 285,000 files – now being digitised by the Military Archives – resulted from the Southern State's decision to compensate revolutionary veterans under a series of pension acts passed between 1923 and 1953.[15] In contrast to the Bureau of Military History (BMH), the light these records shine on the past was a by-product of the MSP's administrative process rather than its purpose. While the government sought primarily to compensate individuals for their service, the scheme (incrementally widened to further categories of recipients) offered a source of political patronage and a means of reintegrating disaffected veterans into society.[16] The process usually involved the submission by applicants of a handwritten account of their activities, supported by references and other evidence including their own oral testimony. Applicants were incentivised to remember actions that constituted 'active service' (although this term was never clearly defined). Kearney, for example, insisted that his role as a prison censor was an intelligence one that required him to be armed. That financial necessity motivated some who would not otherwise have recorded narratives is evident. Applicants were also motivated by other considerations, including a desire to see their role validated. With 66,300 of 82,000 applicants rejected, the process engendered considerable resentment; many of the 15,700 recipients of pensions were also unhappy about the level of award they received.[17]

In a parallel but separate project, the Irish State established the BMH 'to assemble and co-ordinate material to form the basis for the

---

[14] Peadar Kearney, MSPC.
[15] Catriona Crowe (ed.), *Guide to the Military Service (1916–23) Pensions Collection* (Dublin: Óglaigh na hÉireann, 2012).
[16] Marie Coleman, 'Military Service Pensions for Veterans of the Irish Revolution, 1916-123', *War in History* 20 (2013), 201–221.
[17] Crowe, *Pensions Collection*.

compilation of the history of the movement for Independence'.[18] Running from the 1940s to the 1950s, it amassed a large archive of 1,773 first-person 'witness statements'. Released in 2003, it amounted to 36,000 pages of testimony and 150,000 pages of documents. Those who contributed (or refused to submit) statements had many motives. Many felt it important to record the small role they had played in one of the most significant events of their lives, although some sought to settle scores or defend their record for posterity.

Each of the surviving Abbey rebels received a military pension. Although only Molony submitted a witness statement to the BMH, the archive includes correspondence from Nic Shiubhlaigh (relating to her husband Bob Price) and hundreds of references (other people's recorded memories) to the Abbey's rebels. These sources reflect the limitations of retrospective oral evidence: subjectivity, Civil War animosities, the accumulation of subsequent information and impaired memory present obvious difficulties. The investigating officer who recorded Molony's statement noted that her 'memory is not too good. I am of the opinion that she failed to remember many of the activities in which she took part and that in this respect her statement does not do her justice.' Describing her first (oral) attempt at a witness statement (recorded verbatim in March 1949) as 'unintelligible gabble', Molony rewrote much of it before resubmitting it the following May.[19]

Both archives are supplemented by unofficial repositories of memory. Between the 1930s and 1940s, Ernie O'Malley 'criss-crossed Ireland in his old Ford, driving up boreens and searching out old companions in order to record, and in a sense relive, the glory days of the revolution'.[20] His voluminous and near illegible notebooks, detailing interviews with some 450 Volunteers, are now being transcribed and published. In contrast to the BMH, O'Malley's project was motivated more by post-revolutionary

---

[18] Quoted in Fearghal McGarry, *Rebels. Voices from the Easter Rising* (Dublin: Penguin Ireland, 2011), p. xii.

[19] Molony to Kissane, 29 September 1947, BMH S164 (Helena Molony). Although efforts to distinguish between faulty memory, mistaken perceptions and ideologically driven distortion are probably fruitless, discrepancies between recorded testimony and established facts can be readily identified. Molony, for example, downplayed Jim Larkin's republican convictions, misleadingly describing his outlook as 'that of a British Socialist'. She also attributed the ITGWU's lack of support for her efforts to commemorate the Rising in 1917 (by unfurling a banner protesting James Connolly's murder from the roof of Liberty Hall) to Larkin despite the fact that the union was led by Thomas Foran and William O'Brien, an anti-Larkin Connollyite. There are also striking omissions. In a paragraph recounting her opposition to the British war effort, she mentioned that she 'spent the whole of 1914' in France without noting that she worked there (with Maud Gonne MacBride) as a nurse in a French military hospital.

[20] Roy Foster, *Vivid Faces. The Revolutionary Generation in Ireland 1890–1923* (London: Allen Lane, 2014), p. 310.

malaise than a desire for raw material for the State's foundation narrative. Describing his life as a broken one, he was philosophical about the outcome of his revolution: 'I had given allegiance to a certain ideal of freedom as personified by the Irish Republic. It had not been realised except in the mind.'[21] This may have resulted in 'a less sanitized and more embittered memory': while a witness in the BMH recalled that Bob Price 'dearly loved a "half one"', O'Malley's notebooks recorded its consequences.[22]

The impact of these narratives on both historiography and public memory appears to bear out, as Guy Beiner has noted, the claim that 'traditions which have been collected, documented and conserved in an archive can later be resurrected and gain a "second life", once again acquiring social currency'.[23] Since the BMH's digitisation in 2012, over 200,000 users from 178 countries have accessed this collection.[24] Its impact on scholarship, moreover, is evidenced by the recent biographical turn in the historiography. Exploring such themes as education, family, associational activity, intellectual influences and sexuality, biographical studies of leaders, grassroots activists, Easter widows and the children of revolutionaries have deployed personal narrative to recast the revolution, prompting, for example, the revival of a generational explanatory paradigm.[25]

In addition to these recently available sources, there exists a large body of published narratives in the form of autobiographical writing. *The Splendid Years. Recollections of Maire Nic Shiubhlaigh; as Told to Edward Kenny*, published by James Duffy in 1955, was the product of a collaboration between Nic Shiubhlaigh and her nephew. Although written by Kearney's nephew, Seamus de Burca's *The Soldier's Song. The Story of Peadar Kearney*, published in 1957, incorporates Kearney's autobiographical writings and reminiscences.[26] In the late 1960s, Arthur Shields also

[21] Ernie O'Malley, *The Singing Flame* (Dublin: Anvil Books, 1978), p. 213.

[22] Foster, *Vivid Faces*, p. 310; BMH 1572 (Padraig Ó Catháin); Joost Augusteijn, *From Public Defiance to Guerrilla Warfare. The Experience of Ordinary Volunteers in the Irish War of Independence 1916–1921* (Dublin: Irish Academic Press, 1996), p. 142.

[23] Guy Beiner, 'Probing the Boundaries of Irish Memory', *Irish Historical Studies* 39 (2014), 302.

[24] Statistics (August 2012–16 March 2015) kindly provided by Commandant Padraic Kennedy (Irish), Military Archives.

[25] Fearghal McGarry, *The Rising. Ireland. Easter 1916* (Oxford: Oxford University Press, 2010); Foster, *Vivid Faces*, Sinéad McCoole, *Easter Widows. Seven Irish Women who Lived in the Shadow of the 1916 Rising* (Dublin: Doubleday Ireland, 2014).

[26] The chapter on the Rising draws on a narrative by Kearney ('Incidents of Easter Week', Ms 3560/1, Trinity College Dublin) although de Burca, 'with the approval of Uncle Peadar', made minor changes, altering it from third to first person, excising a reference to a rebel whose cowardice Kearney had attributed to his atheism, and adding new material 'which I took down from Peadar verbally'). Aspects of Kearney's original account appear sanitised. He emphasises the Volunteers' reluctance to retaliate against hostile civilians,

began recording his own story, drawing on an extensive archive of diaries, letters and documents. His papers include hundreds of pages of unpublished biographical and autobiographical material (much of it written by his third wife, Laurie, after his death in 1970). Compared to the State projects, which specified which actions and periods should be remembered, autobiography allowed veterans greater latitude as to how to frame their narratives and which events to record (or exclude). They were, however, often shaped by other pressures, such as family participation.

Letters, reminiscences, interviews and a wide range of other first-person material also record the Abbey rebels' memories of 1916. In addition, public figures such as Molony and Shields had further opportunities to shape discourse about the Rising. Even for Connolly, who could leave no record of his own involvement in 1916, extensive material was generated by his comrades, siblings and descendants.[27] In contrast, for rebels without family networks who engaged in forms of public remembering, there exists little material. Prior to the release of the MSP collection, for example, there was no known first-person testimony for Murphy and Bushell.

The 'memory' that this chapter analyses is not that which results from the psychological process of encoding, storing and retrieving information but rather officially recorded or publicly articulated first-person narratives. The accuracy of these accounts is obviously open to question. For example, Nic Shiubhlaigh concluded her memoir by recounting how she and her female comrades were escorted from Jacob's prior to the general surrender by a polite British officer.

We walked down the roadway and turned the corner into Camden Street. It was a route I had taken many times through the years. I cannot remember what we talked about – if we talked at all, for there did not seem very much to say. I felt confused and disappointed. All at once, I had begun to feel very tired … Everything looked strange, even the street was different. It was though I had never seen it before. Despite what was going on inside, Jacob's looked very dark, very empty. Dublin seemed unnaturally still.[28]

Recalling the same episode, however, Min Ryan described a condescending rather than a polite officer, and a distraught rather than a numbed Nic Shiubhlaigh:

We made Maire come with us as she was on the verge of being hysterical. When we came to the door, a high-ranking officer and a young officer were arriving to take

---

whereas Michael Walker (BMH WS 139), describing the same incident, noted that the rebels shot and bayoneted a civilian.

[27] See, for example, the testimony of Niamh O'Sullivan, Sean Connolly's granddaughter, recorded by the Irish Life & Lore oral history project (www.irishlifeandlore.com).

[28] Nic Shiubhlaigh, *Splendid Years*, pp. 185–186.

the surrender. They came in a small two-seater car. I suppose the high-ranking officer was General Lowe. The young officer stood, and we stood too. Louise [Gavan Duffy] stood up with great dignity. One of the officers said: 'We are not taking women, are we?' The other said: 'No'. We went off. Louise said: 'The cheek of him anyway – not taking women'. When we got home to 19 Ranelagh Road, we put Maire Nic Shiubhlaigh to bed. She was worn out completely. We sat again, and sat and sat.[29]

But the focus of this chapter is not the accuracy of these narratives so much as their significance, a historical approach described by Pierre Nora as 'less interested in events themselves than in the construction of events over time, in the disappearance and re-emergence of their significations; less interested in "what actually happened" than in its perpetual reuse and misuse'.[30] For example, why does Nic Shiubhlaigh's story end at Easter Week? Why is the theme of transformation ('Everything looked strange') – characteristic of 1916 narratives – recorded in such a despondent register? In analysing the author's intentions, what is omitted may be as significant as what is included. Despite its devastating impact on her family, Nic Shiubhlaigh does not record that her sister's (non-combatant) fiancé, James Crawford Neil, was killed during Easter Week while returning to the city centre from her family home. Although this event was recorded by contemporary sources, the memory of Neil's death did not resurface as a narrative of 1916 until articulated by Nic Shiubhlaigh's great-nephew almost a century later.[31] This parallels a public silence, only now dissipating, about Easter Week's civilian dead.

This chapter is also concerned with tracing how the rebels' narratives (and their reception) altered over time. Again, the trauma of violence provides a useful example. In an interview (recorded by a radical journalist in 1935), Molony described the killing of Constable James O'Brien (in the opening engagement of the insurrection) in a manner that emphasised both the rebels' restraint and the momentous import of their actions:

They reached the gate of the Castle, and Sean Connolly, who was in command ordered the policeman on duty to stand aside. He refused. Connolly insisted and warned him, presenting the revolver. But this blind tool of imperialism could not believe that the Irish people were demanding their own. Connolly shot him dead, and that bullet destroyed the *status quo* in Ireland.[32]

---

[29] BMH WS 399 (Mrs Richard Mulcahy).
[30] Pierre Nora, 'From Lieux de mémoire to Realms of Memory', p. xxiv, quoted in Joan Coutu, *Persuasion and Propaganda. Monuments and the Eighteenth-Century British Empire* (Quebec: McGill-Queen's University Press, 2006), p. 11.
[31] *Irish Independent*, 11 May 1916; Dave Kenny, 'Gypsy and the Poet', www.writing.ie/tell-your-own-story/gypsy-and-the-poet-by-dave-kenny/.
[32] R. M. Fox, *Rebel Irishwomen* (Dublin: Talbot Press, 1935), pp. 128–129.

Molony's BMH witness statement (recorded fifteen years later in the knowledge that it would remain confidential until her death) describes (as do other accounts) a hastier, less considered killing, in a more sympathetic tone:

> When Connolly went to go past him, the Sergeant put out his arm; and Connolly shot him dead . . . When I saw Connolly draw his revolver, I drew my own. Across the road, there was a policeman with papers. He got away, thank God. I did not like to think of the policeman dead . . . I think the policeman at the gate was killed instantly, because they were quite close. The police did not think the Citizen Army were serious.[33]

What follows is an attempt to identify and interpret key themes and patterns in the Abbey rebels' narratives of rebellion.

IV

A noticeable feature of the rebels' narratives is the importance attached to the period up to, and including, the Rising. Helena Molony's sixty-page witness statement relegates the revolutionary period of 1916–1923 to a three-page postscript. Despite, like Molony, playing a significant role in the wider revolution, two-thirds of Kearney's biography is devoted to the period up to Easter 1916. There is a sense that their stories have climaxed or, as in Nic Shiubhlaigh's case, literally come to an end with the Rising. Rather than marking the beginning of a new Ireland, as in many nationalist histories, and revolutionary memoirs by archetypal IRA leaders such as Tom Barry, who joined the mass movement that emerged after the Rising, 1916 seems more like the end of an era.

The shadow cast by the Civil War may partly account for this. Although the BMH pragmatically encouraged witnesses to end their accounts at the 1921 Truce, this reflected a broader reluctance to discuss (both privately and in public) the events that followed. Although his biography spans Kearney's life, de Burca devotes less than one page to Kearney's reminiscences of the 'fratricidal strife'.[34] However, many veterans were also reluctant to discuss the Tan War, an era when violence was both endured and inflicted. This reticence may also be, in part, a response to the Rising itself, particularly the impact of the execution of men with whom many rebels were intimate. Although Molony does not mention her depression and alcoholism (which preceded 1916), her statement conveys the executions' traumatic impact: 'I heard the shots every morning at dawn', she

---

[33] BMH WS 391 (Helena Molony). See also BMH WS 316 (Peter Folan).
[34] Seamus de Burca, *The Soldier's Song* (Dublin: P. J. Bourke, 1957), p. 219.

recorded: 'Connolly was dragged out, unable to stand, and murdered. After that life seemed to come to an end for me.'[35]

The impact of the Easter Rising on the revolutionary movement may also be a factor. Prior to 1916, the Abbey rebels could view themselves as insiders, never far from the centre of action. As Kearney put it: 'To be admitted into that magic circle, to be one of the chosen company with whom Tom [Clarke] discoursed without restraint, was something to be worthy of, and a memory to be proud of.'[36] Trusted by the Military Council, Molony hid copies of the Proclamation under her pillow at Liberty Hall the night before the Rising. Nic Shiubhlaigh spent Easter Sunday at Eamon Ceannt's house, while Barney Murphy was friendly with Tom Clarke and Seán Mac Diarmada.[37] After 1916, they found themselves at the edge of a more popular movement with a different leadership, their role reduced from actors on the main stage to bit players. This was keenly felt, if not necessarily articulated, by the female activists who had played a more significant role before 1916. In her witness statement, Helena Molony makes no mention of her extensive efforts to secure representation for women within the leadership of Sinn Féin after the Rising, which remained forgotten until discovered by feminist historians half a century later.[38]

Marginalisation was accompanied by other post-revolutionary disappointments. Although a perception that many did well out of 1916 would later emerge, none of the Abbey's rebels – leaving aside their modest military service pensions – benefited materially from their activism, while several suffered as a result of it. In predicting this 'hard service', Yeats had been prescient. Most died in poverty and obscurity. Nic Shiubhlaigh and her husband Bob Price (previously a leading GHQ officer) moved to Laytown in 1929 where the weight of the past hung heavily. An alcoholic who failed to hold down a job, Price did not find a place in post-revolutionary Ireland. Surrounded by mementoes of the 'splendid years' – a George Russell portrait of Máire's performance in *Deirdre of the Sorrows* dominated the living room – their lives were tinged with regret.[39]

In the final years of her life, Nic Shiubhlaigh's circumstances were assessed as 'poor'.[40] A letter written in 1950 by Nic Shiubhlaigh to another (then) forgotten figure, the Ulster playwright Alice Milligan, suggests neglect and hardship: 'Any chance of any broadcasting? I never get

---

[35] BMH WS 391 (Helena Molony).   [36] De Burca, *Soldier's Song*, p. 91.
[37] Sworn statement, 7 July 1937, Bernard Murphy, MSPC.
[38] Margaret Ward, *Unmanageable Revolutionaries: Women and Irish Nationalism* (London: Pluto Press, 1983).
[39] Author's interview with Dave Kenny, 17 February 2015.   [40] Maire Price, MSPC.

anything to do if you can put anything in my way or if there is anything of yours going to be read don't forget Maire nic Shiubhlaigh.' Milligan was no better off: 'I am so glad to have your address at last. I wd have been sending you ... tickets ... only I have no cash at all for a couple of months ... I can get clothes and food on credit till then but not ... newspapers or washing done.'[41] For some veterans, penury made remembering a necessity. A letter from the St Vincent de Paul requesting that Barney Murphy's 1935 pension application be expedited noted that 'the claimant who has a large family is unemployed and utterly destitute'. Despite urgent appeals from veterans' associations – 'This man is rapidly sinking' – Murphy had not received his pension when he died four years later in the Dublin Union Hospital (still described locally as the workhouse).[42] Forced to retire from the Abbey due to ill-health in 1948, Nellie Bushell also died in impoverished and neglected circumstances.[43]

Material considerations aside, the need to remember was bound up with anxiety about being forgotten, although this was not always a straightforward impulse. In submitting her BMH witness statement, Molony appeared torn between her desire to place on record her story and a reticence to articulate it shared by many veterans. She confided to the Bureau's Investigating Officer that she had been teased by her partner (the psychiatrist Evelyn O'Brien): 'It is Miss Kissane who ought to get a special medal as decoration for dragging information out of a lot of unwilling clams like you all. I doubt if any of you were out in the rebellion at all.'[44]

The Splendid Years represented Nic Shiubhlaigh's attempt to write herself back into the 'Story of the Irish National Theatre' (the subtitle of her memoir). The book's origins lay in a process of remembering which had begun with a lecture to female graduates at University College Galway in 1947. Nic Shiubhlaigh, like other Irish National Theatre Society members, believed that her part in founding the Abbey had been overshadowed by 'the origin myth sedulously cultivated' by W. B. Yeats.[45] Her fractious relationship with the poet (which saw her leave the Abbey in acrimonious circumstances) compounded her obscurity: she was overlooked in Yeats's 1923 Nobel prize speech (which identified her rivals, Sarah Allgood and Maire O'Neill, as the 'players of genius' that

[41] Maire Price to Alice Milligan, n.d. [c. 1950], Alice Milligan to Maire Price, n.d. [c. 1950], Ms. 27, 624, National Library of Ireland (NLI).
[42] J. P. L. Murphy, St Vincent de Paul, to Dept. of Defence, 12 October 1936, Bernard Murphy, MSPC.
[43] McGarry, *Abbey Rebels*.
[44] Molony to Kissane, 29 September 1949, BMH S164 (Helena Molony).
[45] Foster, *Vivid Faces*, p. 77.

made the Abbey a success).[46] A key concern of Nic Shiubhlaigh's narrative was to present her departure, which ended her opportunity for a professional career on the stage, as the result of a conscious decision to prioritise politics over art: 'I am glad I left the Abbey Theatre when I did for if I had remained there I might have missed the greatest part of my life's work.'[47] Judging from the extent to which her memoir is now quoted by scholars, she did succeed in writing herself back into the historical record, although she had yet to escape Yeats's shadow by 1966.

The theme of unrewarded service is emphasised in the rebels' narratives. Padraic Colum set the tone in his foreword to Nic Shiubhlaigh's memoir: 'They were austere days for the young men and women who made them splendid. They gave to and they got nothing from the Dublin of those days.'[48] Kearney emphasised how his revolutionary activism impaired his health and reduced his family to charity: 'Twice in my life I left my home never to return to it. Books, manuscripts, prints, furniture lost. Personal mementoes, autographs of Tom Clarke, Sean McDermott and the rest, all destroyed. There was nothing left.'[49] However, rather than being suppressed due to shame, Kearney's poverty and obscurity (which are juxtaposed with the fame of his ballads) were thematised in de Burca's account. His biography also draws attention to the destitution of Paddy Heaney (the composer of the national anthem who was buried in an unmarked grave), and former revolutionaries who fell into poverty after independence. Indeed, de Burca proved so successful in foregrounding these themes that they now dominate popular memory of Kearney.[50]

The Soldier's Song attributed Kearney's poverty to unemployment, his adherence to trade-union principles and ill-health. It does not record – as Kearney informed the Military Service Pensions' board – how his prospects had been damaged by the death of Michael Collins: 'Gen Collins called here on his way south [before his death]. He chatted to me & said that my job was only temporary one but I was to sit tight. I was paid £4-4-0 a week.'[51] According to Martin Walton (the founder of the Dublin music firm who was interned with Kearney at Ballykinlar), Kearney believed that Collins had pledged to support them in founding an Irish School of Music after independence.[52] By the time he applied for a military pension in 1926, Kearney was 'in very needy

---

[46] See www.nobelprize.org/nobel_prizes/literature/laureates/1923/yeats-lecture.html.
[47] Nic Shiubhlaigh memoir, Ms. 27,634, NLI.   [48] Nic Shiubhlaigh, *Splendid Years*, xii.
[49] De Burca, *Soldier's Song*, p. 220.
[50] As is evident from entering 'Peadar Kearney' and 'poverty' into a search engine.
[51] Kearney handwritten statement, Peadar Kearney, MSPC.
[52] Kenneth Griffith and Timothy O'Grady, *Curious Journey. An Oral History of Ireland's Unfinished Revolution* (London: Hutchinson, 1982), p. 321.

circumstances'.[53] Although Collins had reportedly declared that 'Nothing that Ireland could give would be enough for the man who wrote *The Soldier's Song*', the State's refusal to pay him royalties for its use as the national anthem led Kearney to embark on a lengthy legal dispute which eventually embarrassed the government into conceding a payment of £1,000 (to which it did not believed him entitled).[54] This experience understandably engendered resentment. As de Burca noted in a letter in 1962: 'Peadar often said to me: "I got little out of the Soldier's Song, not even fame."'[55] However, this dispute is not mentioned in *The Soldier's Song* which constructs a more stoical narrative: 'There can be no doubt that if Peadar had been a self-seeking man his later life would have been spent in comparative luxury', de Burca observes, 'But he was content with his humble lot'. The biography does, however, pointedly contrast Kearney's plight with those who did benefit from 1916: 'He was never bitter about his lot, which was often hard, though he was bitter against certain old comrades who had turned into self-seeking politicians.'[56]

For Kearney, as with many revolutionaries, the concern was not merely with being forgotten but how he would be remembered. The concept of 'postmemory' (a term initially used to describe 'second generation memory', characterising 'the experience of those who grew up dominated by narratives that preceded their birth' but more recently reconceptualised to encompass living memory) is useful here. It can describe 'those who agonised over how certain domineering events, or causes to which they were deeply devoted, would be perceived by later generations and utilised their privileged position as witnesses of history to assume the role of custodians of memory'.[57] In the case of Kearney, a zealous republican who supported the Treaty, his anxiety about the political victory of the Civil War's military losers seems evident from de Valera's absence from his narrative, and his passionate defence of Collins: 'It is easy for the younger generation to question our motives . . . The generation that will see the Republic will never appreciate the men who gave their all.'[58]

Collectively, these narratives form part of a wider post-revolutionary literature of disillusionment, encompassing writers such as Sean O'Casey and veterans such as P. S. O'Hegarty, which emerged in the 1930s,

---

[53] P. S. Doyle, 20 September 1926, Peadar Kearney, MSPC.
[54] D/Taoiseach S7395A, National Archives (Ireland).
[55] De Burca to John O'Donovan, 3 August 1962, de Burca papers, NLI.
[56] De Burca, *Soldier's Song*, pp. 222, 221.
[57] Beiner, 'Boundaries of Irish Memory', pp. 298–302, 304–305.
[58] Peadar Kearney, *The Soldier's Song & Other Poems* (Dublin: Talbot Press, 1928), p. 220.

alongside a more dominant triumphal Statist narrative of 1916.[59] From this nostalgic vantage point, the optimism of the 'pre-revolution' is framed by the disappointments that followed: writing to Nic Shiubhlaigh in 1950, Padraic Colum recalled 'days that now seem all summer and poetry'.[60] On learning of her final illness some years later, he recalled 'the lovely times ... when we were young and hopeful and enthusiastic'.[61] In her memoir, Nic Shiubhlaigh recalled the Dublin of her youth (when republicans had rarely been more marginalised) as a city 'full of earnest young people, all of them anxious to do something useful for Ireland'. This was, as Diarmaid Ferriter has observed, 'a convenient transference of the personal to the general, but also selective; what were difficult and contested years (reflected in her own theatre career and the intrusion of politics) became instead *The Splendid Years*.'[62]

V

The Abbey rebels formed part of a generation for whom history, particularly historical narratives articulated through drama, literature and biography, was politics. Most had been radicalised through organisations such as the IRB which emerged from, or devoted themselves to sustaining, a commemorative political culture. In particular, remembering 1798 had been crucial to bringing about 1916. To what extent did their own narratives of insurrection reflect an ideological intent?

The individual whose accounts of 1916 most clearly reflected a critique of contemporary society was Helena Molony, who devoted much of her career as an Irish Women Workers' Union official to radical causes such as support for the Soviet Union and, only somewhat less beyond the pale in interwar Ireland, gender equality. Due to the Rising's centrality to discourse in the Irish Free State, female activists often rooted their demands for equality in terms of women's participation in the rebellion and the egalitarianism of the Proclamation of the Republic. At the same time, their narratives of participation often emphasised the gendered dimension of their roles during Easter Week.[63] In contrast, although her revolutionary activities had been typically gendered, Molony emphasised her role as a combatant.[64]

[59] Foster, *Vivid Faces*, pp. 294–302.
[60] Colum to Nic Shiubhlaigh, 1 December 1950, Ms 49,752/21, NLI.
[61] Colum to Gypsy Walker, 28 February 1958, MS 49,752/22, NLI.
[62] Nic Shiubhlaigh, *Splendid Years*, p. xvi; Diarmaid Ferriter, *A Nation and Not a Rabble. The Irish Revolution 1913–23* (London: Profile, 2015), p. 27.
[63] Senia Pašeta, *Irish Nationalist Women 1900–1918* (Cambridge: Cambridge University Press, 2013), p. 187.
[64] 'Sworn Statement', 3 July 1936, Helena Molony, MSPC.

In the mid-1930s, she began a lengthy dispute with the MSP's board of assessors due to its refusal to classify much of her revolutionary activism as military service: 'Women were recruited into the Citizen Army on the same terms as men. They were appointed to the duties most suitable to them – as were men – and these duties fell naturally into dealing with Commissariat, Intelligence, First Aid and advanced Medical Aid, but their duties were not confined to these.'[65] She was 'not primarily concerned with a pension', she told the assessors, 'but with the recognition of women's services rendered to the Republic'.[66] Ill-health, and probably poverty, compelled her to drop her objections but she continued to criticise the board's narrow definition of military service:

when I was presiding at a meeting in O'Connell St ... (under Army orders) one woman was shot dead, and a boy standing beside me shot through his head, and six others wounded. It is difficult for the ordinary person to understand how such things are not classified as 'military service'. In any regular Army in any civilized country, I never heard of such no[n]-combatants as Army Service Corps, or Intelligence Dept. – being classified as non-Military.[67]

The wider context to this dispute was framed by the Irish State's unwillingness to place the revolutionary role played by women on a par with that of men, a stance which reflected an ideological aversion to acknowledging women's equality as citizens. By allowing Irish Citizen Army members to apply for pensions, the terms of the 1923 Army Pensions Act inadvertently included a small number of women. However, when Margaret Skinnider – who was shot three times as she led her male Irish Citizen Army (ICA) comrades in battle during the rebellion – applied on the basis of her injuries, the pensions board ruled that 'the definition of "wound" ... only contemplates the masculine gender'. The Treasury solicitor agreed, in a revealingly tortuous formulation: 'the Army Pensions Act is only applicable to soldiers as generally understood in the masculine gender.'[68] Although service with Cumann na mBan was subsequently deemed eligible for compensation in 1932, it was narrowly defined to exclude much of the revolutionary activism conducted by women. Like Molony, Máire Nic Shiubhlaigh felt slighted by the military pension board's failure to recognise her post-Rising activism as 'Active Service'.[69]

In her submission to the BMH some fifteen years later, Molony continued to emphasise the military role played by women. 'I had my own

---

[65] Molony to Advisory Committee, 14 July 1936, Helena Molony, MSPC.
[66] Ibid., 18 November 1936.   [67] Ibid., 11 October 1937.
[68] Ferriter, *A Nation*, p. 340.
[69] Maire Price to Dept. of Defence, 28 October 1942, Maire Price, MSPC.

revolver and ammunition', she informed the Bureau (and posterity). Even 'before the Russian Army had women soldiers, the Citizen Army had them'.[70] But her insistence that the ICA was 'the first army in the world where men and women were on equal terms' was misleading.[71] The aristocratic, trouser-wearing, cigarette-smoking Countess Markievicz was the only woman formally recorded as a member of the Citizen Army prior to the Rising; the other females belonged to 'the women's section'. Although James Connolly had issued revolvers to some women, including Molony, he did so for defensive purposes, and the ICA's women were, like Cumann na mBan, generally confined to gendered roles such as cooking and first-aid.[72] But the myth proved enduring, and the appealing notion of gender equality within the Irish Citizen Army is still emphasised in popular accounts which present Connolly's radical vision as the road not taken after 1916.

Although the desirability of subordinating women's rights as citizens to the construction of a gendered discourse of nationhood was accepted across the political spectrum of the Irish Free State, Molony pointed to her 1916 record to present the government's efforts to return women to the home as an attack on the ideals of the Rising. Despite fighting for independence, she complained in 1930, women retained 'their inferior status, their lower pay for equal work, their exclusion from juries and certain branches of the civil service, their slum dwellings and crowded, cold and unsanitary schools for their children'.[73] Such rhetoric did not prevent her comrades in the Labour Party and the Irish Trade Union Congress from supporting de Valera's (largely symbolic) efforts to exclude women from certain occupations. In a 1935 interview, Molony attributed the shortcomings of independence to the ideological limitations of the movement that achieved it. 'Perhaps the time was not ripe for success', she reflected: 'Our people had not a widespread economic knowledge to cope with social evils. I should have hated to see Padraic Pearse as President of an Irish Republic if the misery and wretchedness of the tenements had still gone on.' At the same time, she rejected the Pearsean blood sacrifice which had become the dominant narrative of the Rising: '1916 has been represented as a gesture of sacrifice. It is said that those in it knew they would be defeated . . . I know how we all felt . . . Everyone was exalted and caught in the sweep of a great movement. We

---

[70] BMH WS 391 (Helena Molony).
[71] 'Sworn statement by Helena Moloney', 3 July 1936, Helena Molony, MSPC.
[72] Ann Matthews, *Renegades. Irish Republican Women 1900–1922* (Cork: Mercier Press, 2010), pp. 129–130.
[73] Helena Molony, 'James Connolly and Women' in *Dublin Labour Year Book* (Dublin: Dublin Trades' Union and Labour Council, 1930).

saw a vision of Ireland, free, pure, happy. We did not realise this vision. But we saw it.'[74]

In her final years – whether due to the conservatism of Irish society or her own precarious circumstances – Molony ceased to articulate a radical interpretation of 1916. During the 'Emergency', when she was monitored by Irish military intelligence, her alcoholism, poor mental health and support for the IRA saw her forced out of trade-union office. She lived in relative poverty, dependent on friends for support and accommodation. Curiously, she developed an admiration for de Valera (who, as President, delivered a generous tribute at her funeral). Some of her friends, however, attributed this rapprochement to her mental decline: 'she seemed to lose the revolutionary spirit', Máire Comerford recalled: 'she didn't seem to appreciate what was going on'.[75]

Aspects of Peadar Kearney's narrative of 1916 also critique the State. His recollections demonstrate a strong sense of class-consciousness but, in contrast to Molony, without a socialist analysis. He too was aware of his generation's limitations:

We lived as revolutionists in a period of revolution. We had no thought of the morrow. As far as we were concerned, we were simply units in a movement. A fair number of the rank and file were separatists pure and simple, with no idea of economics or the science of politics as such. When the Irish people had the free choice of their own representatives in their own parliament in their own country, our war was ended. Naturally, we hoped it would be a republic.[76]

His writings indicate bitterness at the failure to achieve a united, independent republic. He added an (unnoticed) anti-partitionist stanza to 'The Soldier's Song' in 1937 and identified Irish Protestant supporters of the British army during the Second World War with Freemasonry and the Cromwellian settlement.[77] The consequences of the unfinished revolution, moreover, reverberated within his own family: Kearney's nephew Brendan Behan was serving a fourteen-year sentence for shooting at a policeman when he died in 1942. The Minister for Justice's reported refusal to allow him to attend the funeral unsurprisingly rankled: 'I wouldn't let Brendan Behan out on a chain.'[78]

Shields' remembering of 1916 can also be seen, if more obliquely, as a critique of independence. Although the 'Green Room' of his Hollywood

---

[74] Fox, *Rebel Irishwomen*, pp. 127, 131–132.
[75] Penny Duggan, 'Helena Molony: Actress, Feminist, Nationalist, Socialist and Trade-Unionist' (International Institute for Research and Education Working Paper, 1990), p. 34.
[76] Kearney, *Soldier's Song*, pp. 217–218.
[77] Peadar Ó Cearnaigh, 'Cromwell Rides Again', 4 September 1942, Ms. 39/1125/1, NLI.
[78] E.H. Mikhail (ed.), *The Letters of Brendan Behan* (London: Macmillan, 1992), p. 15.

home was 'full of souvenirs of the Abbey and of Dublin during the Rising', Shields – an unassuming figure – seldom discussed his role in the Rising. His recollection (recorded in his wife's unpublished biographical treatment) of his pacifist socialist father's disappointment at his decision to join the Irish Volunteers indicates a more considered attitude to 1916 than the uncritical interpretations of insurrectionary violence presented in *The Splendid Years* and *The Soldier's Song*.[79] As assistant director of the Abbey's 1926 production of *The Plough and the Stars*, Shields was closely involved in the most contentious re-enactment of the Rising ever staged. It was to prove highly influential, as James Moran has noted: 'those who strove to dramatize the Rising in the period immediately after 1916 helped to influence the way that the insurrection was viewed for the rest of the twentieth century.'[80]

As Lieutenant Langon, Shields carried a tricolour into a pub in one of the play's most inflammatory scenes. Although the presence of a prostitute also provoked outrage, the play's 'real shock-value' lay in its anti-heroic portrayal of the Rising.[81] On the fourth night, it was disrupted by cat-calls, hisses and a physical attack on the cast. Following Yeats's ineffectual attempt to address the republican protesters – 'You have disgraced yourselves again' – sections of the audience broke into the 'Soldier's Song' until the police restored order. As the revolutionary widows and mothers (including Kathleen Clarke, Margaret Pearse and a sister of Sean Connolly) walked out, Hannah Sheehy Skeffington (whose pacifist husband had not fought in the Rising) exclaimed: 'I am one of the widows of Easter Week. It is no wonder that you do not remember the men of Easter Week, because none of you fought on either side.'[82] The show went on, despite an attempt by armed republicans to kidnap Arthur's brother Barry Fitzgerald later in the week. Although many of the Abbey's Catholic actors disliked both the play and O'Casey (with some refusing to speak their lines), Shields consistently backed O'Casey in his escalating disputes with the Abbey. He also remained committed to *The Plough and the Stars*, acting as an assistant director, and appearing as Patrick Pearse, in John Ford's 1936 screen adaptation.

Shields' disillusionment with the Rising's conservative legacy contributed to his decision to leave Ireland in the late 1930s. A bohemian from a

---

[79] 'Outline', p. 4 (1974), T13/A/512, Shields papers, Hardiman Library, National University of Ireland Galway.

[80] James Moran, *Staging the Easter Rising. 1916 as Theatre* (Cork: Cork University Press, 2005), p. 4.

[81] Foster, *Vivid Faces*, p. 301.

[82] Robert Hogan and Richard Burnham, *The Years of O'Casey, 1921–1926: A Documentary History* (Newark, DE: Colin Smythe, 1992), p. 301.

Protestant background, he resented the imposition of a Gaelic Catholic ethos by de Valera's government. He explained his decision to leave the Abbey Theatre, increasingly under the influence of cultural conservatives such as Ernest Blythe, to his unwillingness to say 'his prayers in Gaelic'.[83] In later life, Shields' memories of the Rising were framed by a sense of his otherness. He recalled, for example, how his efforts to remain sane during his imprisonment in 1916 by reciting lines from plays were misinterpreted by the old republican in the cell next to him: 'Ah, aren't you the great one for praying, though. It's night and day you never stop!'[84] On location in India, when independence was proclaimed in 1949, he proudly wore his 1916 medal but – he told the *Irish Press* – when asked by locals, he was unable to translate its Gaelic inscription.[85] While reflecting a genuine sense of difference that he experienced during the Rising and at Frongoch, where the other prisoners recited the Rosary in Gaelic, these ostensibly humorous anecdotes suggest a retrospective projection of his disillusionment with an independent State, which he saw as characterised by 'a narrow nationalism alien to the spirit of the Rising'.[86]

VI

While the Abbey's rebels exercised varying degrees of influence over the narratives they constructed, their subsequent impact was beyond their control. Most obviously, it was conditioned by the changing context in which these narratives circulated, but their transmission (or recycling) was also often a result of efforts by family members. Seamus de Burca's *The Soldier's Song* exemplifies both these points. Decades before its publication, Kearney – or his admirers – had articulated its principal themes. In 1928, for example, the Dublin historian J. W. Hammond prefaced his essay on Kearney with a quotation from Thomas à Kempis: 'Others shall be magnified in the mouths of men, and on you no one shall bestow a word. Such and such an office shall be conferred on others, but you shall be passed by.'[87] Although the *The Soldier's Song* reiterated the same theme of unrewarded service, it was received more sympathetically. While some reviewers presented Kearney as an unproblematic exemplar of 'patriotic fervour', most identified explicitly the biography's critical motifs.[88] 'Peadar Kearney contributed more than his share to the National Revolution, and, unlike many others, he got very little out of

---

[83] *Irish Times*, 28 September 1964.
[84] Homer Swander, 'Shields at the Abbey', *Éire-Ireland* 5 (1970), 29.
[85] *Irish Press*, 29 April 1950.   [86] Swander, 'Shields at the Abbey', 39.
[87] J. W. Hammond, 'Introduction' in Kearney, *Soldier's Song*, p. 6.
[88] Ivrea, 'The Soldier's Song', *Midland Tribune*, n.d., Ms. 39,125 /5, NLI.

it', Seamus G. O'Kelly observed. He 'died as he had lived, a poor man'.[89] Kearney, another reviewed noted, 'made little or nothing from his many poetic works and . . . gained equally little from a lifetime of service devoted to the cause of Irish freedom.' The themes of anonymity and neglect, which were also articulated publicly by relatives such as Behan, were emphasised by reviewers.

Clearly, *The Soldier's Song*'s narrative of unrewarded selflessness struck a chord; Kearney personified a trope whose day had come. The biography's subtext was articulated most explicitly by a reviewer in the *Irish Times*, a newspaper that had never sympathised with the Statist republican orthodoxy:

Young people growing up in Ireland at the moment cannot be blamed for thinking that some time in the early twenties a few hundred men carried out a rebellion, were partly successful, took over 26 counties, have been running the country ever since, and now look on it more or less as their private property. This view is not altogether accurate. Quite a few took part in the revolution of 1916–23, who sought nothing for themselves and who received nothing in return for their fight except poverty, derision and broken lives. Such a man was Peadar Kearney, the Dublin house painter who composed the 'Soldier's Song'.[90]

Here was a narrative of 1916 that chimed with the malaise of 1950s Ireland, and growing resentment of the deployment of the Rising's sterile legacy to reinforce the power of a political elite for over two generations. There is a sense here of a shift in the 'memory horizon',[91] as Kearney's disillusioned postmemory narrative is deployed against an increasingly hollow triumphalist State narrative of 1916.

Something similar can be discerned in a letter sent to de Burca from Monte Carlo's Le Grand Hotel du Cap Ferra by his niece's husband, the BBC broadcaster, Eamonn Andrews:

I had a strange surge of reactions in the reading of it. Perhaps it was because it lay so strangely against a foreign background of sunshine and blue sky . . . I was deeply moved by the ending. Odd is it not that to have read it in England would have put me closer to it? Of course we realise again the awful apathy that greeted the revolution. We are I'm afraid no different from other nations . . . This is one reason it's wrong to have hate against whole nations . . . It's only sad that it takes war to stimulate heroes.

Andrews' further ruminations about how patriotism can become 'corrupted to excessive nationalism and love of country to bigotry' are striking,

---

[89] Press cutting, Ms. 39,125 /5, NLI.
[90] P[roinsias]. MacA[onghusa], *Irish Times*, 1957, Ms. 39,125 /5, NLI.
[91] Alison Ribeiro de Menezes, *Embodying Memory in Contemporary Spain* (Basingstoke: Palgrave Macmillan, 2014).

as these ideas do not form any part of *The Soldier's Song*'s unreconstructed Gaelicist Fenian narrative. As with the *Irish Times*' review, there is a sense in this letter that the story – both Kearney's and the State's – has not ended as it should: 'Did Peadar end his days a saddened man? Was he disillusioned by the small men who hide their smallness behind the loud talk of wordy patriotism or those who think a language is to make a nation small instead of big?'[92]

The success of *The Soldier's Song* also highlights the centrality of family networks in constructing, disseminating and reviving veterans' narratives. Kearney's nephew, de Burca, wrote and published the biography. He also kept it in print, subsidising, publishing and distributing a second edition. Máire Nic Shiubhlaigh would not have recorded her memoirs, or found a publisher, without the help of her co-author and nephew Ted Kenny (whose son, Dave, is preparing a new edition for publication). The biographical treatment, interviews and reminiscences among Shields' papers were written, recorded or transcribed and – most importantly – preserved and archived by his wife Laurie. Their efforts demonstrate the importance of the mechanisms that sustained and transmitted narratives, as well as the changing context that shaped their reception. In the 1970s, when the appetite for remembering 1916 had waned, Laurie Shields failed to persuade Gill & Macmillan to publish her biography.[93] During the same period, de Burca also failed to publish a third edition of *The Soldier's Song*, despite considerable efforts.

These books represented just the most visible facet of a broader familial remembering. Working with like-minded organisations such as the Old Dublin Society, de Burca solicited reminiscences of Kearney, published his correspondence, erected plaques to his memory and ensured they were maintained by (or – when necessary – protected from) Dublin Corporation. He organised book launches, fund-raising campaigns, parades and other commemorative events; embarked on international lecture tours; presented copies of his biography to writers, diplomats and politicians; secured interviews with journalists; chastised the press, when necessary, for inattention to Kearney's memory; provided sources and interviews to scholars; secured the preservation of papers and recordings in archives; placed books in libraries; donated artefacts to museums and galleries; policed copyright infringements; and rebuked those who slighted the family name. A Royal Irish Academy of Music lecturer who misattributed the authorship of the National Anthem was met with a demand for 'an apology to the sons of Peadar Kearney and the nephews of Peadar Kearney of

---

[92] Eamonn Andrews to de Burca, 21 June 1958, Ms. 39,133, NLI.
[93] Michael Gill to T. Taplinger, 10 December 1974, T13/A/513, Shields papers.

whom I am one'.[94] Remembering, for some, was an act of love. Laurie Shields sought to stitch the memory of her husband into the fabric of history by arranging for academics to interview him; urging scholars to study her husband's life; encouraging writers to place biographical features with magazines such as *Life* and archiving his memories.[95]

De Burca's efforts formed part of a process of familial commemoration which is maintained by a fourth generation. In 2013, family members inaugurated a new tradition at Kearney's graveside at Glasnevin Cemetery 'in memory of all who served in Easter week' involving government ministers, British diplomats, the French embassy and the Defence Forces.[96] For some relatives, such a legacy could be a psychological burden as well as a source of cultural capital. As Marianne Hirsch has noted: 'To grow up with overwhelming inherited memories, to be dominated by narratives that preceded one's birth or one's consciousness, is to risk having one's own life stories displaced, even evacuated, by our ancestors.'[97] While the rebels' achievements and status could be identified with, or their papers sold off to American universities, relatives also inherited their disappointments, slights and unfulfilled hopes. In his preface to Máire Nic Shiubhlaigh's memoir, Ted Kenny described his aunt's story as one of 'hard work, for little material reward; of a constant striving for recognition', a description that could apply to his own efforts. When their memoir fell out of print, following a dispute with his publisher, he felt keenly his failure to restore the family name to prominence.

VII

Few will be surprised to learn that the stories people tell about their past change over the course of their lives; the knowledge that the sources which form the building blocks of history require careful handling has long defined the professional practice of history. Nonetheless, the current deluge of archived 'memory', which is transforming the historiography of the revolution, presents challenges. Disillusioned 'postmemory' offers a useful source for historians who, writing within a new 'memory horizon', wish to revise unsatisfying old narratives. It facilitates the retrieval of the radicalism that existed before 'the sharply conservative aftermath of the revolution, when nascent ideas of certain kinds of liberation were

[94] De Burca to O'Donovan, 3 August 1962, Ms 39/130/5, NLI.
[95] Homer Swander to George Hunt, managing editor, *Life*, Time Inc, 7 February 1966, T13/A/22, Shields papers.
[96] www.decadeofcentenaries.com/forthcoming-easter-rising-commemoration-glasnevin-cemetery-20-april-2014/
[97] See www.postmemory.net/.

aggressively subordinated to the national project of restabilization and clericalization'.[98] It also facilitates analysis of subjects such as violence and sexuality, which lay submerged for generations. But while undoubtedly of contemporary resonance, how representative are these narratives? The Abbey rebels formed part of a small, urban, radical network; their sensibilities differed from the younger, more rural and more conservative foot-soldiers of the post-1916 revolution, as well as the more representative members of their own cohort typified by figures such as de Valera, whose lives were not framed by disappointment. A contemporary analogy is the reliance of historians of the Troubles on the disillusioned narratives of ex-IRA activists, which are probably more candid than representative of the wider republican experience.

The effective use of these personal narratives requires consideration of why and how they were constructed, preserved and revived. The features that render such 'memory' problematic as sources offer insights into the construction of historical narratives, and why the meanings attached to seminal events change over time. Ireland's revolution may, or may not be, 'the best-documented modern revolution in the world', but there can be little doubt that it has among the most comprehensively documented bodies of memory.[99] This case study points to the potential, as Guy Beiner has elsewhere identified, for a more systematic 'archaeology of social memory' to trace systematically the ebb and flow of such narratives across generations, not least given the emergence of memory as 'the central organizing concept of historical study, a position once occupied by the notions of class, race, and gender'.[100] The impact of the current 'memory boom', moreover, extends well beyond the universities. Memory, Alison Ribeiro de Menezes suggests,

constitutes a new epistemological approach to the relationship between individual and society, and to our perceptions of the relations between the past, present and the future. Memory is not simply individual; it is also social and collective, and it has manifold cultural dimensions that are embedded in our sense of shared identities. Memories – personal, collective, and cultural – are thus part of how we see ourselves and others, and these intersections have a currency beyond the academic sphere, in national and transnational debates concerning the burden of traumatic and unmastered pasts.

The focus of memory, de Menezes argues, has shifted from physical sites such as battlegrounds and cemeteries to 'embodied memory', and its

---

[98] Foster, *Vivid Faces*, p. 117. On retrospective sources, see pp. xix–xx.

[99] Peter Hart, 'The Social Structure of the IRA, 1916-23', *Historical Journal* 42 (1999), 207–231.

[100] Beiner, 'Boundaries of Irish Memory', pp. 302–304; Jay Winter, 'The Memory Boom in Contemporary Historical Studies', *Raritan* 21 (2001), 52.

transmission across the generations. This notion of history as trauma, or therapy, rather than intellectual endeavour, in the age of identity is exemplified by the increasingly commonplace deployment in historical discourse of medical terminology, such as amnesia, to diagnose and heal society's disordered past.[101]

The closer one looks at the ceremony that frames this essay, the more unstable it appears. It formed part of a wider process in 1966 that subordinated problematic aspects of 1916 – such as the agency of women and the rebellion's radical impulses – to a conservative vision of revolution.[102] That Yeats's myths required delicate handling was, of course, understood by the politicians and Abbey cognoscenti who participated in the event. The State's organising committee had already declared its opposition to 'the inclusion of O'Casey's plays as part of any 1916 Commemorative Programme', while a government minister had urged his colleagues to steer clear of Yeats's poetry. Despite praising publicly the theatre's commitment to 'free expression', Lemass had told his Minister for Posts and Telegraphs to instruct the State's cultural institutions to offer 'suitable' content in 1966: 'This means in particular no O'Casey', he clarified.[103] The shadow of past conflicts with the State could be discerned in Lemass's hope that the memorial would remind all 'of the national purpose which the founders had in mind', coupled with his insistence on the need for greater State representation on the Abbey's board to ensure 'that their advice and guidance might be at the disposal of the directors'.[104] For its part, the Abbey had its own reasons for reasserting its patriotic credentials on the opening of its new State-funded building.[105]

However, as Roisín Higgins has noted, the 'significance of the Easter Rising has not been primarily in its official commemoration'.[106] Reading too much into the significance of the ceremony at the Abbey obscures the importance of other, less visible, forms of remembering such as collective, cultural and family memory, which are often 'characterised as much by debate, division and contestation as they are by homogenous and overarching narrative perspectives'.[107] By the late 1980s, when the State's

---

[101] Ribeiro de Menezes, *Embodying Memory in Contemporary Spain*, pp. 1–2.
[102] Moran, *Staging the Easter Rising*; Higgins, *Transforming 1916*.
[103] Higgins, *Transforming 1916*, pp. 162–163, 122. Denounced by Blythe, the committee's statement was memorably described by the *Sligo Champion* as 'possibly the most stupid statement to be issued in the Jubilee year' (James Moran, *The Theatre of Sean O'Casey* (London: Bloomsbury, 2013), p. 171).
[104] *Sunday Independent*, 24 July 1966; *Irish Press*, 25 July 1966.
[105] For the Abbey's deployment of its history, see Holly Maples, 'Producing Memory: A History of Commemoration and the Abbey Theatre' in Oona Frawley (ed.), *Memory Ireland. Volume 1. History and Modernity* (Syracuse: Syracuse University Press, 2011).
[106] Higgins, *Transforming 1916*, p. 12.   [107] De Menezes, *Embodying Memory*, p. 5.

appetite for remembering 1916 had diminished, the Yeatsian narrative that framed the Abbey's memorial no longer seemed so compelling, prompting Paul Muldoon to wonder mischievously: 'If Yeats had saved his pencil-lead/would certain men have stayed in bed?'[108] But, even in 1966, many in the audience were sceptical about the commemorative ritual in which they participated. Christine Shields, who delivered a speech on behalf of her father, subsequently confided to him her irreverent thoughts:

> We . . . also met Ernest Blythe . . . Horrid man! He refuses to read or listen to all the criticisms of himself & is still holding on with the firm grip. Well anyway the production was pretty bad. Daddy, you would have been terribly disgusted with the whole bloody mess! 'Recall the Years' is nothing more than two or three lines from practically every play the Abbey ever put on & started with Lady Gregory and Yeats signing the agreement for the theatre & ended with firemen racing across the stage . . . Well, last nite, the opening, everybody was there & to tell you the truth, I think everyone was a bit disappointed. Dev. made the opening speech . . . Well, both Jack and I both were surprised that there was no party or anything. That's Blythe's doing . . . P.S. Sean Barlow rang the gong at the beginning of the show – got best reception of all'.[109]

Others who attended, or stayed away, resented how they, or their relations, had been excluded from the memorial. This is not to set opportunistic 'official' memory against virtuous 'family' memory: each shapes the other, as does the wider social context. Revealingly, the impetus that 'led to the erection of the 1916 commemorative plaque' came from de Burca's *Soldier's Song*, itself a critique of official commemorative impulses.[110] By the 1980s, when the plaque had become such a well-known feature that it had begun to generate its own historiography, observers had begun to complain that the names on the memorial now conveyed 'very little'.[111] More recently, as a result of the Decade of Centenaries, a transformed political context, and the retrieval by historians of a lost generation of radicals, figures like Helen Molony have increasingly been restored to public memory. The recycling of their narratives, and the meanings attached to them, will continue to evolve as the rewriting and reimagining of the past advances relentlessly into the future.

---

[108] Paul Muldoon, '7, Middagh Street' in *Poems 1968–1998* (London: Faber, 2001).

[109] Christine to Arthur Shields, 19 July 1966, T13/A/486 (2), Shields papers.

[110] Gabriel Fallon, cited in *Abbey Theatre – Dublin 1904–1966* (Dublin: National Theatre Society, 1966).

[111] Seamus Scully, 'The Abbey Theatre 1916 Plaque', *Dublin Historical Record* 41 (1988), 157; James Wren, 'Barney Murphy and the Abbey Theatre Plaque', *Dublin Historical Record* 51 (1998), 81–83; idem, 'The Abbey Theatre 1916 Plaque', *Dublin Historical Record* 52 (1999), 108–109.

6   Beyond the Ulster Division: West Belfast members of the Ulster Volunteer Force and Service in the First World War

Richard S. Grayson

Introduction: popular memory

The centrality of the 36th (Ulster) Division, 'an unambiguously unionist and Protestant formation',[1] to unionist/loyalist commemoration of the First World War is well-established. Indeed, it goes beyond that: some school curricula which cover the First World War as part of wider issues sometimes pick out the division as just one, or one of a few aspects of the war, which are mentioned in any depth.[2] For unionists/loyalists, the experiences of the 36th Division on the Somme are central to commemoration, even exclusive. Marking the division's role on 1 July 1916, the first day of the battle of the Somme began almost as soon as it became public knowledge. Although many events on 12 July 1916 had been cancelled in response to a request from the Ministry of Munitions to keep production flowing, there was a five minutes' silence in Belfast in memory of the dead at 12 noon, and this set the pattern that in future years, 12 July would be linked by many to the Somme.[3] A specific link

I am grateful to David Fitzpatrick for pointing out to me the value of regimental medal rolls in the case of Isaac Hughes. Prior to digitisation, these rolls (WO 329 at the National Archives) were exceptionally time-consuming to use given their varied forms of organisation, and only sporadically yielded information of significant value on units of service. However, now that they are digitised (available on www.ancestry.co.uk or on CD-ROM from the Naval and Military Press) they can be far more easily utilised. They yielded information on the range of units served in beyond those cited in newspapers for Hughes and several others.

[1] Keith Jeffery, *Ireland and the Great War* (Cambridge: Cambridge University Press, 2000), p. 39.

[2] For Key Stage 3, see Sheelagh Dean, Vivien Kelly and Julie Taggart, *History for NI Key Stage 3: A Study after 1900* (London: Hodder Education, 2009), pp. 22–23. Three pages cover the war, one on the Ulster Division, one on 1 July 1916 largely focused on the division and not mentioning others, and one page is on technological change. For A-Level, see Henry A. Jefferies, *History: Partition of Ireland 1900–25 (Option 4)* (Deddington: Philip Allan, 2011), pp. 33–34. In a course that is focused on political matters, the war features primarily in terms of recruitment to the 36th and 16th Divisions with a clear sense that 'the Ulster Volunteer Force was organised into an "Ulster Division"'.

[3] David Officer, '"For God and Ulster": The Ulsterman on the Somme' in Ian McBride (ed.), *History and Memory in Modern Ireland* (Cambridge: Cambridge University Press,

between Somme commemoration and the Ulster Volunteer Force (UVF) has similar long-standing roots. Gillian McIntosh observes of writers such as Cyril Falls in the immediate post-war years that 'celebrating the achievements of the 36th Division was in its own way a celebration of the Ulster Volunteer Force'.[4] Meanwhile, Graham and Shirlow point to a particular growth of Somme commemoration after the 1994 paramilitary ceasefires with the modern UVF's 'appropriation' of the Somme. They argue that 'The Somme is a defining motif of unionist history and identity and the UVF – past and present – is an essential part of that unofficial history.'[5] This view is widely accepted by academic writers, even if there is more debate over Graham and Shirlow's belief that this is 'an unofficial history of the protestant people denied to them by the Stormont state and the cult of Britishness'.[6] In contrast, Kris Brown argues that 'Loyalist commemorations [of the Somme], by word, action and use of symbols, express only a continued attachment to Britishness.'[7]

Whatever view one takes of that debate, there is no question that among unionists/loyalists, Somme commemoration (and specifically the role of the 36th (Ulster) Division) dominates all other commemoration of the First World War. Similarly, there is little to debate about the centrality of the UVF to the formation of the 36th (Ulster) Division. Though by 1918 the 36th (Ulster) Division contained thousands of Catholics and four Jesuit chaplains[8] due to reorganisations in January and February of that year, the relationship between the UVF and the division in 1914–1916 (and arguably 1917) was strong. Of course, that flowed from the fact that it had been Sir Edward Carson who had secured the establishment of the division, specifically for the purpose of transferring the UVF into the British army. This then manifested itself in UVF formations joining the division *en masse* in early September 1914. In Belfast, each part of the UVF was allocated different days on which to enlist. The North came first

2001), pp. 160–183 (pp. 174–175); Catherine Switzer, *Unionists and Great War Commemoration in the North of Ireland 1914–1918* (Dublin: Irish Academic Press, 2007), pp. 30–37.

[4] Gillian McIntosh, *The Force of Culture: Unionist Identities in Twentieth Century Ireland* (Cork: Cork University Press, 1999), p. 11.

[5] Brian Graham and Peter Shirlow, 'The Battle of the Somme in Ulster Memory and Identity', *Political Geography* 21 (2002), 881–904 [891 & 897].

[6] Ibid., 897.

[7] Kris Brown, '"Our Father Organization": The Cult of the Somme and the Unionist "Golden Age" in Modern Ulster Loyalist Commemoration', *The Round Table* 96, 393 (2007), 707–723 [718].

[8] Richard S. Grayson, *Belfast Boys: How Unionists and Nationalists Fought and Died Together in the First World War* (London: Continuum, 2009), pp. 128–129. See also, Philip Orr, *The Road to the Somme: Men of the Ulster Division Tell Their Story* (Belfast: Blackstaff, 1987, 2008 edn), pp. 42–62.

on 4th September, followed on subsequent days by the East, West and South.[9]

Quite how far the 36th (Ulster) Division did equal the UVF is difficult to measure precisely. The source that would help us most is the collection of applications to the UVF Patriotic Fund, which is held at the Somme Heritage Centre. However, other than for specific small-scale enquiries, the archive is closed for data protection reasons and it is not possible to trawl through a large quantity of papers to see how many members of the initial division were members of the UVF (or at least later claimed to be). As discussed below, newspapers are the only significant source to mention UVF membership. Of course, the widely reported mass enlistment, as already noted for Belfast, is a strong indicator, especially because some battalions appear to have been filled rapidly by such volunteers. It is also known, as Tim Bowman points out, that the formation of the division 'saw many UVF units effectively cease to exist by autumn 1914'.[10] But there are some caveats to that. In December 1914, the division was still said to be 1,955 understrength, while by February 1915, it was recruiting in Liverpool.[11] We cannot know whether all those who had joined by December were UVF members, nor can we know that those who joined afterwards were not, but these figures do challenge the idea that the division was filled from the initial rush of volunteering from the UVF. Meanwhile, Cyril Falls claimed that the divisional artillery 'was raised, six months after the rest of the Division, in the suburbs of London' and offered very precise information on where specific Royal Field Artillery units came from around the city.[12]

Yet, despite these caveats, it is understandable that commemoration of the 36th Division has dominated in the way that it continues to do. As Keith Jeffery says, 'the 36th exemplified on a grand scale the "pals" battalions of some other divisions'.[13] Consequently,

The particularly concentrated nature of the Ulster Division, not just socially but also in terms of its religion and politics, meant that its losses on the first day of the Somme, grievous enough in themselves, had a disproportionately great impact back home.[14]

It was the UVF contribution to the division which brought those pals' battalion characteristics. So it is quite natural that, in specific local areas,

---

[9] Grayson, *Belfast Boys*, pp. 11–12.
[10] Timothy Bowman, *Carson's Army: The Ulster Volunteer Force, 1910–22* (Manchester: Manchester University Press, 2007), p. 167.
[11] Bowman, *Carson's Army*, pp. 177, 179.
[12] Cyril Falls, *The History of the 36th (Ulster) Division* (Belfast: McCaw, Steven & Orr, 1922), p. 8.
[13] Jeffery, *Ireland*, p. 56.   [14] Jeffery, *Ireland*, p. 57.

it is the UVF connection with the division which is most commemorated. Taking today's West Belfast as a case study, it can be seen in a number of different murals/memorials, often combined with commemoration of the post-1966 UVF. In the nature of murals, these are not all still in existence, but they have been recorded on the CAIN (Conflict Archive on the Internet) website.[15] Some simply make general references to First World War service, through displays of images of First World War soldiers alongside more contemporary references. Examples can be found on Ainsworth Avenue and Glenwood Street.[16] Others make more specific Ulster Division references, linked to the UVF. Two in Disraeli Street remember 1989 and 1994 UVF deaths through imagery linking the contemporary UVF to the 36th Division through displaying the 14th Royal Irish Rifles flag (which, of course, is more accurately linked to the Young Citizen Volunteers (YCV) than the UVF).[17] Most markedly, a mural not on the CAIN website but photographed by the author in September 2008 is situated at Canmore Street's junction with the

Figure 6.1: Shankill Mural, 28 September 2008 (photo: with permission of Richard S. Grayson).

[15] See also similar murals in North Belfast (http://cain.ulst.ac.uk/viggiani/north_mural.html#130; and http://cain.ulst.ac.uk/viggiani/north_memorial.html#85) and East Belfast (http://cain.ulst.ac.uk/viggiani/east_mural.html#126, http://cain.ulst.ac.uk/viggiani/east_mural.html#127 and http://cain.ulst.ac.uk/viggiani/east_memorial.html#76).
[16] http://cain.ulst.ac.uk/viggiani/west_plaque.html#149 and http://cain.ulst.ac.uk/viggiani/west_mural.html#114.
[17] http://cain.ulst.ac.uk/viggiani/west_mural.html#110 and http://cain.ulst.ac.uk/viggiani/west_mural.html#111.

Shankill Road (Figure 6.1). It depicts an evolutionary narrative that begins with the 'Shankill Volunteers' drilling at Fernhill. That is then followed by the 9th Royal Irish Rifles – specifically given the nomenclature of 'West Belfast UVF' in brackets, rather than the more correct West Belfast Volunteers – on the Somme in 1916. This is followed by images of the UVF in 1969 and 2002, with a title 'The Peoples Army – 1912–2002 – 90 years of resistance'.

This mural is a vivid example of a narrative that begins with the Shankill's involvement in resistance to Home Rule. In this chain of events, having been formed (actually in early 1913 rather than 1912 as is commonly held), the men of the UVF expected to take part in some kind of conflict over Home Rule. Instead, in September 1914, those men found themselves marching *en masse* into the British Army as part of the 36th (Ulster) Division, the formation which Edward Carson had persuaded the British government to establish to receive members of the UVF. The next year was spent in training before the Division was sent to France in October 1915, with further acclimatisation and training on arrival. Many battalions did not find themselves engaged in serious action until the summer of 1916, and the first major attempt at engaging the enemy was, of course, the first day of the Battle of the Somme, 1 July 1916. That date is forever etched in the annals of the British Army as its bloodiest day ever. It is also widely held to be the primary manifestation of Ulster's contribution to the war effort with a widely accepted figure of around 5,500 casualties in the entire Ulster Division (which would have totalled about 16,000) on those two days, with approximately 2,000 of those being killed. That narrative generally ends on 2 July 1916 and we see in the mural how it rapidly moves on to the modern UVF.

Of course, Figure 6.1 cannot be taken to imply that its makers think that all of those from the Shankill who joined up were in the 9th Royal Irish Rifles. However, it is part of a narrative which links the West Belfast UVF only to one battalion and/or the Ulster Division. This can also be seen in a tourist information board outside the Shankill Memorial Garden, photographed in June 2008 (the board is still in place) (see Figure 6.2).

The section of text relevant to this discussion reads:

During World War One, members of the Ulster Volunteer Force, who had been instrumental in resisting Home Rule, joined the 36th Ulster Division of the British Army. Almost an entire generation of Shankill men was wiped out on 1 July 1916 at the Battle of the Somme. Of the 760 men who fought for the regiment, only 76 returned.

Figure 6.2: Tourist Information Board, Shankill Road, 25 June 2008
(photo: with permission of Richard S. Grayson).

These breath-taking figures, with 'of the 760 who fought only 76 returned' picked out in large letters on the information board, were the original inspiration for my book *Belfast Boys*.[18] I had first seen them displayed in the Shankill Heritage Centre at Fernhill House when on holiday in Northern Ireland in 1999. Some years later, I resolved to try to tell the story of those men, with the addition of the parallel story of Catholic men from the Falls, who also heeded their political leaders and joined the British Army believing that it would help to advance their cause – just as Unionists believed they could advance a different case through enlisting. The book became a story of West Belfast[19] as a whole.

Yet, this text is problematic on a number of levels which have been addressed elsewhere in depth but require some short summary here. In the first place, if it is meant to set out how many from the Shankill served and were killed, then it massively understates both figures. In *Belfast Boys*, this author identified at least 6,431 from the wider Shankill area who served, and at least 1,358 who were killed.[20] Due to records being destroyed in the Second World War, the actual level of service (if not those killed) is likely to be much higher.[21] Moreover, there is some confusion over what is meant by the term 'regiment'. In the British army, this correctly refers to a grouping of a number of battalions but, despite common usage by soldiers saying they are being 'posted to their regiment', what is actually meant is battalion. We can be fairly sure that 'battalion' is what is actually meant here because of the numbers, short of a thousand, with that being the maximum size of a battalion. Given the West Belfast connection, this is likely to mean the 9th Royal Irish

---

[18] Grayson, *Belfast Boys*.

[19] The area's basis is five electoral wards: Shankill, Woodvale, Court, Smithfield and Falls. Also included are sections of the Donegall Road and Grosvenor Road west of the railway line. These were in St Anne's ward, but formed part of what might be called 'Greater Falls' in 1914 in terms of living, working and socialising. The result is an area bounded by the Crumlin Road to the north, the Donegall Road and railway line to the south, Upper Library Street and Smithfield Market to the east, and the city boundary to the west. For further information on the area covered, see Richard S. Grayson, *Belfast Boys*, pp. 189–190.

[20] That would suggest a fatality rate of over 20 per cent. However, as already stated, many records were not possible to locate and, once that is factored in, the fatality rate for the whole Shankill area is unlikely to be much higher than the overall figure of approximately 12 per cent of those who served across the United Kingdom. One would expect this to be higher in specific infantry units like the 9th Royal Irish Rifles which were in more danger on a regular basis than, say, the Army Service Corps. But no figure which it is possible to reach – even that compiled from newspaper reports which focus on the dead – comes anywhere near the 90 per cent of the popular narrative.

[21] Grayson, *Belfast Boys*, pp. 194–195. For discussion of a debate around the estimate of higher figures, see Richard S. Grayson, 'Military History from the Street: New Methods for Researching First World War Service in the British Military', *War in History*, 21 (2014), 465–495 (481–482 n. 63).

Rifles, but again, as has been argued elsewhere, these figures would severely overstate the level of fatalities in that one battalion, probably based on a misreading of the memoirs of the battalion's commanding officer, F. P. Crozier.[22]

None of this is to diminish the Shankill's sacrifice on the Somme. In addition to those in the 9th Royal Irish Rifles, at least another 61 Shankill men were killed on 1 and 2 July 1916, a total of 173 dead in just two days of the war. That means that nearly 13 per cent of the Shankill's wartime fatalities occurred on 0.1 per cent of the days of the war, which is a massive concentration.[23] Such a figure explains how that battle, and the deaths which flowed from it, were so traumatic at the time, and rightly are still given greater prominence in remembrance than any other part of the war.

The extent to which this narrative only offers a very partial of the Shankill's service in the war does not need further discussion here. However, what has not been discussed for West Belfast is whether the dominant UVF narrative even offers an accurate picture of war service by UVF members. In his study of the UVF, Tim Bowman has pointed out 'the extent to which UVF members were not predisposed to join the 36th (Ulster) Division'. Using a sample of seventy-six members of one unit ('E' (Bushmills) Company, 2nd North Antrim Regiment), he shows that while fifty-four had joined the 12th Royal Irish Rifles who were formed from their area's UVF, another twenty had gone elsewhere, including some outside the Ulster Division.[24] Why might West Belfast men have served outside the Ulster Division?

The UVF and enlistment

The West Belfast UVF had been seen by some to be among the elite of the UVF and one would expect therefore that there would be no trouble in filling the ranks of the 9th Royal Irish Rifles, the battalion which was to take men from the west. However, more than any other former Belfast UVF battalion in the British Army, it was the 9th which had problems meeting its targets. Partly, this would have been because the West Belfast

---

[22] Grayson, *Belfast Boys*, p. 200. In fact, the official *Soldiers Died* records show 255 dead among 'Other Ranks' in the 9th Royal Irish Rifles. That is from 700 to 900 at any one time, and probably a few thousand in total due to soldiers being wounded and drafted. Officer fatalities are harder to gauge as a battalion is not always listed. Source: *Soldiers Died in the Great War* [Published in paper form in 1921 but now available online at 'UK, Soldiers Died in the Great War, 1914–1919', http://search.ancestry.co.uk/search/db.as px?dbid=1543, and on CD-ROM from the Naval and Military Press.] There were another 44 dead when the merged 8/9th Royal Irish Rifles are added.

[23] Grayson, *Belfast Boys*, pp. 200–201.   [24] Bowman, *Carson's Army*, p. 173.

UVF was smaller than other Belfast parts of the UVF but it would also have been affected by so many men having already enlisted or been called up as reservists.[25]

The most important factor in joining the UVF would have been to hold broadly 'Unionist' political sympathies (with the term 'Loyalist' seldom if ever being in use at that time). Some who joined might not have thought through the precise consequences of what they could be asked to do, such as fighting against the British Army in rebellion against an act passed by the Westminster government. But others would have been well aware of what was expected, and as such, the UVF would have had strong attractions for those with some kind of military experience. That might have meant former service in the British Army, or it might have meant men who were serving as reservists in the Army. As the equivalent of today's Territorial Army, those who served in the reserve were liable to be called up to their regiments on the outbreak of war. In most cases, that would have involved being called into one of the regular battalions of the British Army, the 1st and 2nd battalions of each regiment. For Belfast men, that would usually be the Royal Irish Rifles, but it might also be the Royal Irish Fusiliers or the Royal Inniskilling Fusiliers, and potentially any other unit of the British Army, especially if men had previously served elsewhere. The consequence of this was that any UVF man who was a reservist was called up immediately on the outbreak of war and was not able to join the Ulster Division.

We also have to note that the Ulster Division was not formed until early September 1914, a full month after the outbreak of war. If one makes a reasonable assumption that members of the UVF would have been relatively keen to heed the call to fight for King and Country, some would not have wished to wait until 'big house Unionists' had done deals in London to set up the Ulster Division. Instead, they would join a unit already in existence, or being formed more quickly. In some cases, that meant battalions of the 10th (Irish) Division, which was formed on 21 August 1914. Like the later 16th (Irish) Division, it recruited across Ireland, but unlike the 16th, which was broadly nationalist in its politics, the 10th was non-political. Neither Carson nor Redmond was calling on supporters to join it.

There were other reasons for UVF members to enlist prior to the formation of the Ulster Division. Individuals might make personal decisions over which regiments to join, perhaps due to some family connection with a particular regiment. There were also economic factors. In the first few days of the war, a number of employers in West Belfast lost

[25] Grayson, *Belfast Boys*, pp. 11–12.

continental orders and men were laid off. Faced with unemployment, and the hardship it would bring to their families, taking the King's shilling was an obvious solution.

Therefore, while we might imagine that the West Belfast UVF simply became the 9th Royal Irish Rifles, the reality is far more complicated than that. As will be discussed, its members served throughout the British Army. That means that even if one is primarily interested in the history of the UVF during the First World War, rather than others from Ulster who served, it is problematic to focus only on the Ulster Division.

The UVF in the British Army

Where did UVF members from West Belfast serve? The discussion offered here is far from being a complete story and the numbers should not be taken as definitive. Relevant information for most who served is either not in existence or is not accessible for reasons already stated. Indeed, references to UVF membership can only frequently be found in newspapers, and the only men mentioned in newspapers were those who were unusual in some way: for example, by virtue of being killed or wounded, winning a medal, or occasionally, by sending an interesting letter home. But most men were not killed or wounded or awarded gallantry medals, and of those who wrote interesting letters home, only a small number appeared in newspapers. Moreover, men might have been mentioned in a newspaper without their UVF membership being specified. However, the cases identified do at least serve as a pointer to where men served and what they did having moved from the UVF to the British Army.

In the course of writing *Belfast Boys*, references in newspapers were identified for 138 West Belfast men who served having been members of the UVF. This data is now online for public viewing.[26] Sixty-eight of the men were dead, which is nearly half of the sample, but to reiterate, only those to whom something remarkable happens are mentioned in newspapers, so the actual fatality rate would be far below that. Newspapers are the sole consistent source for UVF membership. It was not recorded on official service records, and the closure of the UVF Patriotic Fund records was mentioned earlier. However, in this research, medal rolls have been used (both the WO 372 index and the WO 329 regimental records) along with service pensions records (WO 363 and 364) to supplement service

---

[26] http://queensub.maps.arcgis.com/apps/webappviewer/index.html?id=9a444246f92b4f6bb2f3deffc85b9b24.

information on soldiers reported in the newspapers as being members of the UVF and living in West Belfast.

It will come as no surprise that the largest single number of men (59 of the 138) were in the 9th Royal Irish Rifles, as shown in Table 6.1. The table indicates home addresses, and in which part of the UVF they served if it is known. It should be noted that because part of the Shankill was in the North Belfast parliamentary constituency, it was covered by the North Belfast UVF, even though such areas would have been thought of by many as 'West'. One of these men, Richard Mussen, had first served in the 1st Royal Irish Rifles, so was probably not deployed for the first time with the Ulster Division (his date of embarkation is not apparent). However, of the remaining fifty-eight, there are dates of first date of embarkation available for forty-nine. All of these men first embarked between 2 and 5 October 1915, and all (except one for whom no 'theatre' exists) landed in France. This suggests that at least all these forty-eight were part of the original 36th Division.

One point is striking about the deaths in the 9th Royal Irish Rifles: of the twenty-eight for whom there is a date of death, only four lost their lives on 1 July 1916. Fifteen had been killed before the battle began; one was killed a week later;[27] while eight were killed in 1917. This is a small sample and should be treated with the relevant caveats. It is quite likely that the high volume of news of deaths on 1 and 2 July 1916 left journalists unable to investigate personal stories of those killed simply because there were so many at one time. That would lead to an under-reporting of UVF membership. However, the presence of information on many deaths before and after the Somme does point to the problems of assuming shared characteristics across a cohort of men with an apparently shared story. Of these twenty-eight UVF men, twenty-four did not fall in action on 1 July 1916. Of course, any or all of the others who were killed in the battalion that day could have been UVF members, meaning that a vast majority of the dead fit the popular narrative. However, the sample available suggests that caution should be taken in assuming this.

Meanwhile, although the link between West Belfast and the 9th Royal Irish Rifles is well known, twenty-six UVF members from the area also served in other units of the 36th Division. Twenty-one were in other infantry units with five outside the infantry. YCVs were drafted into the 14th Royal Irish Rifles from across Belfast, and that might explain how Herbert Lynch and Hugh Neely came to be in that battalion, as they were

---

[27] Samuel Bryans, who is listed in *Soldiers Died* as KIA, rather than being DoW received in a previous action. However, the battalion war diary suggests that the unit was behind the lines at Rubempré that day, so he was possibly a victim of artillery. See WO 95/2503.

Table 6.1: *UVF members from West Belfast serving in 9th Royal Irish Rifles*

Name	Road	House	UVF Regiment+	Death date
Allen, John[a]	Acton Street	17	North	
Barnes, Samuel	Wilson Street	20	West	
Beattie, Albert[b]	Canmore Street	165	West	
Beattie, Robert	Palmer Street	8	North	
Bell, John K	Carlow Street	25	West	29-3-1916
Bell, William J	Cumberland Street	33	West	8-3-1916
Bingam, Alfred	Sugarfield Street	51	West	5-2-1916
Bryans, Samuel	Sugarfield Street	39	West	8-7-1916
Campbell, Hugh	Kirk Street	12	*UVF	
Campbell, James A	Upper Townsend Street	31	North	
Carlisle, Samuel[c]	Aberdeen Street	62& 74	West	
Cassidy, William[d]	Springfield Road	247	West	
Crilly, Daniel	Francis Street	7	West	8-12-1915
Crone, Joseph[e]	Brookmount Street	122	West	
Currie, Thomas	Derry Street	7	West	21-10-1915
Doherty, Isaac	Leopold Street	107	*UVF	
Dunning, Thomas John	Haddow Street	16	West	2-3-1916
Eccles, John	Sixth Street	35	West	
Fleming, Thomas	Boundary Street	160	West	
Gallagher, James	Cambrai Street	264	North	24-12-1915
Gault, James[f]	Riga Street	62	West	
Glenn, James	Canmore Street	76	West	
Gray, John	Springfield Road	280	West	
Harvey, John	Sugarfield Street	33	West	
Hill, Arthur	Enfield Street	89	North	24-8-1919
Jenkins, Edward[g]	Sixth Street	5	West	17-8-1917
Johnston, Alexander	Bristol Street	79	North	
Larmour, William	Glenfarne Street	38	West	1-7-1916
Magee, William	Clovelly Street	None	West	21-6-1917
Malcolm, James[h]	Sixth Street	49	West	
Marsden, James	Eighth Street	3	West	17-1-1916
Martin, John	Northland Street	1	West	25-12-1915
Martin, Joseph	Parkview Terr., Woodvale Rd	3	North	1-7-1916
Matier, Samuel	Ainsworth Avenue	171	West	7-6-1917
McComb, William	North Howard Street	23	West	5-8-1917
McDowell, James[i]	Third Street	49	West	
Mooney, Edward	Third Street	11	West	6-6-1916
Moore, Jackson	Cupar Street	290	West	
Moore, John W	Eastland Street	27	West	

Table 6.1. *(cont.)*

Name	Road	House	UVF Regiment+	Death date
Moore, Robert McConnell[j]	Springfield Road	227	West	27-3-1918
Morrison, David	Southland Street	13	*UVF	16-1-1916
Mussen, Richard	Dundee Street	41	West	21-3-1918
Parker, George	Dover Street	96	West	
Pratt, Samuel	Geoffrey Street	48	North	
Quinn, William James	Little Sackville Street	27	West	6-6-1916
Russell, William Lester	Westland Street	30	West	
Smyth, Matthew	Gardiner Street	5	West	3-1-1916
Smyth, Robert	Perth Street	42	West	1-7-1916
Swain, Samuel[k]	Urney Street	1	West	17-8-1917
Spence, Thomas H	Wilton Square North	14	West	1-7-1916
Stockman, Hugh	Conway Street	298	West	
Thompson, John	Divis Drive, Glen Road	14	West	
Tinsley, John	Sugarfield Street	113	West	
Todd, Edward[l]	Trelford Street	8	West	
Verner, John A[m]	Canmore Street	63	West	
Wilkinson, Robert[n]	Haddow Street	4	West	
Williamson, William	Canmore Street	179a	West	10-5-1916
Wright, John	Fifth Street	29	West	18-3-1916
Young, Thomas	Sugarfield Street	162	West	

*Denotes no specific UVF Regiment stated.
+North, South, East and West are references to Belfast UVF Regiments.
[a]Later served in the 8th and 15th Royal Irish Rifles.
[b]Later served in the 15th Royal Irish Rifles.
[c]Later served in the 8th Royal Irish Rifles.
[d]Later served in the Royal Flying Corps.
[e]Later served in the 2nd Royal Irish Rifles.
[f]Later served in the 15th Royal Irish Rifles.
[g]Later served in the 8th Royal Rifles.
[h]Later served in the 8/9th and 15th Royal Irish Rifles.
[i]Later served in the 8th, 13th & 15th Royal Irish Rifles.
[j]Later commissioned as a 2nd Lieutenant in the 1st Royal Irish Rifles, in which unit he met his death.
[k]Killed while serving later with the 107th Machine Gun Corps, in the Ulster Division.
[l]Later served in the 14th Royal Irish Rifles.
[m]Later served with 17th Royal Irish Rifles, 3rd Garrison Battalion Northumberland Fusiliers, and 3rd Garrison Battalion Royal Irish Fusiliers.
[n]Later served in the 8th Royal Irish Rifles.

also members of the YCV. However, there were also two others in it who did not have any stated YCV affiliation, as detailed in Table 6.2. There were also some among the divisional or brigade troops, as set out in Table 6.3. In these tables, Inniskillings denotes the Royal Inniskilling Fusiliers, RIRifles the Royal Irish Rifles and RIFusiliers the Royal Irish Fusiliers.

Taken together, 85 of the 138 men identified served in the Ulster Division. As with those in Table 6.1, the vast majority of the men listed in Tables 6.2 and 6.3 who lost their lives did not do so on 1 July 1916. Indeed, only one man, Alfred Bryans, did so. Another, Andrew Bell, was reported as having died on 15 July, while a prisoner, of wounds incurred on 1 July. Of the remaining twelve, one was killed in June 1916, three in October or November 1916, while eight lost their lives in 1917.

There are also a further eight in Table 6.4 whose specific battalions or other units have not been possible (yet, at least) to identify, and it has not been possible to prove that they were *not* in the Ulster Division. Certainly both Samuel Beattie and Thomas Crellin deployed in France at exactly the time the Ulster Division arrived there, and Hugh Cathcart just a few weeks after. Only one lost his life. His cause of death was listed as 'Died, Home' at the time the Ulster Division was landing in France, though he could have been 'home' having served with it initially.

Intriguingly, that leaves another forty-five men (nearly one-third of all those found) who definitely did not serve in the Ulster Division as it was first constituted (noting that, of course, the 2nd Royal Irish Rifles did transfer into the division towards the end of the war). It is these men who add the most significant 'lost' dimensions to the story of what happened to UVF members during the war. In the vast majority of cases (30), as Table 6.5 shows, such men served in the 1st and 2nd battalions of various Irish regiments. That would indicate that they had either enlisted as regular soldiers prior to the war breaking out or, more likely, that they were reservists who were obliged to join their regiments on the outbreak of war. In such battalions, UVF members would have served alongside nationalists, including members of the Irish National Volunteers.[28]

From those listed in Table 6.5, we can add many new dimensions to the UVF's war story, simply by looking at where men were killed. The first fatality was Frank Todd from March Street who was killed on 22 October 1914 serving with the 1st Royal Irish Fusiliers. Others killed at that time, as the British Army fought to stop the Germans taking France's channel coast, were serving with regular battalions of the

[28] Grayson, *Belfast Boys*, pp. 27–28.

Table 6.2: *UVF members from West Belfast serving in 36th (Ulster) Division infantry other than 9th Royal Irish Rifles*

Name	Unit	Road	House	UVF Regiment+	Death
Bryans, Alfred	9th Inniskillings	Sugarfield Street	39	West	1-7-1916
Cunningham, William	8th RIRifles	Shankill Road	330	West	5-8-1917
Hill, David[a]	8th RIRifles	Wilton Street	30	West	
Kyle, Thomas	8th RIRifles	Mountcashel Street	27	West	7-6-1917
Shields, Robert	8th RIRifles	North Boundary Street	32	West	
Milne, Ernest[b]	10th & 8th RIRifles	Roden Street	107	South	
Bell, Andrew	11th RIRifles	McTier Street	80	Randalstown	15-7-1916
Henderson, William	13th RIRifles	Warkworth Street	44	Bangor	25-8-1917
Mills, Harry	13th RIRifles	Sixth Street	47	West	
Bell, James McD	14th RIRifles	McTier Street	80	Randalstown	10-10-1916
Lynch, Herbert VR	14th RIRifles	Carlisle Street	66	North	1-11-1916
Neely, Hugh W	14th RIRifles	Shankill Road	218	*UVF	
Robinson, James G[c]	14th RIRifles	Springfield Road	342	*UVF	9-10-1916
Beattie, Herbert	15th RIRifles	Palmer Street	8	North	
Brickley, William[d]	15th RIRifles	Disraeli Street	20	North	
Burns, Isaac	15th RIRifles	Brownlow Street	63	North	22-11-1917
Grant, Malcolm	15th RIRifles	Hudson Street	10	*UVF	3-1-1917
Hewitt, James[e]	15th RIRifles	Cambrai Street	171	West	
Hughes, Fred	15th RIRifles	Cambrai Street	179	North	
Stewart, Samuel	15th RIRifles	Wolfhill Lane	35	*UVF	10-1-1917
Smith, John	16th RIRifles	Kendal Street	7	West	

*Denotes no specific UVF Regiment stated.
+North, South, East and West are references to Belfast UVF Regiments.
[a]Later served in the 2nd Royal Irish Rifles.
[b]Later served in the 8th Royal Irish Rifles.
[c]Described as Robert Graham Robinson in *Soldiers Died* but as James G. Robinson in newspapers and the CWGC records.
[d]Later served in a non-infantry unit of the 36th Division, the 107th Machine Gun Corps.
[e]Later served in the 12th Royal Irish Rifles and the Labour Corps.

Table 6.3: *UVF members from West Belfast serving in non-infantry units of 36th (Ulster) Division*

Name	Unit	Road	House	UVF Regiment+	Death
Cranston, William	109th R.Army Medical Corps	Boundary Street	130	West	2-8-1917
Maconachie, Samuel	110th R.Army Medical Corps[a]	Ballygomartin Road	1 Greenmount	West	2-9-1915
Neill, John	121st & 150th R. Engineers	Westmoreland Street	28	West	
McClean, Ramsey[b]	36th Div. Army Service Corps	Ohio Street	5 or 6	North	11-6-1916
Stitt, John	36th Div. Trench Mortar Battery	Sixth Street	20	West	7-1-1917

+North, South, East and West are references to Belfast UVF Regiments.
[a]Later served in Army Service Corps in 36th Division.
[b]Discharged from the ASC on 1 February 1915 as unfitted for the duties of the corps, and reenlisted subsequently in the 16th Royal Irish Rifles in time to land with them in France on 4 October 1915.

Table 6.4: *UVF members from West Belfast serving where specific unit has not been identified*

Name	Unit	Road	House	UVF Regiment+	Death
Booth, Thomas	Army Service Corps	Sidney Street West	5	*UVF	19 10 1915
Beattie, Henry	RAMC & ASC	Palmer Street	8	North	
Beattie, Samuel	Royal Army Medical Corps	Palmer Street	8	North	
Crellin, Thomas	Royal Army Medical Corps	Milltown	Eno Cottage	West	
Cathcart, Hugh	Royal Field Artillery	Lime Street	14	North	
Logan, John	RIRifles	Leopold Street	107	West	
Shaw, Charles	RIRifles	Rathlin Street	14	North	
Smyth, John B	RIRifles	Glenwood Street	92	West	

*Denotes no specific UVF Regiment stated.
+North, South, East and West are references to Belfast UVF Regiments.

Table 6.5: *UVF members from West Belfast serving in regular infantry units*

Name	Unit	Road	House	UVF Regiment+	Death
Jameson, William John	1st Irish Guards	Argyle Street	18 or 13	West	6-11-1914
McRoberts, James	1st Irish Guards	Lanark Street	61	West	14-1-1915
Reid, Joseph	1st Irish Guards	Argyle Street	121	West	20-2-1915
Bennett, Hugh	1st Inniskillings	Springfield Village	35	West	1-7-1916
Moreland, Thomas	1st Inniskillings	Bellevue Street	145	West	19-6-1915
Morrison, William John	1st Inniskillings	Glenwood Street	26	West	1-2-1917
Robinson, William	1st Inniskillings	Beresford Street	6 & 8	West	
Rosson, William	1st Inniskillings	Wilton Street	131	West	
Seeds, Thomas	1st Inniskillings	Crosby Street	13	West	21-8-1915
Alexander, John	1st RIFusiliers	Riga Street	94	North	
Bell, Charles	1st RIFusiliers	Upton Cottages, Glen Road	11	West	25-4-1915
Owens, James	1st RIFusiliers	Esmond Street	17	West	9-5-1915
Todd, Frank	1st RIFusiliers	March Street	5	West	22-10-1914
Boyles, John	2nd Inniskillings	Wall Street	77	North	
Martin, Daniel	2nd Inniskillings	Wilton Street	80	West	
McComb, Archibald	2nd Inniskillings	Fourth Street	12	West	
McNeice, William	2nd Inniskillings	Silvio Street	146	North	
Porter, Thomas	2nd Inniskillings	Sugarfield Street	111	West	16-5-1915
Reid, William	2nd Inniskillings	Emerson Street	31	West	7-11-1914
McIlroy, William[a]	1st & 2nd RIRifles	Aberdeen Street	31	West	16-6-1915
Beattie, William	2nd RIRifles	Seventh Street	40	West	
Boyd, Alexander	2nd RIRifles	Lawnbrook Avenue	63	West	27-10-1914
Fleming, G	2nd RIRifles	Lawnbrook Avenue	63	West	

Table 6.5: (*cont.*)

Name	Unit	Road	House	UVF Regiment+	Death
Fleming, John	2nd RIRifles	Lawnbrook Avenue	63	West	
Gillespie, Samuel J	2nd RIRifles	Lanark Street	65	West	21-2-1915
McComb, Leonard	2nd RIRifles	Broadbent Street	19	North	7-7-1916
McCrory, Hugh	2nd RIRifles	Urney Street	45	West	2-4-1915
Scott, TJ	2nd RIRifles	Fifth Street	25	West	
Shearer, William	2nd RIRifles	Seventh Street	29	*UVF	25-9-1915
Sinclair, George	2nd RIRifles	Fourth Street	12	West	

*Denotes no specific UVF Regiment stated.
+North, South, East and West are references to Belfast UVF Regiments.
ªFirst served in 1st, later in the 2nd Royal Irish Rifles.

Royal Irish Rifles and Royal Inniskilling Fusiliers, and the Irish Guards. Taking the story further on, we can see deaths at Gallipoli in 1915 with the 1st Inniskillings. Such UVF members had been in action, and in some cases had died, long before the Ulster Division even arrived in France.

In addition to those who served in these regular battalions, fifteen were found in other units, as listed in Table 6.6. The largest body of these men (6) were in the 6th Royal Irish Rifles, which was part of the 10th (Irish) Division. As stated earlier, that had been formed before the 36th and it is possible that an ardent member of the UVF, keen to enlist, would join the 10th Division rather than wait around for the 36th to be formed. Indeed, Carson was told in mid-August that around 500 members of the Tyrone UVF and forty Belfast UVF members had joined the 10th (Irish) Division since there had not been any agreement on the formation of an Ulster Division, although this only appears to have been talked about in the context of men joining the Royal Inniskilling Fusiliers.[29] Some of those men could also have been reservists in the Royal Irish Rifles who were despatched to the 6th to add some experience to the newly formed battalion. Those who served in non-Irish regiments would have done so for a

---

[29] Stephen Sandford, *Neither Unionist nor Nationalist: The 10th (Irish) Division in the Great War* (Dublin: Irish Academic Press, 2015), p. 14.

Table 6.6: *UVF members from West Belfast serving in other units*

Name	Unit	Road	House	UVF Regiment+	Death
McCready, George	2nd Royal Sussex Regiment	Glenwood Street	90	West	30-10-1914
Bell, Robert Rea	16th & 5/6th Royal Scots	Ambleside Street	13	South	11-8-1918
Ferguson, William G	6th East Lancashire Regiment	Esmond Street	22	West	
Edgar, James	6th RIRifles	Broom Street	2	West	11-8-1915
Haydock, Thomas[a]	6th RIRifles	Fortingale Street	84	North	
Lindsay, William[b]	6th RIRifles	Lawnbrook Avenue	56	West	8-7-1916
McAuley, Robert J	6th RIRifles	Canmore Street	3	North	
McClune, Harry	6th RIRifles	Bellevue Street	173	North	27-9-1915
McMeekin, Thomas	6th RIRifles	Brownlow Street	58 or 59	North	11-8-1915
Lyons, Henry James	7th King's Own Royal Lancaster	Riga Street	75	North	23-9-1917
Hughes, Isaac	6th & 8th Royal Inniskilling Fusiliers	Cambrai Street	179	North	29-6-1916
McBurney, Ernest	Canadian Forces	Eastland Street	35	West	
Harper, John L	Military Mounted Police	Beverley Street	67	North	
Cairns, George	4th Seaforth Highlanders	Roden Street	174	South	8-4-1917
Thomas, Fred[c]	Royal Field Artillery	Roden Street		South	

+North, South, East and West are references to Belfast UVF Regiments.
[a]Later served in the 2nd Royal Irish Rifles.
[b]Later served in the 2nd Royal Irish Rifles.
[c]Although it has not been possible to identify the specific RFA unit in which Fred Thomas served, a letter published in a newspaper shows that he was in France over Christmas 1914, so he was not initially part of the 36th Division. *Belfast Telegraph*, 5 January 1915, p. 3.

variety of reasons, ranging from family traditions to just having been in another part of the United Kingdom when they enlisted.

Just like the listing for regular battalions, Table 6.6 includes Gallipoli deaths. It also includes the last identified UVF man from West Belfast to be killed in the war: Robert Rea Bell, on 11th August 1918, serving with the 5/6th Royal Scots. Bell, a Shankill-born shipyard labourer, had not enlisted until June 1917 when, aged 20, he was initially posted to the 3rd reserve battalion of the Royal Scots, joining the 16th battalion of the regiment in France in October 1917. Wounded in March 1918, he was in hospital for a time before he joined the 5/6th in late June, serving for around six weeks before his death.[30] But the most intriguing case is that of Isaac Hughes. He was killed on the Western Front while serving with the 8th Inniskillings, part of the 16th (Irish) Division. How did this former UVF member come to be serving in a nationalist unit? As mentioned above, some of the Belfast UVF had joined the 10th (Irish) Division rather than wait for the Ulster Division to be formed. Hughes himself had first served in that division, in the 6th Inniskillings, and his first overseas service was noted as 'Balkans' on 11 July 1915, which would be the date he was deemed to have been deployed en route for Gallipoli. At some point, he transferred from the 6th to the 8th Inniskillings, and consequently, from the non-aligned 10th to the nationalist 16th division. His service record has not survived so we might never know exactly when or why, but the case does point to the dangers of making assumptions about the men who served in 'political' divisions.

Conclusion: remembering service and loss

The information presented here only begins to tell the story of what happened to UVF members during the war. But it does point to some of the complexities of service in the war. The telling of 'lost' histories of the war is very much the vogue and a staple of some popular history publications. However, it is often the case that such stories have not been lost in the strictest sense of the term, just not told very often. Yet, the story of UVF members outside the 36th Division is a genuinely lost aspect of the war because it has been displaced by a powerful narrative of what happened on the Somme in July 1916. It has not been lost because people in the Shankill, or those interested in West Belfast history, were not interested in the minutiae of the history of their forebears' service in the war. Rather, it has been buried because the local history of the 1913–1914 UVF was used as a way of telling a particular story of that period, which linked the original UVF to that of the Troubles. It can be argued that this represented an effort to place 'service' in an illegal paramilitary organisation as part of an evolutionary process, following on from similar 'service' in an earlier legal paramilitary group which, of course, effectively became

[30] WO 363: 46396 Robert Bell.

part of the British army in 1914. Certainly the narrative presented in Figure 6.1 above presents exactly that timeline. The most graphic part of the history of that unit of the army (formed from the West Belfast UVF), 1 and 2 July 1916, therefore became the dominant representation not only of the Shankill's service but of West Belfast UVF service in the war.

While those two days are *much* of the story of West Belfast's UVF members in the war, they are far from *all* of it. Such men fought and died from 1914 through to 1918, not only on the Western Front but also at Gallipoli. With nearly 13 per cent of the Shankill's wartime fatalities coming on 1 and 2 July, it is no surprise that there should be so much concentration on the anniversary of those two days. Nothing here suggests there should not be such a focus because there is no other moment of the war when losses were experienced so intensively. However, to imagine that it is *all* the story of those who serve is to neglect much of the service of those who enlisted from the Shankill. Surprisingly, as figures presented here suggest, a preoccupation with service in the 36th (Ulster) Division overlooks the experiences of around one-third of those from West Belfast who were members of the UVF and who served. Even in the iconic 9th Royal Irish Rifles, formed directly from the West Belfast UVF, attention to fatalities on 1 July overlooks the vast majority of known UVF members who lost their lives during the war. All these others who died at other times, beyond the Ulster Division and beyond 1 July 1916, including a sizeable body of UVF members, deserve their place in public memory. They deserve to be remembered in addition to those who gave their lives in the Ulster Division on the Somme. It is time for those with an interest in the history and commemoration of the UVF to consider whether they are doing as much as they might to remember the full depth and breadth of its members' service in the First World War.

Appendix *Newspaper sources for individuals*

Name	Belfast Telegraph	Belfast Weekly News	News Letter
Alexander, John	25-5-1915, p. 6	27-5-1915, p. 7	
Allen, John			29-5-1915, p. 10
Barnes, Samuel	21-6-1916, p. 4		16-6-1916, p. 3
Beattie, Albert	31-12-1915, p. 6		15-12-1915, p. 10
Beattie, Henry	21-1-1918, p. 6		
Beattie, Herbert	17-1-1918, p. 5 & 21-1-1918, p. 6		
Beattie, Robert	21-1-1918, p. 6		21-7-1916, p. 8
Beattie, Samuel	21-1-1918, p. 6		

Appendix (*cont.*)

Name	Belfast Telegraph	Belfast Weekly News	News Letter
Beattie, William	25-5-1915, p. 6	20-5-1915, p. 7	
Bell, Andrew	11-11-1916, p. 6		9-8-1916, p. 8 & 28-10-1916, p. 8
Bell, Charles	4-6-1915, p. 6		3-6-1915, p. 7 & 10-6-1915, p. 7
Bell, James McD	11-11-1916, p. 6		28-10-1916, p. 8
Bell, John K	11-4-1916, p. 4		7-4-1916, p. 8 & 4-12-1916, p. 3
Bell, Robert Rea	11-9-1918, p. 3		
Bell, William J	18-3-1916, p. 4		17-3-1916, p. 10
Bennett, Hugh			22-9-1915, p. 10 & 26-6-1917, p. 8
Bingam, Alfred	16-2-1916, p. 6		12-2-1916, p. 8
Booth, Thomas			21-10-1915, p. 10
Boyd, Alexander			26-4-1916, p. 3
Boyles, John		24-6-1915, p. 7	
Brickley, William	19-4-1918, p. 3 & 27-4-1918, p. 4		
Bryans, Alfred	20-3-1917, p. 6		10-3-1917, p. 8
Bryans, Samuel	20-3-1917, p. 6		10-3-1917, p. 8
Burns, Isaac			4-10-1916, p. 8 & 6-8-1917, p. 6
Cairns, George	4-5-1917, p. 4		4-11-1915, p. 10 & 1-5-1917, p. 8
Campbell, Hugh	25-1-1916, p. 6		19-1-1916, p. 10
Campbell, James A	8-7-1916, p. 3		10-7-1916, p. 7
Carlisle, Samuel	17-11-1915, p. 6		2-11-1915, p. 7
Cassidy, William			18-12-1915, p. 10
Cathcart, Hugh			14-4-1916, p. 10
Cranston, William James	24-8-1917, p. 6		20-8-1917, p. 6
Crellin, Thomas	13-7-1916, p. 4		
Crilly, Daniel	12-2-1916, p. 6		22-12-1915, p. 10
Crone, Joseph			16-11-1916, p. 8
Cunningham, William Andrew	31-8-1917, p. 5 & 13-9-1917, p. 4		1-9-1917, p. 5
Currie, Thomas	22-11-1915, p. 6		11-11-1915, p. 10
Doherty, Isaac	19-6-1916, p. 4		22-5-1916, p. 8
Dunning, Thomas John	27-3-1916, p. 4		22-3-1916, p. 8

Appendix (cont.)

Name	Belfast Telegraph	Belfast Weekly News	News Letter
Eccles, John	28-2-1916, p. 6		22-2-1916, p. 8
Edgar, James	17-9-1915, p. 6		13-9-1915, p. 10
Ferguson, William George	21-1-1915, p. 6		24-5-1916, p. 8
Fleming, G	15-1-1915, p. 6		
Fleming, John		14-1-1915, p. 7	
Fleming, Thomas	11-11-1916, p. 6		6-10-1916, p. 10
Gallagher, James	5-1-1916, p. 8		4-1-1916, p. 10
Gault, James			16-12-1915, p. 12
Gillespie, Samuel James	12-3-1915, p. 6 & 21-2-1917, p. 4	18-3-1915, p. 7	
Glenn, James	13-4-1916, p. 4		10-4-1916, p. 8
Grant, Malcolm	23-1-1917, p. 3 & 2-1-1917, p. 6		24-1-1917, p. 8
Gray, John	9-12-1916, p. 3		28-11-1916, p. 8
Harper, John L	5-1-1916, p. 8		31-12-1915, p. 10 & 20-11-1916, p. 8
Harvey, John	21-2-1916, p. 6		18-2-1916, p. 10
Haydock, Thomas	29-9-1915, p. 3 & 1-10-1915, p. 3		6-9-1915, p. 10
Henderson, William	8-9-1917, p. 6		8-9-1917, p. 6
Hewitt, James	27-10-1916, p. 3		27-8-1917, p. 6
Hill, Arthur	18-7-1916, p. 3 & 27-8-1919, p. 4		19-7-1916, p. 8 & 15-8-1916, p. 8
Hill, David	2-10-1915, p. 6		10-9-1915, p. 10
Hughes, Fred	6-7-1916, p. 4		
Hughes, Isaac	6-7-1916, p. 4		
Jameson, Wiliam John		24-6-1915, p. 7	
Jenkins, Edward	21-1-1916, p. 8 & 25-9-1917, p. 6		15-1-1916, p. 10 & 12-9-1917, p. 6
Johnston, Alexander (Sandy)	1-11-1916, p. 3		31-10-1916, p. 8
Kyle, Thomas	2-7-1917, p. 7 & 7-7-1917, p. 6		3-7-1917, p. 8
Larmour, William	24-7-1916, p. 3		25-7-1916, p. 8
Lindsay, William	18-1-1916, p. 8 & 25-7-1916, p. 3		26-7-1916, p. 8
Logan, John			24-5-1916, p. 8

Appendix (*cont.*)

Name	Belfast Telegraph	Belfast Weekly News	News Letter
Lynch, Herbert Valentine Mitchell	2 12-1916, p. 6		10-11-1916, p. 10
Lyons, Henry James	2-10-1917, p. 6		
Maconachie, Samuel			3-9-1915, p. 10
Magee, William	30-6-1917, p. 7, 4-7-1917, p. 6, 11-7-1916, p. 3, & 11-9-1916, p. 3		
Malcolm, James	5-2-1916, p. 6		31-1-1916, p. 10
Marsden, James			2-2-1916, p. 10
Martin, Daniel	1-6-1915, p. 6	27-5-1915, p. 7	
Martin, John	11-1-1916, p. 6		7-1-1916, p. 10
Martin, Joseph	25-7-1916, p. 3 & 2-8-1916, p. 3		26-7-1916, p. 8
Matier, Samuel	18-7-1916, p. 3, 30-6-1917, p. 7		19-7-1916, p. 8
McAuley, Robert J	15-9-1915, p. 6		3-9-1915, p. 10
McBurney, Ernest	27-7-1916, p. 3		28-7-1916, p. 8
McClean, Ramsey	11-7-1916, p. 4		
McClune, Harry			12-10-1915, p. 10
McComb, Archibald	30-7-1915, p. 6 & 6-5-1918, p. 4	8-7-1915, p. 7	
McComb, Leonard	8 11-1916, p. 3		5-10-1916, p. 8
McComb, William			29-8-1917, p. 6
McCready, George	11-12-1914, p. 6	17-12-1914, p. 7	
McCrory, Hugh	27-4-1915, p. 6	22-4-1915, p. 7	
McDowell, James	9-1-1918, p. 5 & 21-1-1918, p. 6		
McIlroy, William	1-7-1915, p. 5 & 12-8-1915, p. 6		8-7-1915, p. 7 & 20-9-1915, p. 10
McMeekin, Thomas	29-9-1915, p. 3		8-9-1915, p. 10
McNeice, William	16-8-1916, p. 3		10-6-1915, p. 7 & 26-7-1916, p. 8
McRoberts, James	3-2-1915, p. 6	4-2-1915, p. 7	
Mills, Harry	9-6-1916, p. 4		31-5-1916, p. 8

Appendix (*cont.*)

Name	Belfast Telegraph	Belfast Weekly News	News Letter
Milne, Ernest			23-12-1915, p. 10 & 26-6-1917, p. 8
Mooney, Edward	21-6-1916, p. 4		15-6-1916, p. 8
Moore, Jackson	22-12-1915, p. 6		26-11-1915, p. 10
Moore, John W	11-11-1915, p. 6		4-11-1915, p. 10 & 11-11-1915, p. 10
Moore, Robert McConnell	21-11-1916, p. 4		20-11-1916, p. 8
Moreland, Thomas	6-8-1915, p. 6		21-7-1915, p. 10
Morrison, David	27-1-1916, p. 6		19-1-1916, p. 10
Morrison, William John			5-3-1917, p. 8
Mussen, Richard	14-5-1918, p. 4		
Neely, HW	2-8-1916, p. 3		22-7-1916, p. 8 & 18-10-1916, p. 10
Neill, John	7-7-1916, p. 3		10-7-1916, p. 7
Owens, James	22-7-1915, p. 6		8-7-1915, p. 7 & 7-9-1915, p. 10
Parker, George	16-12-1915, p. 8		30-11-1915, p. 10
Porter, Thomas			1-7-1915, p. 7 16-6-1916, p. 3
Pratt, Samuel	25-11-1915, p. 6		6-11-1915, p. 10
Quinn, William James	6-6-1917, p. 5 & 17-6-1916, p. 4		1-11-1915p, p. 9 & 14-1916, p. 8
Reid, Joseph	24-2-1915, p. 6	25-2-1915, p. 7	
Reid, William	27-11-1914, p. 3	17-12-1914, p. 7	
Robinson, James G	30-10-1916, p. 6		28-10-1916, p. 8
Robinson, William	2-2-1916, p. 6 & 9-5-1918, p. 4		24-1-1916, p. 10
Rosson, William	20-5-1915, p. 8	13-5-1915, p.10	
Russell, William Lester	4-12-1916, p. 6		18-11-1916, p. 10
Scott, TJ		8-7-1915, p. 7	
Seeds, Thomas	11-11-1915, p. 6		4-10-1915, p. 10
Shaw, Charles			20-11-1916, p. 8
Shearer, William	15-10-1915, p. 7 & 23-10-1915, p. 2		16-10-1915, p. 10

Appendix (*cont.*)

Name	Belfast Telegraph	Belfast Weekly News	News Letter
Shields, Robert	5-7-1916 & 27-12-1917, p. 4		20-12-1917, p. 8
Sinclair, George	30-7-1915, p. 6 & 30-4-1917, p. 4		9-7-1915, p. 10 & 23-4-1917, p. 8
Smith, John	25-1-1916, p. 6		18-1-1916, p. 10
Smyth, John B	9-1-1918, p. 5 & 28-1-1918, p. 6		
Smyth, Matthew			25-1-1916, p. 10
Smyth, Robert	3-9-1917, p. 6		27-8-1917, p. 6
Spence, Thomas H			9-8-1917, p. 6
Stewart, Samuel			31-1-1917, p. 8
Stitt, John	16-1-1917, p. 6		12-1-1917, p. 7
Stockman, Hugh	17-4-1916, p. 4		15-4-1916, p. 8 & 10-5-1916, p. 5
Swain, Samuel	26-9-1917, p. 6		17-9-1917, p. 8
Thomas, Fred	5-1-1915, p. 3		
Thompson, John			16-2-1916, p. 10
Tinsley, John	20-4-1918, p. 3 & 27-4-1918, p. 4		
Todd, (William Francis) Frank	27-11-1914, p. 6		3-12-1914, p. 8 & 10-12-1914, p. 5
Todd, Edward	7-7-1916, p. 3		10-7-1916, p. 7
Verner, John A	27-6-1916, p. 4		6-6-1916, p. 8 & 20-6-1916, p. 8
Wilkinson, Robert	7-1-1916, p. 6		5-1-1916, p. 10
Williamson, William	26-5-1916, p. 4		20-5-1916, p. 8
Wright, John	7-4-1916, p. 6		4-4-1916, p. 8
Young, Thomas	7-8-1917, p. 4		4-8-1917, p. 6 & 20-8-1917, p. 6

7   Remembering 1916 in America: the Easter Rising's many faces, 1919–1963

David Brundage

The goal of this chapter is to focus some attention on a period that has been relatively neglected by historians of the Irish in America: the years from the end of mass immigration in the 1920s through the early 1960s. How, by whom, and with what effect was the Easter Rising remembered in this period? Providing some answers to these questions may tell us something about a wide range of memory practices, while also shedding light on important aspects of Irish-American life – and American life more generally – in these decades. The argument can be briefly stated: though a once powerful Irish-American republican movement shrank dramatically in this period, the Easter Rising continued to be remembered (in different ways and for different purposes) by figures as varied as ecclesiastical sculptors, Irish-American labour leaders, and African-American nationalists. Remembering 1916 in America involved a diverse array of people, mediums, and motives, and its analysis has the potential to shed light on important mid-twentieth-century topics ranging from African-American political activism to the ethnic diversity within American Catholicism.

The period from the 1920s to the 1960s remains one of the least studied in Irish-American history, and this is one reason for this chapter's temporal focus. The rich body of nineteenth- and early-twentieth-century research suddenly thins out (as evidenced, for example, by the 1921 end date of Kerby Miller's landmark study, *Emigrants and Exiles*). The situation improves somewhat when we reach the mid-1960s and beyond: historical scholarship on the 'American connection' to the Northern Irish conflict, along with a strong tradition of research and writing by sociologists, political scientists, and (more recently) cultural studies scholars, focusing on Irish-American ethnic, racial, and political identities, has rendered this later era somewhat more familiar. It is the 'in-between' years that are most in need of research. As Kevin Kenny, one of the leading historians of Irish America, has noted, 'the post-1920 period

I would like to thank Fearghal McGarry, Jonah Stuart Brundage, and participants in the 2015 Wiles Colloquium and the UCSC History Department's works-in-progress series for their helpful suggestions on this chapter.

138

has not been entirely neglected, but it remains largely unstudied and presents the best opportunities for new scholarship'.[1]

There is a second reason to focus on this period, one more directly connected to the specific concerns of this volume: it has a coherence that stems from its proximity in time to the Rising itself. Unlike later years, this is a period that can be understood, following Eric Hobsbawm, as a kind of 'twilight zone between memory and history'. For the individuals that I discuss below (Marcus Garvey, Mike Quill, and Seamus Murphy – all born between 1887 and 1907), the Easter Rising was not yet 'history' ('a generalized record which is open to relatively dispassionate inspection', in Hobsbawm's words). It was rather thoroughly interwoven with the events of their own lives, connected inextricably to varied personal memories and individual timelines. Despite the fact that none of these individuals had direct personal experience (or, as a result, first-hand recollections) of the Easter Rising, these connections gave the event a special kind of intensity that shaped the way they told its story.[2]

In discussing these figures and their work, I am conscious of two major criticisms that have been directed at the field of memory studies. One of these critiques its tendency to elevate memory itself 'to the status of an historical agent', leading, in Kerwin Lee Klein's biting words, to 'a new age in which archives remember and statues forget'. In an effort to avoid this hazard, I try as best I can to identify the agency of specific persons and to delineate their particular contributions to the narratives of the Rising that I examine. A second criticism turns on the question of reception. 'Many studies of memory are content to describe the representation of the past without bothering to explore the transmission, diffusion, and ulti-mately, the meaning of this representation', writes Alon Confino; 'Yet to make a difference in society, it is not enough for a certain past to be selected. It must steer emotions, motivate people to act, be received.' In

---

[1] Kevin Kenny, 'Introduction to Section 4' in Kevin Kenny (ed.), *New Directions in Irish-American History* (Madison: University of Wisconsin Press, 2003), p. 245; Kerby A. Miller, *Emigrants and Exiles: Ireland and the Irish Exodus to North America* (New York: Oxford University Press, 1985). For the post-1960 period, see Andrew J. Wilson, *Irish America and the Ulster Conflict, 1968–1995* (Washington, DC: Catholic University of America Press, 1995); Nathan Glazer and Daniel P. Moynihan, *Beyond the Melting Pot: The Negroes, Puerto Ricans, Jews, Italians, and Irish of New York City*, 2nd edn (Cambridge, MA: M.I.T. Press, 1970); and Diane Negra (ed.), *The Irish in Us: Irishness, Performativity, and Popular Culture* (Durham, NC: Duke University Press, 2006).

[2] E. J. Hobsbawm, *The Age of Empire, 1875–1914* (London: Weidenfeld and Nicolson, 1987), p. 3. In making this point, I do not intend to endorse the sharp distinction between 'history' and 'memory' that has characterised some of the work on this topic. The examples that Hobsbawm provides illustrate the point I wish to make: "I met him shortly before the end of the war"; "Kennedy must have died in 1963, because it was when I was still in Boston".'

response to this complaint, I present evidence not only on the ways in which Garvey, Quill, and Murphy interpreted the Rising, emphasising some of its features and ignoring others, but also on how such interpretations were received by wider audiences. This is a considerably more difficult task, and much of my analysis on this point should be taken as suggestive rather than definitive.[3]

Just as in Ireland, the group most obviously inclined to commemorate the Easter Rising in the United States were Irish republicans. Yet for most of the period under consideration, this group was relatively insignificant. The debate over the Anglo-Irish Treaty and the subsequent Irish Civil War provided the immediate cause for the declining fortunes of Irish-American republicanism. The American Association for the Recognition of the Irish Republic (AARIR), which had been founded by Eamon de Valera in 1920 and had reached a membership of nearly 700,000 by the following year, remained strongly anti-Treaty, but only by purging two of its national presidents and triggering a mass exodus of its rank and file. By 1922, it was, in the words of one of its stalwarts, 'absolutely shot to pieces'. The ageing John Devoy's 1925 quip that the AARIR had more letters in its name than members was not that far off the mark. However, Devoy's own organisation, the pro-Treaty Friends of Irish Freedom (FOIF), fared little better. By 1931, the FOIF, which had embraced nearly 100,000 members a decade earlier, had been reduced to a mere 539, formally disbanding in 1935. Meanwhile, the secretive republican body known as Clan na Gael, founded in 1870 (and thus the longest continuously active Irish nationalist organisation in American history), split into pro- and anti-Treaty wings, neither of which could be considered significant by the 1930s.[4]

Though the Irish Civil War and other later Irish political events (the Irish Republican Army's (IRA) 1939 bombing campaign in Britain and Éire's neutrality in the Second World War, for example) badly damaged

---

[3] Kerwin Lee Klein, 'On the Emergence of Memory in Historical Discourse', *Representations* 69 (2000), 136; Alon Cofino, 'Collective Memory and Cultural History: Problems of Method', *American Historical Review* 102 (1997), 1395, 1390. For a concise discussion of these criticisms and for useful suggestions on methods and approaches, see Joan Tumblety, 'Introduction: Working with Memory as Source and Subject' in Joan Tumblety (ed.), *Memory and History: Understanding Memory as Source and Subject* (New York: Routledge, 2013), pp. 7–10, 13–14.

[4] M. H. Hopkinson, 'Irish Americans and the Anglo-Irish Treaty of 1921' in John Bossy and Peter Jupp (eds.), *Essays Presented to Michael Roberts* (Belfast: Blackstaff, 1976), p. 136; F. M. Carroll, *American Opinion and the Irish Question, 1910–23: A Study in Opinion and Policy* (New York: St. Martin's, 1978), p. 181; Brian Hanley, 'Irish Republicans in Interwar New York', *IJASonline* 1 (2009), para. 3; *Gaelic American*, 28 April 1923; Michael Doorley, *Irish-American Diaspora Nationalism: The Friends of Irish Freedom, 1916–1935* (Dublin: Four Courts, 2005), pp. 152–154, 200.

Irish republicanism in the United States, there were also deeper trends in American society that contributed to this outcome, including significantly lower levels of migration from Ireland after 1930, the gradual improvement of material conditions for Irish-American working people in the post-Second World War era, and the concomitant suburbanisation of a significant proportion of the Irish-American population. As they left the concentrated Irish neighbourhoods of large cities, mining towns, or industrial mill villages, many Irish-Americans also left behind the dense web of ethnic and religious institutions that had provided a crucial social context for both Irish nationalists and their memories of their own history. The reflections on 'historical amnesia' by Tom Hayden provide a useful illustration of this last point. Hayden, a third-generation Irish-American and future leader of the American New Left, who was born in Detroit in 1939 but grew up in suburban Royal Oak, Michigan, would later describe his childhood as 'growing up unconscious' in relation to the history of Irish nationalism. Though he had been told that his middle name came from the name of a famous Irish political martyr, for example, young Thomas Emmet Hayden had not a clue as to whom that figure might be. Although it is beyond the scope of this chapter, Hayden's comments on suburban 'amnesia' suggest interesting avenues for research on the dynamics of social forgetting.[5]

Not surprisingly, and in spite of these trends, local groups of Irish republicans continued to commemorate the Easter Rising throughout this period. In the heavily Irish mining town of Butte, Montana, for example, a socialist republican organisation called the Pearse-Connolly Irish Independence Club (founded in late 1916 after a visit to Butte by the Irish labour leader Jim Larkin) held annual commemorations of the Rising into the 1920s, enlivened by rousing performances of the club's Pearse and Connolly Fife and Drum Band. Commemorations like this could be found in other strongly republican centres, such as Philadelphia, San Francisco, and New York, where a significant number of anti-Treaty immigrants, some of them IRA veterans, settled after their defeat in the Irish Civil War. By the early 1960s, this group of self-defined political exiles had thinned considerably but had not been entirely silenced. In April 1961, an organisation called the IRA Veterans of America, Inc. marked 'the greatest Easter of our time – Easter Week 1916' by

---

[5] Tom Hayden, *Irish on the Inside: In Search of the Soul of Irish America* (London: Verso, 2001), pp. 10, 30–31. See also Kevin Kenny, *The American Irish: A History* (Harlow: Longman, 2000), pp. 226–267, for a discussion of some of these trends. For an approach to the history of social forgetting, see Guy Beiner, 'Disremembering 1798? An Archaeology of Social Forgetting and Remembrance in Ulster', *History & Memory* 25 (2013), 9–50.

publishing a pamphlet that its unnamed authors must have viewed as an inspiring statement to the youth of Ireland, a passing of the torch from elderly Irish political exiles to a younger generation. 'As St Patrick lighted the fire of Christianity on the hill of Tara, so Patrick Pearse lighted the fire of Irish Nationalism in Dublin City on Easter Monday 1916', they wrote, reminding 'young Irishmen' that 'you are the standard-bearers of the Flag of the Irish Republic'.[6]

However, the day when such rhetoric could inspire large numbers of residents of the United States had passed. In November 1963, the IRA Chief of Staff Cathal Goulding travelled to Philadelphia to attend a Clan na Gael convention, but the organisation that he found there was in disarray, weak in members, funds, and energy. When the Irish Taoiseach Seán Lemass visited Philadelphia that year, only five Clan supporters turned out to protest his visit, and a protest at United Nations headquarters in New York the following year brought out only fifteen. In the early 1960s, the US Federal Bureau of Investigation cut back its surveillance of the organisation, referring in a memo to its 'lack of activity'. Few serious students of American life would have disagreed with the sociologist Daniel Patrick Moynihan, when he penned his epitaph for Irish-American republicanism in 1963: 'Its dogmas no longer dominate; its divisions no longer interest; its institutions no longer direct the patterns of life.'[7]

Nonetheless, Irish-American republicans had no monopoly on the remembrance of 1916. Indeed, once we turn our attention from the relatively small and self-enclosed world that they inhabited, we find an array of diverse and in some cases much more consequential ways of remembering the Rising. For example, a powerful narrative of martyrdom and sacrifice associated with the Easter Rising played a significant role in Marcus Garvey's Universal Negro Improvement Association and African Communities League (UNIA), a relatively short-lived but extremely significant example of diasporic nationalism that achieved prominence in the United States in the years after the First World War. Garvey had founded the UNIA in his native Jamaica in 1914, moving it to the Harlem neighbourhood of New York two years later. Over the next few years, the UNIA grew dramatically, partly because of Garvey's own talents as a charismatic orator and forceful writer (using his weekly newspaper, the

---

[6] *Irish Republican Bulletin* (Easter 1961), in Gerard Tighe Papers, Ms 28,894, folder 2, National Library of Ireland. For Butte's Pearse-Connolly Club, see David M. Emmons, *The Butte Irish: Class and Ethnicity in an American Mining Town, 1875–1925* (Urbana: University of Illinois Press, 1989), pp. 359–360, 404.

[7] Brian Hanley and Scott Millar, *The Lost Revolution: The Story of the Official IRA and the Workers' Party* (Dublin: Penguin Ireland, 2009), pp. 48–49; Glazer and Moynihan, *Beyond the Melting Pot*, p. 253.

Negro World, as his forum). The movement also benefited from the activism of African-American soldiers returning from the war to find a dispiriting resurgence of white racism, and by the location of Garvey's headquarters in the increasingly important African-American political and cultural centre of Harlem. By the early 1920s, the UNIA had chapters in thirty American cities, 65,000–75,000 dues-paying members, and African-American supporters that some historians estimate to number in the millions. The movement, moreover, had direct linkages to later currents of Black Nationalism in the United States; both of Malcolm X's parents had been Garveyites, for example, and it was at a Harlem festival honouring Garvey in 1957 that Malcolm first began gaining followers for his own brand of Black Nationalism.[8]

As Robert A. Hill has demonstrated, the example provided by Irish nationalism played a pivotal role in shaping Garvey's political outlook. Born in 1887, Garvey's first encounter with Irish nationalism came in 1910, when he became the assistant secretary of the National Club of Jamaica. S. A. G. Cox, the National Club's founder, had absorbed the political programme of Sinn Féin while studying law in London and he chose the name *Our Own* (a very rough translation of 'Sinn Féin') for the club's newspaper. More important was Garvey's own experience in London, where he studied from 1912 to 1914, the years of the Home Rule crisis, when the 'Irish question' was in the news almost continuously. The subsequent development of the Irish revolutionary struggle had a tremendous impact on Garvey's political thinking, providing the major ideological example for his dramatic shift from apostle of self-help to African-American nationalist and anti-colonialist.[9]

Garvey was not the only African-American political leader to look to Ireland for political guidance or inspiration in these years. Hubert Harrison, the intellectual and activist sometimes described as 'the father of Harlem radicalism', drew on several international models, including that of Ireland, in his 1917 campaign for black electoral representation. Anyone who sought 'to lead the Negro race', Harrison argued, had to 'follow the path of the Swadesha movement of India and the Sinn Fein movement of Ireland', building an independent political party for 'ourselves first'. In organising the secret African Blood Brotherhood for

---

[8] For the UNIA's significance in its own time and its influence on later movements, see especially Theodore G. Vincent, *Black Power and the Garvey Movement* (Berkeley, CA: Ramparts, 1971). See also Manning Marable, *Malcolm X: A Life of Reinvention* (New York: Viking, 2011), pp. 16–18, 131.

[9] Robert A. Hill, 'General Introduction' in Robert A. Hill (ed.), *The Marcus Garvey and Universal Negro Improvement Association Papers*, 10 vols. (Berkeley: University of California Press, 1983–2006), vol. I, pp. lxx–lxxviii.

African Liberation and Redemption two years later, Cyril V. Briggs drew explicitly on the model of the Irish Republican Brotherhood. In February 1921, Briggs hailed 'the Irish fight for liberty' as 'the greatest epic of modern times and a sight to inspire to emulation all oppressed groups'. The poet Claude McKay, a central figure in what would become known as the Harlem Renaissance, was another black intellectual who sympathised with the Irish revolution. 'I think I understand the Irish', he declared in 1921. 'My belonging to a subject race entitles me to some understanding of them.'[10]

Garvey's emphasis, however, was slightly different. For him, it was not only the practical salience of Irish revolutionary political models (whether provided by Sinn Féin or the IRB) or a sympathetic connection that existed between two colonised peoples. Garvey was mainly drawn, it appears, to the 'blood sacrifice' of the Easter Rising. It was the willingness of the Rising's leaders to give up their lives for the sake of a larger cause that he found most compelling and that he sought to convey to his followers. In his formal dedication of Liberty Hall, the UNIA's new headquarters on 138th Street in Harlem, on 27 July 1919, Garvey proclaimed that 'the time had come for the Negro race to offer up its martyrs upon the altar of liberty even as the Irish had given a long list from Robert Emmet to Roger Casement'. The very name 'Liberty Hall' reflected Garvey's appreciation for this sacrifice, for he had named it after Liberty Hall, Dublin, the headquarters of the Irish Transport and General Workers Union and of James Connolly's Citizen Army, one of the sites from which the Easter Rising had been launched. In a Carnegie Hall speech the following month, Garvey returned to this theme: 'From the time when Robert Emmett [*sic*], when he lost his head, to the time of Roger Casement, Ireland has been fighting, agitating and offering up her sons as martyrs', he proclaimed. As such, men 'bled and died for Ireland, so we who are leading Universal Negro Improvement Association, are prepared at any time to free Africa and free the negroes of the world'. Garvey continued to use the Irish independence struggle, and especially the self-sacrificing idealism he found in the Rising and in the Irish War of Independence, as a kind of rhetorical touchstone throughout the early 1920s. In September 1920, for example, he sent a telegram to the confessor of Terence MacSwiney, the republican Lord Mayor of Cork, who was then on hunger strike and nearing death in Brixton prison: 'Convey to McSwiney [*sic*] sympathy of 400,000,000 Negroes.' In a

---

[10] Jeffrey B. Perry (ed.), *A Hubert Harrison Reader* (Middletown, CT: Wesleyan University Press, 2001), p. 139; Tyrone Tillery, *Claude McKay: A Black Poet's Struggle for Identity* (Amherst: University of Massachusetts Press, 1992), p. 51.

speech on 'Ireland and Africa' a year later, Garvey lauded MacSwiney's self-sacrifice, expressing his belief that it 'did more for the freedom of Ireland today than probably anything they did for 600 years prior to his death'. But MacSwiney's sacrifice was just one of many: in Garvey's impassioned words, 'hundreds and thousands of Irishmen have died as martyrs to the cause of Irish freedom'.[11]

How did African-American members and supporters of the UNIA respond to words like these? Did Garvey's efforts to honour the Easter rebels as inspiring figures in a long line of Irish political martyrs that stretched from Emmet to MacSwiney have any significant impact on his followers? This is a difficult question to answer, and the fact that the *Negro World* noted 'applause' at Garvey's Irish-themed speeches or 'boos and hisses' at his references to British Prime Minister Lloyd George takes us only so far, as does the fact that UNIA branches across the country followed Garvey's lead in establishing meeting places called 'Liberty Halls' in their own communities. Black activism associated with a three-week boycott of British ships by New York's Irish-American dockworkers in support of MacSwiney's hunger strike provides more direct evidence on the reception of Garvey's ideas: when a group of 250 rank-and-file African-American longshoremen on Manhattan's west side docks agreed to support 'the Irishman in the strike for liberty by virtue of it being a Common Cause akin to that of the Aethiopian people' – in spite of a long and bitter history of Irish-American racism and conflict between Irish and black dock workers there – it indicated at least their provisional support for Garvey's interpretation of the Irish struggle.[12]

What can be stated with confidence is this: in America, the Easter Rising story took on a life of its own. That is, narratives of 1916, marked by what seemed to many to be stirring examples of idealism, dedication, courage, and sacrifice, could be lifted out of their specifically Irish context and used to legitimise or inspire other sorts of movements and causes. A second example of this phenomenon is provided by the emergence of industrial unionism and the organisation of large numbers of unskilled workers in American mass production industries in the 1930s. US labour historians have long been aware of the ethnic dimension to the emergence of industrial unionism in the 1930s, which was energised by the activism

---

[11] Hill (ed.), *The Marcus Garvey Papers*, vol. I, pp. 472, 506–507, vol. II, p. 649; vol. IV, p. 259.

[12] 'Decision of Colored Longshoremen Engaged in the Breaking of the Irish Patriotic Strike, 13 September 1920' in Peter Golden Papers, Ms. 3,141, folder 6, National Library of Ireland. For the fullest account of the boycott, see Joe Doyle, 'Striking for Ireland on the New York Docks' in Ronald H. Bayor and Timothy J. Meagher (eds.), *The New York Irish* (Baltimore: Johns Hopkins University Press, 1996), pp. 357–373.

of Jews and Italians in the East, Poles and Slavs in the Midwest, and Mexicans and Filipinos in California. Nonetheless, it was frequently Irish-Americans who led the new unions of the Congress of Industrial Organizations (CIO), becoming, as one of them, James Carey, put it, 'missionaries of industrial unionism'. The roster of CIO leaders with Irish backgrounds included John Brophy, Mike Quill, Joseph Curran, Philip Murray, Harry Bridges, and numerous others.[13]

A variety of intellectual influences, ranging from Catholic social thought to Communism, helped shape the often-lifelong commitment of such leaders, but an early exposure to the political vision of Irish nationalism (in Ireland or the diaspora) played a critical role for many of them. The Lancashire-born Brophy, for example, who would become the national director of the CIO and a key figure in many of its organising drives, was strongly affected by the political outlook of his Irish immigrant father, a coal miner and enthusiastic supporter of the Irish Land League in the early 1880s. The Melbourne-born Bridges, a leader of the 1934 west coast waterfront strike that gave birth to the CIO-affiliated International Longshore and Warehouse Union, was influenced by the republican sympathies of his Irish-born mother and by the First World War-era anti-conscription activism of Archbishop Daniel Mannix (the 'Australian Sinn Féiner').[14]

But for the impact of the Easter Rising in particular on US labour leaders, there is no better example than that of Mike Quill. Born in County Kerry in 1905, Quill grew up in a strongly republican family, reared on stories of Wolfe Tone, Robert Emmet (the youngster would weep when his father recited Emmet's speech from the dock to him), and Michael Davitt and the Land League. 'Years later I understood that the Land League was actually a trade union of Irish tenants', he told his wife, Shirley, in the 1960s. As a youth, Quill joined the Fianna Éireann, the nationalist youth organisation founded by Countess Markievicz, and he later fought with the IRA in both the War of Independence and the Civil War. Like many other anti-Treatyites who foresaw a bleak economic and political future in the Irish Free State, he emigrated to the United States, settling in New York, where he eventually found work on the city's subway system. He joined the anti-Treaty Clan na Gael along with a number of other Irish societies, and when layoffs and pay cuts in the early 1930s

---

[13] Walter P. Reuther and James B. Carey, 'Forward' in John Brophy, *A Miner's Life* (Madison: University of Wisconsin Press, 1964), p. v. For the ethnic dimension to the CIO, see Thomas Göbel, 'Becoming American: Ethnic Workers and the Rise of the CIO', *Labor History* 29 (1988), 173–198.

[14] Brophy, *A Miner's Life*, pp. 3, 7, 10, 31, 78; Robert W. Cherny, 'The Making of a Labor Radical: Harry Bridges, 1901-1934', *Pacific Historical Review* 64 (1995), 363–366.

triggered discontent among New York transit workers, Quill quickly emerged as the key union organiser, working closely with the Communist Party activists who initiated the union drive, while effectively reaching out to the many Irish transit workers he knew from the Clan and other Irish organisations. The Transport Workers Union (TWU) was founded in April 1934, and the following December, Quill was elected president, bringing the union into the CIO in 1937. Heading a union with 30,000 members and with a series of successfully negotiated union contracts behind him, Quill became an important political figure in New York and was elected to the New York City Council from the Bronx in November 1937. Though he consistently denied being a member of the Communist Party, he remained ideologically close to the party into the post-war years, once proclaiming that he would 'rather be called a Red by the rats than a rat by the Reds'.[15]

Quill had been just ten years old, and far from Dublin, when the Easter rebellion broke out, though, as his widow Shirley Quill wrote in her 1985 book, *Mike Quill-Himself: A Memoir*, 'even the younger children sensed the excitement in the talk around the fire' and understood 'that something big and important was happening to their country'. The subsequent executions of the Rising's leaders made a strong impression on the child as well: 'Michael remembered that the family was shocked when James Connolly, his body wracked by wounds, was strapped to a chair and carried to the courtyard of Kilmainham jail, where he faced his English executioners without a blindfold.' The figure of Connolly (and especially his combination of militant trade unionism, socialism, and Irish republicanism) would loom large over Quill's entire labour and political career. His left-wing views were a product of his contact with socialist republicans in New York's Clan na Gael and with his fellow TWU organiser Gerald O'Reilly, who attributed his own radicalisation to his encounter with Connolly's writings, as well as of the American Communist Party's efforts to recruit Irish immigrant workers in the 1930s by claiming that it was fighting for 'Connolly's Republic, the Republic of the Working Class of Ireland and America'. Describing Quill's excitement at the rapid progress of industrial union organising after 1935, Shirley Quill noted his view that 'James Connolly's vision had become the CIO's battle cry: "One boss, one payroll, one union"'. When Quill won re-election to the New York City Council in 1943, it was 'a smashing reaffirmation' of Connolly's view 'that industrial and political democracy are two sides of

[15] Shirley Quill, *Mike Quill-Himself: A Memoir* (Greenwich, CT: Devin-Adair, 1985), pp. 13–14; Joshua B. Freeman, *In Transit: The Transport Workers Union in New York City, 1933–1966* (New York: Oxford University Press, 1989), p. 137.

the same coin'. Shirley also recalled that Mike kept a framed copy of the TWU's 1937 charter from the CIO on his office wall for twenty years – flanked by portraits of Abraham Lincoln and James Connolly.[16]

While there is no reason to doubt the importance of Connolly's ideas for Quill – these were common currency for the Irish and Irish-American republican left – the question of agency and authorship of *Mike Quill-Himself* is highly problematic. Though Shirley claimed that much of her material came from vignettes that Mike ('a storyteller in the Gaelic tradition' with 'a marvellous sense of language, a lusty, sometimes acerbic sense of humor and a remarkable memory') had told her, the work was also filtered through her own life experiences, recollections, and political commitments. Indeed, the book was partly, in her own words, a 'love story of a radicalized Jewish divorcee and an Irish Catholic subway worker'. Already a left-wing activist when she met Mike Quill, Shirley Quill remained so after his death; her 1991 obituary in the *New York Times* referred to her as a 'tenant organizer'. And it was Shirley, not Mike, who made the decisions regarding the content and organisation of *Mike Quill-Himself* (subtitling the chapter on his upbringing 'A Terrible Beauty is Born', for example, or including photographs of James Connolly and Dublin's Liberty Hall among the book's illustrations). Mike Quill had died nearly two decades before its publication.[17]

If authorship and agency are slippery in the case of Mike Quill's memories of the Rising, it is questions of audience and reception that pose the most interesting problems in another example of remembering 1916 in America: the statuary of St Brigid's church in San Francisco, California. St Brigid's had been established as a parish in 1863, when San Francisco was a city of just 50,000. Though Archbishop Joseph Sadoc Alemany, a native of Spain, had dedicated the church, St Brigid's first priest and many of his successors were Irish-born, reflecting the Irish immigrant neighbourhood in which the parish was located. In 1904, the original wooden structure was replaced with an impressive granite building, constructed in the Romanesque Revival style, which remarkably survived the 1906 earthquake with only minimal damage. Located on the busy corner of Broadway and Van Ness Avenue, a major north-south artery, St Brigid's occupied an important place in San Francisco's Irish community, second only to St Peter's, long-regarded as the city's quintessentially Irish parish.[18]

[16] Quill, *Mike Quill-Himself*, pp. 16–17, 81, 160, 90; Freeman, *In Transit*, pp. 47, 52–53.
[17] Quill, *Mike Quill-Himself*, pp. xi, 16; *New York Times*, 28 September 1991.
[18] Julian Guthrie, *The Grace of Everyday Saints: How a Band of Believers Lost Their Church and Found Their Faith* (Boston: Houghton Mifflin Harcourt, 2011), p. 8; Jeffrey M. Burns, 'St. Peter's Parish in San Francisco: The Rise and Eclipse of an Irish Parish,

In 1948, St Brigid's pastor, the Tipperary-born Monsignor James Cantwell, commissioned the noted Irish sculptor Seamus Murphy to carve St Brigid and the Twelve Apostles, fitted into thirteen niches across the church's façade. While the factors behind Cantwell's decision to commission Murphy are not clear, it is likely that these involved mainly a celebration of the parish's Irish ethnic identity, along with a demonstration of its strong financial resources. At the same time that he commissioned the statues, for example, Cantwell arranged to have new stained glass windows installed in the church, designed and manufactured in the famous Dublin studios of Harry Clarke. He also imported carpets woven and embroidered in Donegal by the Dun Emer Guild, one of Ireland's pioneering Arts and Crafts ventures. As a visiting journalist from Cork observed in the mid-1980s, Cantwell 'would have been a fine representative for the "guaranteed Irish" campaign'.[19]

The statues that Murphy carved for the San Francisco church represent some of his finest work and continue to be highly regarded by art critics and historians. But whatever Cantwell's motives may have been, Murphy brought to his task not only the talents of one of Ireland's most accomplished sculptors (some consider his 'Virgin of the Twilight' to be the most important Irish carving of the twentieth century) but also the sensibilities of an Irish political and cultural nationalist. Born in 1907 near Mallow, County Cork, Murphy had attended St Patrick's National School in Cork city, where his teacher was Daniel Corkery, the writer and cultural nationalist who gave him his first drawing lessons and encouraged him to pursue advanced studies in art. Murphy was a deeply religious person and much of his work reflected this, but a great deal of it reflected his commitment to Irish republicanism. One of his first public works, for example, was the Clonmult Memorial, at the scene of a famous 1921 ambush of East Cork IRA volunteers by Black and Tans, and he later carved monuments to Countess Markievicz and the Fenian Jeremiah O'Donovan Rossa in Dublin's St Stephen's Green. One of his last commissions before his death in 1975 was a headstone for the grave of the War of Independence hero Dan Breen, in County Tipperary.[20]

These nationalist sensibilities appear to have led Murphy to take as his models for the apostles who flank his statue of St Brigid those he called

1913-1964' in Donald Jordan and Timothy J. O'Keefe (eds.), *The Irish in the San Francisco Bay Area: Essays on Good Fortune* (San Francisco, CA: Executive Council of the Irish Literary and Historical Society, 2005), pp. 85–101.
[19] Alan Counihan, 'The Twelve Irish Apostles', *Cork Examiner*, 3 December 1985.
[20] Bebhinn Marten (ed.), *Seamus Murphy, 1907–1975: The Work of Seamus Murphy, Sculptor* (Cork: Crawford Municipal Art Gallery, 1982), pp. 20, 23; Rebecca Minch, 'Murphy, Seamus' in *Dictionary of Irish Biography* (Cambridge: Cambridge University Press, 2009), vol. VI, pp. 218–219.

'the boys' – the leaders of the 1916 Easter Rising. Though characterised by boldly carved features, and recognisably Irish, the faces of the statues are not identifiable as particular individuals. This, however, has not prevented one observer from suggesting that 'the clean shaven figure of St. Philip could possibly be Pearse', or others from recognising 'the likenesses of Plunkett, Clarke, Childers and Connolly'. Despite their lack of definitive identities (and the fact that one recent scholar has dismissed any connection between Murphy's apostles and 'the men of 1916' as 'urban folklore'), many in San Francisco's Irish-American community seem to have embraced the statues as an effective blending of their ethnic, religious, and national identities. The authors of a recent 'coffee table' book on San Francisco's Irish heritage, for example, confidently assert that Murphy 'used the heroes of the 1916 Easter Uprising as his models'.[21]

But what about St Brigid's parishioners, surely the primary 'audience' that Murphy had in mind when he carved his statues? How did they respond to the 'twelve Irish apostles' that now graced their church? The answer to this question is complicated, for even in 1948, St Brigid's was beginning to lose its distinctively Irish character. Exemplifying a pattern long familiar to urban sociologists, Italian immigrants, who had originally settled in the San Francisco neighbourhood of North Beach, began moving south and west over the course of the 1920s and 1930s; by 1940, North Beach contained just a quarter of the city's Italian-born residents. As Italians and second-generation Italian-Americans put down roots in the blocks around Broadway and Van Ness, many transferred their membership from Ss Peter and Paul's, the well-known 'Italian church' in the heart of North Beach, to St Brigid's. Indeed, in the very year that Murphy was creating his statues, the pupils of St Brigid's school included a young Italian-American named George Moscone, who would go on to become one of San Francisco's most popular mayors. Nor, of course, did this process of demographic change come to an end in the 1940s. In 1994, when the San Francisco archdiocese closed St Brigid's (citing earthquake fears and a city-wide decline in the Catholic population), the parish still embraced a number of Irish-American families, as well as a young assistant priest, Father Cyril O'Sullivan, who had been born and raised in Cork. But its parishioners now also included immigrants from Burma, Mexico, Poland, Singapore, and the Philippines, and masses were being celebrated in five different languages. In response to the archdiocese's

---

[21] Counihan, 'The Twelve Irish Apostles'; Robert Tracy, 'Irish Saints in San Francisco', *Irish Literary Supplement* 29 (2010), 21; John Garvey and Karen Hanning, *Irish San Francisco* (Charleston, SC: Arcadia, 2008), p. 82. See also Guthrie, *The Grace of Everyday Saints*, p. xiii. Guthrie, a *San Francisco Chronicle* reporter, also reports the Easter Rising inspiration for the statues as an established fact.

decision to close St Brigid's, this multiethnic group of parishioners launched an impressive, though ultimately unsuccessful, campaign to keep it open. Without a doubt, the physical beauty of their church (including Seamus Murphy's statuary) played an important part in their determination to do so. But any specific traces of honouring 'the men of 1916' would be hard to find.[22]

Two concluding points can be drawn from this admittedly selective array of examples. First, remembering the Easter Rising in America (unlike in Ireland) was a multiethnic and sometimes multiracial affair; given the diversity of the US population in the twentieth century, it could hardly have been otherwise. Statues honouring Irish republican heroes adorned churches where masses were celebrated in Italian, Spanish, and Tagalog. Irish nationalist martyrdom was embraced and championed by African-American nationalists. James Connolly's ideas about socialism and labour rights were summarised in print by Jewish-American radicals and deployed to legitimise an American industrial union movement that was multiethnic at its very core. In this context, the term 'Irish diaspora', recently criticised for its overly-expansive boundaries, may actually suggest implications that are too narrow. Remembering 1916 in America could never be the property of Irish America alone.[23]

Second, the highly contested character of commemorating the Rising, a focus of some of the best research on this topic in an Irish setting, appears much less salient on the western side of the Atlantic. In comparison to the bitter ideological disagreements between 'mainstream' and 'republican' political actors (or between unionists and nationalists) that commemoration long entailed in Ireland, remembering 1916 in America was considerably less charged and argumentative. This is not to deny the existence of bitter social and political conflicts in mid-twentieth-century America. The US government worked effectively to destroy the UNIA in the mid-1920s, for example, and many employers tried desperately to fight off unionisation in the 1930s; but no one ever bothered to argue that a

---

[22] Rose Doris Scherini, *The Italian American Community of San Francisco: A Descriptive Study* (New York: Arno, 1980), pp. 18–26; Guthrie, *The Grace of Everyday Saints*, pp. 6, 11, 12–13, 24. The Committee to Save St Brigid Church was, however, successful in winning its designation as a historic landmark in 2005, which is why the church still stands today. In announcing its decision, the San Francisco Board of Supervisors mentioned 'the statuary by the noted Irish sculptor Seamus Murphy', as well as the fact that Mayor Moscone had 'received the sacraments in St Brigid Church, attended St Brigid School, and was a life-long parishioner'. Moscone had been assassinated along with San Francisco Supervisor Harvey Milk in 1978. See 'San Francisco Landmarks: Landmark #252: St. Brigid Church', http://noehill.com/SF/LANDMARKS/sf252.asp.

[23] See Kevin Kenny, *Diaspora: A Very Short Introduction* (New York: Oxford University Press, 2013).

Marcus Garvey or a Mike Quill misunderstood or misrepresented the lessons of the Easter Rising.[24]

With the eruption of the conflict in Northern Ireland after 1968, however, a more characteristically 'Irish' pattern of commemoration came into prominence in the United States. Near San Francisco, for example, which emerged as a leading support centre, first for the Northern Irish civil rights movement and, subsequently, for both Official and Provisional wings of the IRA, members of the local Clan na Gael commissioned an elaborate new gravestone for a long-dead Fenian and local politician named Thomas Desmond in Holy Cross Cemetery in 1976. Here they began a tradition, which continues to this day, of an annual Easter Sunday 'Commemoration of Ireland's Patriot Dead'. Marked by a reading of the Proclamation of the Irish Republic, music provided by the Pearse and Connolly Fife and Drum band (which had moved from Butte to San Francisco in the later 1920s), and, in the years since the beginning of the Northern Irish peace process, occasional speeches by visiting Sinn Féin politicians, the annual event would not seem out of place in parts of Belfast, Derry, or Dublin. A full analysis of important commemorative events like this, with undoubted parallels in other Irish-American republican centres, however, would take us into a later, and substantially different, phase of remembering 1916.[25]

---

[24] For the contested character of Easter Rising commemorations in Ireland, see Gabriel Doherty, 'The Commemoration of the Ninetieth Anniversary of the Easter Rising' in Gabriel Doherty and Dermot Keogh (eds.), *1916: The Long Revolution* (Cork: Mercier, 2007), pp. 376–407; Mary E. Daly and Margaret O'Callaghan (eds.), *1916 in 1966: Commemorating the Easter Rising* (Dublin: Royal Irish Academy, 2007); and Roisín Higgins, *Transforming 1916: Meaning, Memory and the Fiftieth Anniversary of the Easter Rising* (Cork: Cork University Press, 2012).

[25] Desmond had been a key figure in John Devoy's 1876 *Catalpa* voyage that rescued six IRB prisoners from Western Australia. He was elected San Francisco Sheriff on the Workingmen's Ticket in 1880 and served through 1881. He died in 1910. For a YouTube video of the 2011 commemoration, see 'SF Irish Remember Fenian Thomas Desmond', www.youtube.com/watch?v=0JEWyxQU4FE. I am indebted to Sean Prendiville for sharing information with me about this annual event.

Part III

Literary and material cultures

8　The Rising generation and the memory of 1798

Heather L. Roberts

The centrality of 1916 and the succeeding revolutionary period to the current Irish commemorative impulse makes it difficult to recall that this has not always been the case. In the final years of the nineteenth century and the period leading up to the Rising in the early twentieth century, the biggest commemorative events recalled the Manchester Martyrs of 1867 and, especially, the rebellion of 1798. The widespread flurry of excitement and activity surrounding the latter's centenary commemoration in 1898 contributed to the politicisation of a generation of young people, many of whom would go on to organise, execute, and witness the Easter Rising – the so-called 'Rising generation'. But their very successes contributed to a decline in enthusiasm for commemorating the rebellion that inspired them. This chapter traces the relationship between this generation of young people and the social memory of the rebellion of 1798. It argues that the '98 centenary helped to politicise many of the young and to model revolution for them, but that the succeeding revolutionary period of 1916–1923 nevertheless occasioned a shift in the Irish memorial tradition away from the 1798 rebellion and towards the Easter Rising. The chapter first outlines the politicising effects of the centenary and the public enthusiasm it generated on the generation of young people who witnessed it, before turning to examine the memorial turn away from 1798. Throughout, the 'lifecycle' of one monument in particular, the Kerry '98 memorial in Tralee, will be particularly illustrative and serve to demonstrate the three principal reasons underlying the shift. First, the violence of the intervening years and the bleak outlook of the early Free State raised questions about the valorisation of violent national mythology; second, the grass-roots movements that initially spurred the commemorative fervour had been calcified into processes of state and bureaucracy that no longer held the same power to rally great interest; and finally, the Rising itself and the memory of the 'Rising generation' mingled with and ultimately displaced '98 in the commemorative landscape.

In the increasingly tense political environment of the Home Rule debate and land reforms at the end of the nineteenth century, the '98 centenary offered an occasion to draw together disparate factions of Irish nationalists in support of unified commemorative efforts and to introduce young people to the politics of national remembrance. Throughout the course of the nineteenth century, Ireland, like most of Europe, witnessed a flood of commemorative activity, and by mid-century, memorial statues began to appear on an unprecedented scale.[1] The vast majority of these newly erected monuments recalled great personages and events of importance to the British Empire, with Irish nationalist memorials only beginning to emerge in the latter half of the century and remaining greatly outnumbered until after independence.[2] The tides first began to turn in the late 1890s, prompted by the occasion of the centenary of the 1798 rebellion, the greatest of the failed Irish uprisings. Although Emmet's rebellion in 1803 and the Fenian attempt of 1867 were more recent, both paled in comparison to that of 1798 in terms of scale and successive cultural impact.[3] A grass-roots movement arose surrounding the centenary – spearheaded by a central committee in Dublin and dozens of local committees stretching across the country – to design, fund, and erect numerous commemorative statues and monuments dedicated to the '98 rising and to celebrate the centenary in the public eye. The highly visible activities of these groups – often established and organised by aging Fenians – and the exhaustive discussion of both the centenary and the rebellion itself in the ever-expanding print culture created an atmosphere in which young people in particular would be socialised and politicised in support of a new revolutionary cause.

These young people, many of whom would go on to take part in events of Easter Week in 1916, form what scholars have called the 'Rising generation'. Fearghal McGarry has shown how a distinct set of factors including 'family background, social memory, local community influence, education, the expansion of print culture, and the growth of associational activity' in Ireland at the beginning of the twentieth century influenced the development of a generation 'emboldened rather than placated by the social, economic, and political reforms which it had benefited from'.[4] Narratives, sentiments, and opinions about the 1798

---

[1] For an overview of Irish public statuary in general and its increased appearance in the nineteenth century, see Judith Hill, *Irish Public Sculpture: A History* (Dublin: Four Courts Press, 1998). On 'statuemania' in Europe in the same period, Maurice Agulhon, 'La "statuomanie" et l'histoire', *Ethnologie Française* 8 (1978), 145–172.

[2] Gary Owens, 'Nationalist Monuments in Ireland, 1870–1914: Symbolism and Ritual' in R. Gillespie and B. P. Kennedy (eds.), *Ireland: Art into History* (Dublin: Town House, 1994), pp. 103, 117.

[3] See Guy Beiner's excellent history of the social memory of 1798 in modern Ireland, *Remembering the Year of the French* (Madison: University of Wisconsin Press, 2009).

[4] Fearghal McGarry, *The Rising: Ireland: Easter 1916* (Oxford: Oxford University Press, 2010), pp. 41–42. See also R. F. Foster, *Vivid Faces: The Revolutionary Generation in Ireland 1890–1923* (London: Allen Lane, 2014), especially chapter 9.

rising and its current political import were transmitted to young people through each of these factors to varying degrees during the centenary period. Sean Moylan, a young Volunteer during the Rising, who would later go on to join the Irish government, recalled how the '98 centenary brought his 'first vivid lessons in Irish history'. As a boy, Moylan would attend fireside gatherings to hear the local schoolteacher read the histories of the rebellion that appeared then in the newspapers in weekly instalments for wide circulation. The excitement seemed to travel from the page through the voice of the schoolmaster to the eager ears of those gathered by the fire:

In my mind's eye I saw the Wexford pikemen and the swift fierce onslaught of the French; went breathless with Dwyer from Wicklow to slip down Marshalsea Lane; sorrowed at Downpatrick for the man from Dromohane, while only subconsciously I heard the fierce comments of men who relived the scenes of their youth and in whose hearts the fiery Fenian sap had risen again.[5]

As a child, Moylan could not appreciate that these severe men, many of whom were old Fenian veterans of 1867 who often visited his father's home, shared an experience of national politics unknown to his own generation. 'Looking back now on the many elderly men whom I knew', he recalled as Minister of Education in the early 1950s,

I can understand that they were disillusioned, bewildered, hopeless; depressed because of failure, subdued because they had had their fill of victimisation, reticent because of training and distrustful of politics because they realised the futility of words.[6]

Those like Moylan, however, who experienced the flurry of activity surrounding the '98 centenary with the excitement and intrigue of youth, remained disconnected from the disillusionment of the past and inspired by the example of '98. It would take several years of debilitating violence and the horrors of war to renew those feelings of disenchanted bewilderment for a new generation.

---

[5] Bureau of Military History (BMH) witness statement (WS) 838 (Sean Moylan), (Irish) Military Archives. These sentiments are echoed in the childhood experience of Eamon Broy, IRA double agent within the Dublin Metropolitan Police during the War of Independence: 'In my very young days the centenary of the 1798 Rebellion had revived the spirit of Irish nationalism and the old people recited stories of the Battle of Rathangan in '98 ... Whether through [the memory of] local battles or the centenary celebrations of 1898, a very vivid realisation of the facts of the 1798 Rebellion was widespread.' BMH WS 1280 (Eamon Broy). For similar accounts, see Sean Prendergast, BMH WS 775, and Patrick McCartan, BMH WS 766.

[6] BMH WS 838 (Sean Moylan).

Republican agitators active on the wider scene, such as Maud Gonne, utilised the occasion of the centenary to their advantage. Gonne's auto-biographical account of her own extensive involvement in the centenary celebrations – although recounted much later and infused with the ego-tism typical of such memoirs – reveals several of the mechanisms at work in the politicisation of the young. As a member of the '98 Central Committee in Dublin, Gonne planned many of the city's commemorative activities, but she spent a great deal of time visiting committees and speaking at events elsewhere on the island as well. Although the focus of this activity was ostensibly on the events themselves, the preparations were of greater political importance to her as they afforded the 'opportu-nity to bring the hope of complete independence and the means of its attainment – Wolfe Tone's means – slumbering in the hearts of the whole Irish race, to the surface consciousness of the people'.[7] She visited towns planning to erect '98 memorials and spoke at groundbreaking and foun-dation stone-laying ceremonies across the country, always infusing revo-lutionary politics with the 'national love for dead heroes'.[8] Although the Central Committee wanted all the fundraising efforts directed at a national memorial to Wolfe Tone to be erected in Dublin, Gonne sup-ported the efforts of the local committees to memorialise their own local heroes 'because of the greater opportunities it gave for preaching Wolfe Tone's doctrines throughout the country'.[9] As thousands of people con-tributed funds and turned out for such commemorative ceremonies in town after town, Gonne's speeches connected the historical and social memory of '98 with her own revolutionary agenda in the present.

The centenary nevertheless functioned to bring nationalists together in the commemorative enterprise. One local region's efforts to erect their own '98 monument form a particularly illustrative example, to which we shall return later. Like many communities propelled by the centenary celebrations, nationalists in Kerry formed a series of local '98 memorial committees and began to plan for the creation of a statue to be erected in the county's principal town of Tralee. A prominent member of the main committee, Mr T. J. McCarthy – who would later be interned for his involvement as a Volunteer in Dublin during Easter Week – recalled that the idea arose during the centenary year at a meeting of Fenians held in

---

[7] Maud Gonne, *The Autobiography of Maud Gonne: A Servant of the Queen*, ed. A. Norman Jaffares and Ann MacBride White (Chicago: University of Chicago Press, 1994), p. 259.
[8] Gonne, *Autobiography*, p. 260.
[9] The political impact of her commemorative activities naturally fortified her against the accusations of W. B. Yeats, also a member of the Central Committee, who protested that in supporting the county efforts she bore 'responsibility for encouraging much bad art'. Gonne, *Autobiography*, p. 261.

the old premises of the Young Ireland Society in Tralee, whereupon a '98 Memorial Committee was swiftly formed to begin planning and collecting public subscriptions.[10] The monument would be the first sculpted memorial in the town and would represent a pikeman poised atop a thirty-foot pedestal, which would bear inscriptions on its four sides commemorating not only the 1798 rising but also those of 1803, 1848, and 1867.

Throughout the period prior to its erection, the proposed monument drew support from nationalists across the political spectrum: the constitutionalist North Kerry M. P. Michael J. Flavin, who spoke at the county's annual Manchester Martyrs celebration in order to solicit funds for the statue; Republican Maud Gonne, who characteristically advocated physical-force resistance at her speech at the monument's foundation stone-laying ceremony in 1902; and Charlie Doran, an elderly Fenian veteran of 1867, who, at the monument's eventual unveiling ceremony in 1907, advocated a middle-ground strategy of acquiring from the government whatever one could while holding out for a more opportune time to rebel. *The Kerryman* newspaper reported the observation of the memorial committee chairman, Maurice Moynihan, that

Kerryman of every shade of Nationalist opinion had contributed generously towards the monument, and they had people of every class and creed represented on the platform, and no matter how divergent their views may be as to the best means of achieving the freedom of Ireland, there was absolute unanimity displayed there in honour of the men who died for Ireland.[11]

These statements were borne out through the sheer volume of small sums contributed by individuals and organisations across the county and the unified sense of purpose demonstrated by the speeches of Flavin – a constitutionalist member of the British Parliament, Gonne – a staunch advocate of violent rebellion, and Doran – a Fenian veteran with a willingness to play the long game. All supported the erection of the monument, praised the efforts of the local people of Kerry, and were wildly supported in this endeavour by audiences assembled for broad nationalist commemorations, either for Manchester Martyrdom celebrations or for the '98 memorial events in Tralee.

For some of the young who made up these vast audiences, and whom would later participate in the Easter Rising, the experience of witnessing the '98 commemorations also brought a first taste of political violence. Séamus Robinson, for instance, who as a Volunteer was stationed on

[10] 'Kerry '98 Memorial: Suggestion That Pedestal be Removed', *The Kerryman*, 29 January 1938.
[11] 'The Memory of the Dead', *The Kerryman*, 30 November 1907.

O'Connell Bridge during Easter Week, recalled how his first 'active service' began in 1898 while he was living in Glasgow, where the Irish population also took up the commemorative activities of the centenary. That year, 'with more audacity than wit, I joined in a counter attack (made by an advance party of a Nationalist procession celebrating the '98 centenary) on a charging crowd of Orangemen'.[12] Others participated in violent clashes in Dublin itself. Some, for instance, including several members of the '98 county committees, participated in what came to be known as the Jubilee Day riot in 1897. In a calculated political move, the Central Committee in Dublin arranged to hold a convention of delegates from the local county committees on the same day as the celebration of Queen Victoria's Diamond Jubilee. James Connolly organised a nationalist protest of the jubilee events, centred on a public procession headed by a brass band and bearing a coffin to represent the fate of the British Empire. John O'Leary, as head of the Central Committee, presided over the county convention in City Hall all afternoon, while Connolly arranged his event. O'Leary continued the meeting until the participants could hear the band outside in the evening, which signalled the approach of the Jubilee protest procession. Then, at the urging of Maud Gonne, he instructed the delegates to stand outside on the steps in order that they might all watch Connolly's procession together – another participatory event designed to promote nationalist unity. Gonne recollected the riot that ensued:

Willie Yeats and I and many of the '98 Centenary delegates joined the procession as it moved off down Dame Street to the strain of a Dead March on the cracked instruments of the band. The police were only beginning to realise the meaning of the procession and rushed for reinforcements from the Castle and other police stations. The crowd was so dense they could not attempt to break us up till they were in force. Then foot and horse police arrived and there were charges by mounted police and baton charges and people began to be carried off in ambulances. Connolly was not a man to be easily stopped and the procession arrived in fair order at O'Connell Bridge. Here the fighting was furious and, seeing the coffin in danger of being captured by the police, Connolly gave the order to throw it in the Liffey. The whole crowd shouted: 'Here goes the coffin of the British Empire! To hell with the British Empire!' Connolly was arrested.[13]

Through provocative strategies such as this, the commemorative activities of the '98 committees often became intertwined with the more radical nationalist agenda; in this case, even drawing many of the county committee members themselves into the violent political fray. In the case of the Jubilee Day riot, as also in that of the large, public memorial

---

[12] BMH WS 1721 (Séamus Robinson).   [13] Gonne, *Autobiography*, pp. 216–217.

unveiling and dedication ceremonies, the politicising effects spread to spectators as well as participants. Volunteer Frank Henderson, for instance, identified the Jubilee Day riot, along with the '98 centenary more generally, as two factors by which he was influenced, 'along with many other young people', and which strengthened the 'early separatist and physical force outlook' that led to his involvement in later revolutionary activities.[14]

Despite the groundswell of enthusiasm for commemorating 1798 in the years surrounding the turn of the twentieth century, and the influence of these efforts on the 'Rising generation', interest in remembering the famed rebellion suffered after the new revolutionary period that generation initiated. In the intervening years, the Great War and the Easter Rising itself, followed by a bloody war for independence and an even bloodier civil war, brought on a certain memorial malaise that turned the youthful idealism of men like Sean Moylan into the 'disillusioned' and 'bewildered' reflections of the older men he knew as a child, albeit in a different fashion. A crisis of memory had been created by factionalism and the fracturing of the nationalist commemorative unity developed through the 1898 centenary into oppositional groups with conflicting 'memories' of recent events. To whom did the memory of the Easter Rising belong, for instance? To Free Staters or Republicans? By the time the Irish Free State had been firmly established and the rebuilding of the nation's infrastructure replaced the violence of the revolutionary years, there began to emerge a disillusionment with the past altogether and, for some, the sensation that the national memory-myth itself may bear part of the blame for the destruction.

In this newly developing political landscape, three major factors contributed to the decline of interest in continuing to commemorate the rebellion whose memory had galvanised so many young people at the turn of the century. First, several years of devastating violence and the bleak outlook of the early Free State raised questions about the valorisation of war. The impact of this recent reminder of the human costs of battle served better the impulse to remember the fallen and to fitly mark their sacrifices rather than to celebrate an earlier instantiation of bloody rebellion, especially when its own commemoration had helped to spark the new revolution. Celebratory enthusiasm dulled as the political situation shifted such that calls for solidarity with fighters for Ireland's freedom held less purchase in the Free State than they had during the '98 centenary. Commemoration fever had been interrupted by actual revolution.

[14] BMH WS 249 (Frank Henderson).

These sentiments began to emerge in the dramatic world even before the fighting had come to an end. Theatre-going remained a popular activity for Dubliners and the success or failure of dramatic productions served as a barometer for public opinion, especially at the Abbey Theatre. The Abbey had been founded as the National Theatre of Ireland during the revival of interest in Irish language, literature, and culture that dominated the end of the nineteenth and beginning of the twentieth centuries, and which provided momentum for the nationalist commemorative enterprise of the same period. In the midst of this cultural environment, the theatre's staging of many of the plays of W. B. Yeats, J. M. Synge, Lady Gregory, and the Dublin trilogy of Sean O'Casey attested to more than a passing interest in foregrounding issues of nationalism and national sentiment.[15] *Cathleen Ní Houlihan*, the wildly popular collaboration by Yeats and Gregory, had openly glorified the '98 rebellion in both its setting and its deployment of the national memory-mythology, and had garnered much success when it was first produced in 1902 at the height of the centenary fervour – and still later when it topped the bill for the Abbey's first performance on its opening day in December 1904.

But, by 1919, Yeats had begun to question the relationship between national memory and violence. Twenty years later, the poet would famously contemplate the aftermath of the Rising and the revolutionary period in his self-conscious lament to the success of *Cathleen Ní Houlihan*: 'Did that play of mine / Send out certain men the English shot?'[16] But Yeats had been questioning the wisdom of the national mythology long before he composed 'The Man and the Echo' shortly before his death in 1939. At the beginning of the War of Independence (1919–1921), Yeats composed *The Dreaming of the Bones*, set in the aftermath of Easter Week, which follows a young man who had fought in the GPO as he escapes into the countryside.[17] He encounters the ghosts of Diarmuid and Dervorgilla, figures associated in the national mythology with inadvertently facilitating Ireland's conquest by the Normans, who warn the youth against overly zealous commitment to the memory of the past. Dervorgilla

---

[15] Several of the Abbey's staff participated in the Rising itself; see Fearghal McGarry's essay (Chapter 5) in the present volume. On the history of the theatre, see Robert Welch, *The Abbey Theatre, 1899–1999: Form and Pressure* (Oxford: Oxford University Press, 2003). For the Abbey and the nationalist theatrical zeitgeist, Máire Nic Shiubhlaigh and Edward Kenny, *The Splendid Years: Recollections of Máire Nic Shiubhlaigh* (Dublin: Duffy and Co., 1955).

[16] W. B. Yeats, 'The Man and the Echo', in *Last Poems and Two Plays* (Dublin: The Cuala Press, 1939), pp. 27–29.

[17] By the end of the war in 1921, Yeats would publish his haunting poem 'Easter, 1916', an emotionally fraught reaction to the Rising that he claimed to have written in the summer months immediately thereafter.

tells him of her cursed existence with Diarmuid and that 'the memory of their crime flows up between/and drives them apart'. It is not the act itself that causes their suffering, but the perpetual remembering of it. If the lovers could let go of the memory, it would stop haunting them and they could move on. Yeats contrasts the idealism of the young rebel with contemporary reflections on national memory as a potentially negative force. If old grievances could be forgotten, if the memory of crimes past could be expunged, the future would hold less suffering for Ireland, as the appeal to memory had kept violence fresh in the minds of the young and the consequences were beginning to present themselves by 1919. Yeats ends the play with a clear reiteration of this point: 'Dry bones that dream are bitter.'

Sean O'Casey and Denis Johnston echoed this sentiment even more overtly in the years immediately following the Civil War. O'Casey's *Juno and the Paycock* (1924), one of the Abbey Theatre's most successful plays of the 1920s, features a young republican whose involvement in the war left him disabled and disillusioned. Initially, young Johnny insists that he would do it all again, for 'a principle's a principle', but as the play wears on, his resolve weakens. While his father sings of the men of '98 and those 'in the van of the fight for Ireland's freedom', Johnny becomes moody and disinterested. Eventually, angered at the subject of death and killing, he bursts out: 'Is there nothin' betther to be talkin' about but the killin' o' people? My God, isn't it bad enough for these things to happen without talkin' about them!'[18] Johnston's expressionist-influenced *The Old Lady Says No!* (1926) utilises a similarly direct deployment of the memorialising theme and the canonical nationalist mythology. The play opens on the night of 25 August 1803, the night of Robert Emmet's failed rebellion outside Dublin, a familiar episode in the romantic nationalist memory-myth canon. But it soon becomes clear that the character of 'Robert Emmet' is an actor playing the part of Emmet in a play within the play, which soon breaks down into a cloudy, expressionist jumble of uncertain, unclear scenarios. Most of the actors play two conflicting roles and the effect is a constant juxtaposition of elements of the Emmet story with the confusion and chaos of the Free State's efforts at state-building. Johnston summed up the mood in a later preface to the work. 'In 1926', he wrote, 'several years of intermittent and unromantic civil war had soured us all a little towards the woes of Cathleen ní Houlihan. It was inevitable that such a play would be written in Ireland by someone or other at about that time.'[19]

---

[18] Sean O'Casey, *Juno and the Paycock* (1924), Act II.
[19] Denis Johnston, *The Dramatic Works of Denis Johnston, Volume 1* (London: Colin Smythe Limited, 1992), p. 16.

In the monumental landscape, this new disillusionment manifested much less sharply. While 1798 had been the war most worth remembering before the Rising, by 1923, there were fresh war dead from four new conflicts that stimulated varying degrees of popular interest in their commemoration.[20] With each new outbreak of violent conflict, 1798 became more remote. In addition to a general disillusionment, two other factors contributed to the declining interest in '98 commemoration in the landscape in particular. The grass-roots movements that resulted in the organisation of memorial committees and the initial creation of commemorative statues had been calcified into more rigid processes of state and bureaucracy that no longer held the same power to rally great public interest. As Guy Beiner has noted, the state now governed remembrance. 'Consequently', he observes, 'mainstream commemoration lost its oppositional edge, and expressions of militant republicanism were no longer acceptable in commemorative programs backed by the establishment.'[21] Participation in memorial committees, too, came to resemble a service much more so than a revolutionary associational act. In addition, the impulse to remember the recent conflicts came to be entangled with the memory of '98 and, particularly when memorial committees included members of the 'Rising generation', even to supersede it. Let us return to the Pikeman of Tralee, the unusual circumstances of which allow us to observe within the 'lifespan' of a single monument the impact of these factors in the altered political condition of the Irish Free State.

After its unveiling in 1907, the memorial stood in the middle of Denny Street in Tralee for the next fourteen years with little fanfare, much the same as the majority of '98 monuments. However, near the end of the War of Independence, in the spring of 1921, members of the Royal Irish Constabulary Auxiliary division destroyed the statue in a night of severe and violent reprisals against Tralee for recent republican activity in the town. On the night of 19 April, nine houses and businesses were destroyed by bombs and fire, including the home of the local priest, and the printing houses of *The Kerryman* and the Sinn Féin paper, *The*

---

[20] See Anne Dolan, *Commemorating the Irish Civil War: History and Memory, 1923–2000* (Cambridge: Cambridge University Press, 2003); Jane Leonard, 'Lest We Forget' in David Fitzpatrick (ed.), *Ireland and the First World War* (Dublin: Lilliput Press, 1988), pp. 59–67; Jason Myers, *The Great War and Memory in Irish Culture, 1918–2010* (Bethesda: Munsel and Co., 2013); Catherine Switzer, *Unionists and Great War Commemoration in the North of Ireland, 1914–1918* (Dublin: Irish Academic Press, 2007); R. F. Foster, 'Remembering' in *Vivid Faces: The Revolutionary Generation in Ireland, 1890–1923* (London: Allen Lane, 2014); John Horne and Edward Madigan (eds.), *Towards Commemoration: Ireland in War and Revolution, 1912–1923* (Dublin: Royal Irish Academy, 2013).

[21] Beiner, *Remembering the Year of the French*, p. 265.

Liberator. During this night of destruction, the Auxiliary officers of H Company attacked the pedestal of the '98 memorial, ripped the statue down from its position, and smashed it. The figure's pike and head were taken, as were the arms and legs, and the body left lying decapitated in the middle of the street.[22]

At the close of the Civil War two years later, the Kerry '98 committee sought compensation from the Claims Office of the victorious Free State for the destroyed pikeman and, eventually, following the slow rotation of bureaucratic wheels, they received a sum of £110 to be used for its replacement.[23] However, it had become much more difficult to raise additional funds by public subscription than it had been during the nationalist fervour of the early part of the century. By 1927, the pedestal still stood empty in Denny Street and some local people began to complain to the Urban Council of Tralee that it ought to be removed to a location where it would not obstruct the view of the newly refurbished County Hall. Rather than a representation of national pride for the region, the remains of the monument had become an unsightly obstruction in the civic domain. One complainant suggested that the site where a local man had been killed by the Royal Irish Constabulary (RIC) would be an ideal location to 'fitly commemorate the terrible tragedy that happened there'.[24] The writer was unclear on the reason for the pedestal's fitness for that site. Was it because the tradition of national resistance to the British state in which the '98 rebellion existed now extended to include the War of Independence, and thus the commemoration of one rebellion at the site of an event connected to the other would form a natural complement? Or was it merely that the RIC was responsible for both the killing of the local man and the emptiness of the pedestal, thereby connecting the two memorial episodes? In either case, the memories had become intertwined in the complainant's mind to the extent that no explanation for their relationship to each other seemed necessary. For at least some members of the community, the '98 monument was no longer deemed important enough on its own to hold a prime place in the city's landscape, where it blocked a view of the architecture, and could be suitably relocated to a site of alternative but unclear significance.

---

[22] 'National Monuments Destroyed in Tralee', *Freeman's Journal*, 21 April 1921; 'The Irish Situation', *Anglo-Celt*, 23 April 1921. On the RIC and Auxiliaries and their reprisals, see D. M. Leeson, *The Black and Tans: British Police and Auxiliaries in the Irish War of Independence, 1920–21* (Oxford: Oxford University Press, 2011), esp. pp. 170–173 on Tralee.

[23] '98 Memorial: The Question of Removal', *The Kerryman*, 19 March 1927.

[24] 'Tralee Topics', *The Kerryman*, 26 February 1927.

By 1931, after a decade of inaction following the statue's destruction, the aging memorial committee came under pressure from the Urban Council and approved a plan to replace the original limestone pikeman with a bronze figure atop the existing pedestal. Renowned local sculptor Jerome Connor offered his services free of charge and did present a scale model of a charging pikeman to the satisfaction of the committee, but his own displeasure with the design caused such an extended delay that they eventually took him to court, which left Connor bankrupt and the committee without a pikeman.[25] In the absence of the kind of popular momentum and regional interest that drove the memorial's initial development, legal processes and mundane paperwork stalled the project for several more years. The pedestal still remained empty in 1938, when the Urban Council again suggested that the monument be relocated to an alternative site due to another new civic project, the paving of Denny Street.

The '98 Memorial committee, by then composed of only a few elderly founding members and a handful of interested others, expressed its exasperation at the next meeting.[26] It was becoming apparent that the monument maintained significance chiefly for the republicans who erected it and few else. One such member, Mr Henry Spring, suggested that the broken pieces of the original monument might be collected and displayed on the old pedestal 'as a monument to the destruction wrought by the English Auxiliaries'. There, he suggested, they would be 'a reminder to the rising generation and to visitors of the tyranny practised by British agents'. Several others presented arguments for the creation of a new pikeman before the committee ultimately passed a resolution opposing the removal of the pedestal and declaring the monument 'sacred to the Dead, whose memory it perpetuates, and to the men, now deceased, who organised its erection'.[27] The memory of the experiences of the 'Rising generation', both in raising the monument and in the War of Independence in which it fell, now stood unambiguously equal to the 1798 tradition itself. The committee finally contracted Dublin sculptor

---

[25] 'Kerry '98 Memorial: Bronze Figure to be Erected Old Site', *The Kerryman*, 5 September 1931; John Turpin, 'Jerome Connor: Sculptor of Irish America', *Irish Arts Review* 23 (2006), 84–87 (87); Sighle Bhreathnach-Lynch, 'The Pikeman of Tralee: A Tale of Continuity and Change', *History Ireland* 6 (1998), 5–6.

[26] That week saw the death of one such founder, Patrick Power, whose obituary appeared in the local papers on the same day as the committee's response to the Urban Council and noted his commitment to the Land League, Parnell, the G.A.A., Sinn Féin, the I.R.A., Fianna Fáil, and 'restoring the pikeman figure to the pedestal of the '98 memorial in Denny St'. 'Death of Veteran Kerry Patriot', *The Kerryman*, 29 January 1938.

[27] 'Kerry '98 Memorial: Suggestion That Pedestal be Removed', *The Kerryman*, 29 January 1938.

Albert Power to design a new limestone statue as quickly as possible, but they still faced a shortfall in funding even as the completed project lacked only transportation and erection. The new pikeman was incapable of drumming up the kind of support from individual Kerrymen and nationalist organisations that the project initially enjoyed.

At the eventual unveiling of the new statue on 18 June 1939, it was again the 'Rising generation' who held the spotlight. The event was attended by a large crowd, just as before, and, fascinatingly, Maud Gonne McBride was invited to speak again, as she had at the original foundation ceremony thirty-seven years previously, but the tone of the event was much altered. The statue was now draped in a tricolour before its unveiling and the message of the speakers had less to do with the United Irishmen and a common commemorative spirit than the current status of the divided island. Gonne's political views, while modified to accommodate the new outrages she perceived in recent Irish history, continued to reflect her belief that armed conflict, despite the horrors of the intervening years, still held Ireland's best chance for re-unification and complete separation from Britain. She spoke of Wolfe Tone but little of '98 and chose instead to exhort the people to focus their will on renewed violent rebellion.[28] The re-dedication of the monument in the altered political situation of 1939, and the discordant ideological context of post-war Ireland, had little to do with the faces and events inscribed on the pedestal and the limestone croppy boy representing the common rebel fighting for Ireland's freedom in 1798. Rather, it presented an opportunity for the memorial committee and Gonne to attempt to re-kindle the conditions of the centenary fervour in spite of the intervening years.

Interest in commemorating 1798 renewed in the years surrounding the sesquicentenary of 1948, but it would never reach the fever pitch of the turn of the previous century. A combination of apathy towards the glorification of violent national mythology, disinterest in mundane and quotidian bureaucracy, and the appeal to the memory of the 'Rising generation' itself gradually overshadowed 1798 in the Free State years. The '98 centenary served both to provide an impetus for and a model of a revolutionary uprising, and to help politicise a generation that would ultimately eclipse its commemorative tradition with a national legacy of their own.

[28] 'The Pikeman Restored to the '98 Memorial in Tralee', *The Kerryman*, 24 June 1939.

9 Cultural representations of 1916

Nicholas Allen

If from a cultural perspective the idea of 1916 has continuing meaning for contemporary Ireland, it is to provoke critical reflection on the evolving and interconnected processes of aesthetic and historical transformation that act upon it. For some decades now, the cultural history of Ireland has been the subject of sophisticated literary analysis, with more sporadic attention given to the visual arts and music. This history has remained largely the site of established narratives of cause and effect, which have been shaped in turn by ideas of nation and state that have undergone little renovation, for all the more recent turn away from the canonical figures of high politics towards micro-studies of place and community.[1] Recently, a shift towards memory and the transnational as theoretical terms of engagement has brought history closer to a literary study that understands Ireland and its culture as one part of a globally complex equation. To think of the cultural representation of 1916 is to ask questions of production and reception in a twentieth- and twenty-first-century Ireland that continues to be the contested site of far-reaching processes, in empire and after.

Evidence for this registers in the resurgence of 1916 as a public point of interest at key moments in political history. The Easter Rising has not been a constant cause for celebration in the hundred years since its occurrence. The fact of its centenary should not obscure the variable pull of its significance on the public consciousness,[2] and as Anne Dolan has remarked, the civil war lingers still like Banquo's ghost at the

---

[1] The modern field of historical study has been shaped by Charles Townshend in books like *Easter 1916. The Irish Rebellion* (London: Allen Lane, 2005), and more broadly by Keith Jeffery, with *Ireland and the Great War* (Cambridge: Cambridge University Press, 2000). Other core resources include F. McGarry, *The Rising. Ireland: Easter 1916* (Oxford: Oxford University Press, 2010); S. Hegarty and F. O'Toole, *The Irish Times Book of the 1916 Rising* (Dublin: Gill and Macmillan, 2006). An excellent general study of the longer period is Thomas Bartlett's *Ireland: A History* (Cambridge: Cambridge University Press, 2011). For all that, 'The definitive history of the Rising has yet to be written, and many questions have been left unanswered.' Diarmaid Ferriter, *The Transformation of Ireland 1900–2000* (London: Profile, 2004), p. 142.

[2] The formative study of this tangled history is Roisín Higgins, *Transforming 1916: Meaning, Memory and the Fiftieth Anniversary of the Easter Rising* (Cork: Cork University Press, 2012).

commemoration feast. The cultural representation of 1916 north of the border is another matter altogether, given the synthesis of the Somme with particular kinds of unionist identity. There, sacrifice on the Western Front is significant of Ulster's loyalty to the crown, a split history that is inaccurate, partial and significant mostly of subsequent conditions of twentieth-century Ireland, namely partition and violence.

These realities have their common core in the island of Ireland's deep experience of empire. Britain entered a new phase of global hegemony in the nineteenth century. British power was military and commercial, and the cultural effects of this combination registered in Dublin as home to a thriving music hall and cinema culture that integrated popular entertainment with sophisticated synergies of image, music and text.[3] It hosted salon entertainments for charities and societies, public lectures on themes as diverse as classical civilisation and Shakespeare's drama, plays staged by an array of amateur and professional theatre companies. After 1914, the war seeped into each of these activities as it progressed, the drawing rooms of Dublin used to host parties to raise funds for wounded men, the country fetes of its outlying countries host to raffles for comforts for the Irish regiments. The culture of military tattoo was implanted in the public mind by decades of regimental parades in the barrack towns (a fact that gives lie to the common but misled idea that the rebellion introduced the gun to modern Irish politics). It faded with the call up of troops to the front, a space opened in the streets for the Ulster and the Irish Volunteers to fill with their own manoeuvres.

In 1916, all aspects of life were cut with a cultural shrapnel and the background to culture high and low was the deadly grind of the front. Lectures and recitals found war as their subject, whatever the setting. Thomas MacDonagh spoke to Volunteer officers in Kildare Street of the history of conflict from the campaign of Xerxes to the South African campaigns.[4] After MacDonagh's execution and in a ruined Sackville Street, the Little Theatre hosted the Dublin branch of the British Empire Shakespeare Society to hear a Mr S. Fitzpatrick deliver a lecture on 'Shakespeare and War'. The lecturer undertook that, while Shakespeare was alive to human suffering, 'he was still prepared to justify, and even to laud, a war undertaken in a rightful cause and from motives of

---

[3] The year 1916 is remarkable not least for the publication of James Joyce's *A Portrait of the Artist as a Young Man*. Relative to the point of popular culture's influence on the public mind, when Stephen Dedalus is discovered at prayer by two members of the constabulary he breaks 'off his prayer to whistle loudly an air from the last pantomime'. James Joyce, *A Portrait of the Artist as a Young Man*, ed. John Paul Riquelme (New York: Norton, 2007), p. 205.

[4] Bureau of Military History (BMH) Witness Statement (WS) 242 (Liam Tannam), (Irish) Military Archives.

patriotism'.[5] The thinning of Irish ranks in the regular army caused[?]
anxiety over Ireland's commitment to the war even before the rebellion.
Both Stephen Gwynn and Tom Kettle served on the western front, where
Kettle died in September 1916. In 1915 they edited a propagandistic
collection of *Battle Songs for the Irish Brigades*, which included Gwynn's
'The Irish Brigade, 1914', which asked:

> Must English fill the Rangers' ranks? Welsh pad the Munsters' line?
> Where stood the Dublin Fusiliers, Scots give the counter-sign?
> Or when the Inniskillings faint, shall Sikhs the trench re-man?
> Pathan and Gurka finish what the Irish Guards began?[6]

The question mark is an emblematic symbol of punctuation in Irish
poetry of the First World War. The future was so uncertain as to be
unreadable, even to William Butler Yeats, who wrote 'Easter, 1916', the
greatest literary work associated with the rebellion, in a time of personal
and social turmoil. 'Easter, 1916' is one of Yeats's most read poems and
yet his most elusive, at once a memorial to the dead rebels and a recasting
of their various ideals into a single form, the deafening voices of war and
rebellion bound into a mourning song for Ireland. By the time of the
rebellion, Yeats spent much of his time at a series of dinners and *soirées*
that mixed the social *élites* of London with the cultural *avant-garde*. His
high table invitations show the presence of an establishment figure, pen-
sioned by the British state and secure in his intellectual stock.[7] He
invested part of this access in Lady Gregory's campaign for Dublin's
ownership of the Lane pictures. Some, however, was held in reserve and
distributed slowly in acts of favour that belie Yeats's public persona as
restrained and aloof. Pushed along by Pound, Yeats helped win funds for
a destitute James Joyce, having been persuaded of Joyce's ability by
Dubliners, which Pound read to him aloud.[8] As Pound read, the
American poet worked to settle the estate of his dead friend, the sculptor

---

[5] *Irish Times*, 23 November 1916, p. 3.
[6] Stephen Gwynn and T. M. Kettle (eds.), *Battle Songs for the Irish Brigades* (Dublin:
Maunsel and Company, 1915), p. 30.
[7] The major account of Yeats's life and experience in this period, as in all others, is
R. F. Foster, *W. B. Yeats – A Life, II: The Arch-Poet 1915–1939* (Oxford: Oxford
University Press, 2003).
[8] Pound wrote to Joyce on 2 September 1916, informing him that Yeats was lobbying
Asquith's secretary on behalf of Joyce. 'Yeats also wrote a strong letter of recommenda-
tion, but he was in France, and I don't know but what the grant was made before his letter
was rec'd, still you might thank him, and certainly assume that he helped.' Richard
Ellmann (ed.), *Letters of James Joyce. Vol II* (New York: Viking, 1966), p. 384.

Henri Gaudier-Brzeska. The war was everywhere and on a clear night, the guns from the front could be heard across the channel in London.[9]

The rebellion made the war inescapable to Yeats because it brought the world problem of imperial collapse to Ireland. In London, he subscribed to a news cutting service that clipped articles from newspapers on the subject of Ireland. In the wake of the rebellion, he received a set of pages from the *Daily Telegraph* of 2 May 1916. The rising was wrapped up in a global gathering of bad news. The clipping sent to Yeats had seven columns of news whose headlines were 'The Battles at Verdun', 'Defence of Kut', 'Collapse of the Seven Days' Revolt' and 'Tightening of the Military Cordon'.[10] For all its suffering, Ireland was a small part of a world system that was buckling from France to Arabian Peninsula (a fact that informs Yeats's later vision of apocalypse in the desert in 'The Second Coming').

The artistic and social consequences of this adjustment were problematic and unpredictable. At Stone Cottage in Suffolk, Yeats and Pound were touched by the struggle, which intensified as the French began their defence of Verdun in face of a German assault that was designed to bleed their enemy dry. The river of wounded became a flood and Yeats did not escape the wash. The rebellion caught Yeats by surprise, as it did many others. He followed the newspaper reports that followed through his subscription to the General Press Cutting Association Limited in Norfolk Street, London. He received a long clipping from the *Daily Chronicle* dated 9 May 1916. It was written by an anonymous correspondent in the West of Ireland. It read:

Of the men shot this week, I have known three. An unsuccessful schoolmaster with an impossible ideal; a consumptive minor poet – perhaps one would not call him a poet but for this new solemnity; a University lecturer who was also a minor poet. The thought of them is more poignant than if they were greater men. The last time I saw this one it was at a tea-party in a Dublin hotel; the last time I saw that one he was consulting with me about a literary venture. In both cases their memory remains with me: amiable, a little deferential to an older writer. I thought of them as ineffective, negligible. By what strange currents did they, straws upon the stream, drift to this wild ocean?[11]

---

[9] 'A few nights ago dwellers in a north London suburb were kept awake by the sounds of gun-fire, dull but unmistakeable, and, as there is no report of any air raid on that particular night, they came to the conclusion that their ears must have deceived them. But from the researches of French and English scientists, it seems possible that they were really listening to the guns of Ypres, which have apparently been heard, in certain conditions of the atmosphere, as much as 150 miles away.' *Irish Times*, 26 July 1916, p. 4.

[10] *Daily Telegraph*, 2 May 1916, Ms. 30,714, Yeats papers, National Library of Ireland (NLI).

[11] *Daily Chronicle*, 9 May 1916, Ms. 30,714, Yeats papers (NLI).

The three dead men are Pearse, Plunkett and MacDonagh, and this report is the seed of 'Easter, 1916'. The later poem lists the rebels by description, not name, and wonders, too, how great each dead man may have become. It turns late, also, to the strange currents of these straws on the stream. The language is unmistakeable in comparison to 'Easter, 1916'.

> Hearts with one purpose alone
> Through summer and winter seem
> Enchanted to a stone
> To trouble the living stream.[12]

Yeats made one adjustment to the newspaper report, which was to dam the water before it reached the wild ocean. Yeats was not willing yet to consider the Irish problem as reflective of the world condition. His was a poetry of the particular and the precise, and delirium drew from the imagination's contact with material objects, the stream beating against stone. So Yeats absorbed the language of newspapers into his poetry. The *Daily Chronicle* continued:

I have known Irish leaders of revolution – Parnell, Davitt, O'Leary – all outstanding men. I know all that is to be known from books of the men of '98. What have they in common with these university professors, these fledgling poets? Nothing, except the dreams and ideals. Some of these broken on the red wheel of revolution are more piteous than greater men in like case.[13]

'Easter, 1916' echoed:

> We know their dream; enough
> To know they dreamed and are dead ...[14]

The *Daily Chronicle* correspondent knew of Yeats and admired his work with the Abbey. The Irish were dramatic people and the establishment of a national theatre struck a chord with their natural aspirations. Revolution had a liquid force that seeped through the centuries and across national lines.

Has not this revolution in some sense a genesis in the Irish Theatre? Where out of Paris would you find the Countess Markiewicz? That kissing of the revolver now before she handed it up! The terms in which the main body of the insurgents surrendered, 'the members of the Provisional Government', 'the units of the Republican forces', the sounding titles of such men as P. H. Pearse and James Connolly, it is all of the stuff of drama – the heady wine of the French revolution in new bottles.[15]

---

[12] W. B. Yeats, 'Easter, 1916' in A. N. Jeffares (ed.), *Yeats's Poems* (London: Macmillan, 1996), p. 288.
[13] *Daily Chronicle*, 9 May 1916, Ms. 30,714, Yeats papers, NLI.
[14] Yeats, 'Easter, 1916', p. 288.
[15] *Daily Chronicle*, 9 May 1916, Ms. 30,714, Yeats papers, NLI.

In raising armed men to Ireland's streets, the rebels had changed the stage of history. The hazel woods and homesteads of the west were exchanged for burned out city buildings in the contemporary imagination. The consequences of this were uncertain for a generation confirmed in the belief of Ireland's cultural, and so political, significance. Now there were gunboats on the Liffey and warships in Galway Bay the literary representations of the revival were in sudden disarray.

The Abbey Theatre had been a keystone of that cultural revival, despite its struggles for relevance and audience in the years immediately prior to the rebellion. It escaped major physical damage during the insurrection but for a broken lamp outside the stage door and some smashed panes of glass by the pit.[16] The acting company had been on tour in Limerick, and the theatre reopened on 10 May with a series of matinees, which began with productions of *The Building Fund* and *The Coiner*.[17] The Abbey was thrown back on diminished resources, its company traumatised by the death of an actor in the Volunteer forces and its unionist manager, St John Ervine, a short step away from the sack. Now the Abbey Theatre was desperate for survival, and revived John Millington Synge's *Playboy of the Western World* to its stage, which was ironic given the violence that had attended the *Playboy*'s own first production.

The theatre was one part of a broad cultural space that incorporated practically all modes of public behaviour. Churches, schools, universities, libraries, shops, railways, trams, cars and streets were all sites of potential political disturbance. The funeral of Jeremiah O'Donovan Rossa on 1 August 1915 had seen the first public signs of Patrick Pearse's militant radicalisation.[18] Now Pearse had joined the Fenian dead, and O'Donovan

[16] Robert Hogan and Richard Burnham, *The Art of the Amateur 1916–1920: The Modern Irish Drama. A Documentary History V* (Mountrath: Dolmen Press, 1984), p. 21.

[17] 'The Irish Players will not be at the Abbey theatre next week, as they will be fulfilling a long-standing engagement to appear at the Theatre Royal, Limerick, where they will present a variety of plays. They will return to Dublin the following week, and re-open on Tuesday, March 7th, when Mr St John Ervine's four-act play, "Mixed Marriage", will be performed, together with Mr W. B. Yeats's one-act piece, "Kathleen ni Houlihan," *Irish Times*, 26 February, p. 6. Hogan and Burnham, *The Art of the Amateur 1916–1920*, p. 9.

[18] The funeral is famous for Pearse's graveside speech in which he summoned the ghosts of the Fenian dead to enlist in the Volunteer movement. Monsignor Curran arrived late at Glasnevin. He thought the 'funeral was most impressive, skilfully organised and carried out. It was a challenge to Dublin Castle and a deeply significant lesson to the Irish people. The Irish Volunteers and a detachment of the Citizen Army marched in uniform, some with arms. Besides the various organisations allied to Sinn Féin, many municipal and Local Government bodies took part. So too did the GAA in large numbers and the National Volunteers, but these without arms. Pearse's graveside oration has become a classic, but the supremely impressive moment was the triple volley fired by the Volunteers. It was more than a farewell to an old Fenian. It was a defiance to England by a new generation in Ireland. I heard the volleys as I hurried up Iona Road.' BMH WS 687 (Michael Curran).

Rossa's anniversary in 1916 was led by a procession of fifty women from the American alliance of the Ancient Order of Hibernians. There had already been a demonstration 'of sympathy and protest' following the rebellion in New York's Central Park in late June.[19] Even during the height of the war, there is other evidence to suggest that there was a constant stream of Irish returning from America.[20] The vital link between Ireland and America made Britain's suit for co-operation in the war more complicated, and republican activists took full advantage, marching in formation and placing wreaths of flowers on O'Donovan Rossa's grave. The commemoration ended with a fight with the police over a flag.[21]

Despite censorship, lack of materials, a shortage of advertisements and the perennial challenge to attract and retain an audience, the cultural debate that accompanied these public acts of disaffection was conducted in a range of newspapers, journals and pamphlets. A major figure in this context was George Russell, the long-established editor of the *Irish Homestead* and vocal advocate for national self-determination. His co-operative movement taught self-help among the farm and labouring classes, setting itself against the merchant classes that were bedrock to the constitutional Irish Nationalist Party. For Russell, this economic independence required a firm cultural foundation that began in childhood. Young people were the seed bed for a new civility and so discussion of their potential was a source of controversy; in this context, it is no surprise that Patrick Pearse was the leading figure in the rebellion and an educationalist, as were many of his fellow rebels, Thomas MacDonagh among them. As Russell discussed the practice of social integration through civic schooling, Patrick Pearse paraded a generation of boys through St Enda's, steeping each of them in an experience of spectacle and ambition that none ever forgot.

These experiments took place in different forms, and towards very different ends, across the British Empire. The scouting movement, the boys' brigades, the officer training corps were all ways in which young people could be trained in habits of discipline and adventure towards political benefit. This adult reality does not obscure the tragic aspect of family correspondence between fathers and their children during the war. There is terrible evidence of this in Lady Gregory's son Robert's letters to her grandson Richard during the early autumn of 1916. By late September, Robert was stationed in France and his squadron was in

[19] Padraic Colum, 'The Dead Irish Poets', *Poetry: A Magazine of Verse* 8 (1916), 268.
[20] Irish Americans arrived by the hundred each Tuesday in Dublin at the North and South Walls, at least during the summer. They connected by cross-channel steamers from British ports, presumably Liverpool. *Irish Times*, 29 July 1916, p. 3.
[21] *Irish Times*, 12 August 1916, p. 3.

heavy contact with the enemy. They were grounded when it rained heavily because the canvas bodies of the airplanes stretched when wet. So Robert peppered his son with questions:

Did you ever try the chemical experiments? Did they work all right? I wonder if you would like a box of electrical experiments. I used to have one, & could get shocks & sparks – but not big enough to hurt one. Do you like the Boy's own Annuals that I used to read. There are a lot of things in them that you might like. Did you fly a kite this summer? We have kite balloons here – half kite & half balloon – & men go up & watch the enemy from them. We fly round them & look after them, but the men in the balloon are always very frightened that we shall run into them.[22]

Robert Gregory was under no illusion as to the danger of his profession, having made a new will shortly before writing this letter that secured his effects to his wife and promised her full freedom in the bringing up of their children. A loving father, he brought his experience of the war softly to his son. This was an affection bought of actual experience and represented a humanity that was sometimes lost in the epic version of Ireland's struggle with England, and England's struggle with the world.

With the rebellion over in Dublin and Pearse dead in his grave, Henry V took the stage in place of the Irish hero Cuchulain. The first Saturday afternoon in July 1916 saw the boys of the Royal Hibernian Military School recreate the battle of Agincourt in the grounds of a rainy Phoenix Park. The *Irish Times* was delighted with the production that followed:

The sylvan beauty of the spot, the quaint costumes of the performers, the blare of the trumpets, the stirring strains of the band, and, above all, the enthusiasm of the boys throughout the alarums of battle produced that correct atmosphere essential to such performances. Liberties had, of course, to be taken with the text to make the subject suitable for boys, but both its epic and dramatic sides were carefully preserved . . . The soldiers, with their coats of armour, halberds, and casques, 'that did affright the air of Agincourt', looked genuine, while the shields of the nobles, with their fanciful quarterings, were strictly correct. Nothing essential was omitted, and when the blast of war's brazen trumpets had ceased and the chivalric display ended, the troops marched off in procession, headed by surpliced choristers singing a *Te Deum*.[23]

Barely three months before, Phoenix Park had been drawn into bloody rebellion. Now it was home again to the promise of English victory on the fields of France. Shakespeare alone had the power to bring the union and empire back into alignment, and much was made of 1916's significance as

---

[22] Robert Gregory to Richard Gregory, 20 September 1916, Series 6, Box 48, William Robert and Margaret Gregory Papers, Robert W. Woodruff Library, Emory University.
[23] *Irish Times*, 3 July 1916, p. 7.

the tercentenary anniversary of the playwright's death. The military school's pageant closed with tea hosted by the school's governors. Their guest of honour was Major-General Sandbach, who was part of General Maxwell's command and relieved, no doubt, by the distraction after weeks of fighting, imprisonment and execution. Or, as one newspaper put it,

Easter Sunday, so memorable this year as the eve of the tragic events that still appal our minds, would in calmer circumstances have been remembered as the 300th anniversary of Shakespeare's death. Instead of the ghastly views of ruined Dublin, the pictures of the papers in Easter week would have shown us Sir Sidney Lee's pageants, and instead of revolution, blood, and ruin, the theme of topical writers would have been the songs of Arden, the grief of Othello, the wisdom of Prospero, the enigma of Hamlet.[24]

The rebellion had brought a cast of minor characters to the main stage. Caliban and his cohorts had upstaged the leading men. They were disposed of now, but their presence lingered. Hamlet was ghost-haunted and melancholic, as was the memory of Shakespeare in Ireland, the audience for a great imperial drama upset by the taking of the stage by unlicensed actors. The streets of Dublin city were the theatre of rebellion, and the built environment is a still-visible element of the cultural legacy of 1916. Many buildings are marked with the gunfire that cascaded through public spaces, and the escape of rebels from the General Post Office can be traced in the patched-over holes in the interiors of Moore Street. Serious thought was given after the rebellion to the future of the city's social architecture, in particular because of the destruction of so much property and the poverty-driven looting that attended it. In the summer of 1916, the Lord Mayor of Dublin even reported that a deputation had been sent to an exhibition on the future of city architecture in Paris.[25]

Generously, the offer was made to lend French plans for reconstruction to the Dublin Corporation for a month at a later date, and photograph albums of the exhibits were in public circulation. In this respect, the Easter Rising confirmed Ireland's cultural connections with Europe, connections that extend far beyond the political alliances of war and rebellion. The point can be extended further to a reconsideration of the many

[24] *Sunday Independent*, 28 May 1916, p. 2.
[25] 'The Lord Mayor also dealt with the visit of the deputation to the Exposition in Paris. They were, he said, received by one of the Ministers and the Chief of Police of the city, and what struck them very forcibly was the hopefulness of the French people and the way they were preparing to tackle the future ... An offer had been made to the deputation to lend the plans to the Dublin Corporation for a month or so, in order that they might see what was being done in places where reconstruction was a big problem, indeed.' *Irish Times*, 18 July 1916, p. 6.

Figure 9.1: The cricket bat that died for Ireland (photo: with permission of the National Museum of Ireland, reference HE:EW.5142).

miscellaneous objects held in the collections of the national museums, in particular the objects held by the National Museum of Ireland at Collins Barracks. These include a globe owned by Liam Mellows, a bicycle pump from the skirmish at Asbourne, the bolt cutters that broke the lock to free Ernie O'Malley from Kilmainham Gaol and, most suggestively of all, 'The cricket bat (that died for Ireland)' (see Figure 9.1).

The bat was rescued from the shop window of Elvery's, with a bullet embedded in it, and is a reminder of the many ways in which popular culture, including sport, became a metaphor for the social and political associations that led to rebellion. Relevant to this is the passage in James Joyce's *A Portrait of the Artist as a Young Man* in which Stephen Dedalus and his companions complain of school discipline. *Portrait* was first published in 1916 and is a novel built on the foundations of an Irish culture that the war and rebellion destroyed:

At last Fleming said:
– And we are all to be punished for what other fellows did?
– I won't come back, see if I do, Cecil Thunder said. Three days' silence in the refectory and sending us up for six and eight every minute.
– Yes, said Wells. And old Barrett has a new way of twisting the note so that you can't open it and fold it again to see how many ferulae you are to get. I won't come back too.
    Yes, said Cecil Thunder, and the prefect of studies was in second of grammar this morning.
– Let us get up a rebellion, Fleming said. Will we?
    All the fellows were silent. The air was very silent and you could hear the cricket bats but more slowly than before: pick, pock.[26]

Perhaps the most tragic symbol of the complexity of the Easter Rising's impact on Irish culture during a world war that touched the island deeply exists in the military cemetery at Grangegorman, not far from the memorial at Arbour Hill for the dead leaders of the Easter Rising. The cemetery is across the road from what used to be the Marlborough Barracks,

[26] Joyce, *Portrait*, p. 38.

which date to 1888 and are now called McKee Barracks after Richard McKee, a prominent Volunteer in the War of Independence who was arrested in 1920 and killed in custody. Many of the graves in Grangegorman date from the First World War, and many of these are from Irish regiments, in particular, those of the Royal Dublin Fusiliers. There are also other dead from British regiments who died in Irish hospitals, memorials for soldiers buried in the Cork military cemetery, which was closed due to vandalism, and many of the dead from the sinking of the RMS *Leinster* in 1918.

One of the most remarkable graves is that of Company Sergeant Major Martin Doyle, who was awarded the Victoria Cross for his bravery with the Royal Munster Fusiliers at Riencourt in 1918. Doyle rescued a group of soldiers and the crew of a tank under intense fire before holding his position for the remainder of the day. Afterwards, he fought in the War of Independence against the British and for the Free State in the Civil War before he died in Dublin in 1940.[27] Doyle's final resting place in Grangegorman is a reminder of the tangled emotional bonds that made Ireland after 1916, and the cemetery contains many Irish men who served in the British army before independence but were buried there decades after. The Easter Rising changed the public context of these affiliations, and Grangegorman contains some of the rebellion's dead. One headstone reads:

> In loving memory
> Of
> Margaret Naylor
> Née Rowe
> Shot Crossing Ringsend
> Drawbridge, Dublin
> 29th April 1916
> Died from Her Injuries on
> 1st May 1916
> Also Her Loving Husband
> John Naylor
> Pr. Royal Dublin Fusiliers, 14378
> Killed in Action on the Same Day
> 29th April 1916
> In Hulluch, France
> R.I.P.

Margaret was shot in disputed circumstances near Boland's Mills; John succumbed to gas and his name is listed on the memorial at

---

[27] See: www.royalmunsterfusiliers.org/b4doyle.htm.

Loos.[28] If these personal tragedies had little purchase on the later historical narrative of Ireland's struggle for independence, the psychiatric wounds of those who experienced violence, in the rebellion and afterwards, surfaces in literature with some frequency. Elizabeth Bowen's *The Last September* (1929) is remarkable for its sketch of post-traumatic stress in the character of Daventry, and John McGahern's *Amongst Women* (1990) tells the story from the other side, showing the lifelong decline of Michael Moran after his service in the Anglo-Irish war. The old world was made anew in 1916 as the things that held it together were in rearrangement. Trenches dug from St Stephen's Green to the Somme cut a line across Europe that divided human sensibilities before 1916 from the murderous mechanisms of the future.

If the shape of this new order was unclear, its pieces were in play through the private lives of artists and citizens. The largest questions of cultural representation can be answered in the study of the smallest things, the orchestration of objects in the home or in the imagination, significant of a cultural geography that exceeds the insularity of a debate about the past in Ireland that proceeds from ideas of nation. Yeats's work was made from newspaper clippings, Joyce's from the oddments of other cultures, all woven into the patchwork of his prose, which became more extravagant the longer that he wrote. This literary style had its analogue in visual culture, most obviously in the public posting of flyers for recruitment and rebellion, all of which suggests the workings of many forces, economic, social, cultural and geographical, are consigned to the concepts of nation and empire. The events of 1916 remind us of the multiple forces that operate on the cultural text, the variety of which is evidence further of the close proximity between aesthetics and history in a period of political transformation. There is much work still to do in the critical understanding of Irish culture in the period of late empire as intellectually diverse, formally sophisticated and globally inflected.

The cultural representation of 1916 is an image of melancholy however configured, the scales of loss during rebellion and war tipped dramatically towards the death of so many civilians, Volunteers and soldiers. Against this weighs the imaginative capacity of literature, the theatre, the little presses and the public protests to shape a public space for new forms of political and cultural association that could survive the deadly pressures of world conflict as felt sharply at the local scale. There is available now, and widely for the first time, a range of archival resources in the witness

---

[28] The sad case of Margaret and John Naylor is subject of Frank McNally's 'An Irishman's Diary', *Irish Times*, 3 July 2014, as well as in scattered references elsewhere.

statements, pension records and other archives of the rebellion period to draw a new map for this period that is as rich culturally as politically. In this extended landscape there is room, at last, for a cultural history that is widely representative of the diverse experiences and complicated attachments of those individuals who survived a war and rebellion to find a shattered Ireland on their return.

10 Myth, memory and material culture: remembering 1916 at the Ulster Museum

William Blair

Introduction

The centenary of the First World War in Northern Ireland not only involves consideration of our past but also our present and future as a 'post-conflict' society. Northern Ireland is emerging from a thirty-year period of conflict (commonly referred to as 'the Troubles') which erupted in 1969 and ended with paramilitary ceasefires and a political agreement in 1998. However, political tensions and community divisions remain and there is little agreement on how to deal with the difficult legacy of our past. Therefore, as we creatively engage with the impact of the defining period of revolutionary change surrounding the First World War, where can our collective imagination take us? Can a more complex interpretive approach to the First World War and the pivotal events of 1916 become a model for considering our difficult recent history? This chapter will examine the role of the Ulster Museum as it navigates the contemporary social and cultural environment in Northern Ireland and the politics of identity. It will consider the historic role of the Museum in collecting and interpreting the First World War and the Easter Rising, along with its more recent attempts to challenge prevailing myths in pursuit of complex and inclusive narratives.

The greatest challenge for the Museum looking forward lies in dealing with the difficult and divisive legacy of 'the Troubles'. The contemporary relevance of the events of 1916 to the Troubles is exemplified in two objects in the collection made by republican and loyalist prisoners. One is a plaque depicting 'James Connolly 1916 The Irish Rebel' and was made by republican prisoners in the Maidstone prison ship in the early 1970s while it was docked off Belfast (see Figure 10.1). The plaque was signed by the men who made it. The other object commemorates the Battle of the Somme and was painted by Gusty Spence, the former leader of the modern Ulster Volunteer Force (see Figure 10.2).[1] Each consciously

---

[1] Augustus (Gusty) Spence (1933–2011), from the Loyalist Shankill Road area of Belfast, worked in a number of manual jobs before joining the British Army in 1957. Poor health

Figure 10.1: Prison-made plaque commemorating the 1916 Easter Rising and James Connolly (photo: with permission of National Museums Northern Ireland).

seeks to establish a direct link between the modern Irish Republican Army (IRA) and Ulster Volunteer Force (UVF) and the loyalist and republican movements of the early twentieth century. Therein lies the core of the problem around the meaning and commemoration of 1916 – its compression and appropriation to justify political violence and reinforce loyalist and republican claims of legitimacy during Northern Ireland's recent conflict. Therefore, the question is whether recovering a more complex, inclusive narrative around the Decade of Centenaries can offer a model for considering history and identity more generally.

The material culture of the First World War

Fundamentally, war is the transformation of matter through the agency of destruction; the character of modern technological warfare is such that it

led him to leave the army in 1961. In the mid-1960s, the Ulster Volunteer Force (UVF) paramilitary group was formed and Spence soon became a member. In October 1966, he was sentenced to life imprisonment for the murder of a Catholic barman outside a public house on the Shankill Road. Spence has consistently denied committing the crime. Following the outbreak of the Troubles, and his transfer to the Maze Prison, Spence became UVF commander in the prison where he encouraged UVF prisoners to think along political lines. In 1977, he called for reconciliation in Northern Ireland and condemned the use of violence to achieve political aims and subsequently resigned as UVF leader in the Maze. He was released from prison in December 1984. Following his release, he remained active in community politics and was a leading member of the Progressive Unionist Party.

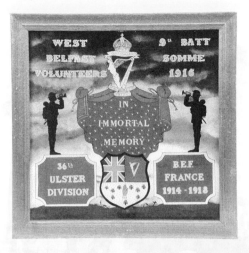

Figure 10.2: Prison-made painted mural commemorating the 36th (Ulster) Division (photo: with permission of National Museums Northern Ireland).

simultaneously creates and destroys more than any previous kind of conflict.[2]

The notion that the First World War simultaneously creates and destroys resonates for many reasons. Its destructive force is evocatively captured in the black-and-white photographs of the battlefield, and the creative work of artists, poets and musicians whose lives were impacted directly by the war. That said, its destructive legacy is reflected most poignantly in the multitude of war memorials, large and small, that bear testament to the thousands of lives lost.

The demands of this new kind of industrialised warfare generated vast armies and quantities of material, leaving behind a physical and cultural legacy which is found not only in museums but within our local communities and, in many instances, within our own homes as part of our family history. In that context, the archaeology of the First World War can be viewed as an anthropological endeavour that involves not only the excavation of battlefield sites and training camps but also reconnecting with personal items contained within our own homes.

The mythology surrounding the Battle of the Somme and the Easter Rising continues to underpin important aspects of contemporary cultural

---

[2] N. J. Saunders, 'Material Culture and Conflict: The Great War, 1914-2003' in N. J. Saunders (ed.), *Matters of Conflict: Material Culture, Memory and the First World War* (London and New York: Routledge, 2004), pp. 5–25 (p. 5).

Figure 10.3: Belfast wall mural commemorating the Battle of the
Somme (photo: with permission of National Museums Northern
Ireland).

and political identity in Northern Ireland today. The popular memory of
the Somme continues to be purposefully evoked through a variety of
cultural forms that range from museums and memorials to commemorative parades and murals.[3] A similar process can be seen in regard to the
1916 Rising and the mythology surrounding its 'martyrs'. Here again, the
forms of remembrance range from official state memorials to banners,
murals and paramilitary displays (Figures 10.3 and 10.4).[4]

Nicholas Saunders has observed how 'the passage of time and generations creates different interpretations of, and responses to, the materialities
of war as they journey through social, geographical and symbolic space'.[5]
The challenge facing museums therefore is to revitalise our interpretive

[3] D. Officer, '"For God and Ulster": The Ulsterman at the Somme' in I. McBride (ed.),
History and Memory in Modern Ireland (Cambridge: Cambridge University Press, 2001),
pp. 160–183 (p. 161).
[4] See, for example, David Fitzpatrick, 'Commemoration in the Irish Free State: A
Chronicle of Embarrassment' in McBride (ed.), *History and Memory in Modern Ireland*,
pp. 185–203.
[5] Saunders, 'Material Culture and Conflict', pp. 5–25 (p. 6).

Figure 10.4: Belfast wall mural commemorating the Easter Rising
(photo: with permission of National Museums Northern Ireland).

approach through new research; the creative application of new media; and
the promotion of greater understanding of the relevance of material culture
to contemporary society. The relative importance of objects held in
museum collections is not static – it changes in line with the evolving social,
cultural and political context. The shift from anonymity to newly ascribed

significance largely defines the biography of objects, and the reverse can occur as items recede in perceived importance. (The Ulster Museum's large collection of stamps is an example of institutional interest mirroring a popular interest in philately, which has now declined.) Therefore, the continued acquisition of the history collections in the Ulster Museum over time reflects changes in both museology and wider society.

The Ulster Museum was established in 1962 by the Government of Northern Ireland, when responsibility for the Belfast Municipal Museum and Art Gallery was formally transferred to a new Board of Trustees. The municipal museum had its early origins in an institution established in 1832 by the Belfast Natural History and Philosophical Society. The primary focus in the nineteenth century was on natural history and science, along with fine and decorative art. History was initially characterised by a large collection of Irish archaeology and a small ethnological collection. Anything other than archaeology was traditionally presented as 'historical antiquities' and later as 'local history'. Many of the major acquisitions relating to historical collections were made in the early twentieth century, for example, a collection of eighteenth-century volunteer material from F. J. Bigger, a prominent antiquarian, and a collection of 5,000 glass plate-negatives taken by the Belfast photographer R. J. Welch from the Belfast Naturalists Field Club. However, the Museum accession registers record a surprising range and quantity of contemporary nineteenth and twentieth-century acquisitions, with the material collected during and after the First World War, a case in point. Collectively, this helped to establish greater prominence for modern history within the Museum's curatorial structure. A Keeper of Local History and Industrial Archaeology was appointed in the mid-1970s, and a new gallery was opened in 1978 that presented the history of Ulster from 1500 to 1921 (see Figure 10.5).

This gallery marked the first attempt on the part of the Museum to present a meta-narrative of modern Irish history. It is perhaps significant that this happened at the time of 'direct rule' for Northern Ireland, as its parliament at Stormont had been prorogued in 1972 in response to the violent civil conflict that erupted in 1969 and reached a peak in 1972, generally regarded as the worst year of the Troubles due to the death toll. The independence offered by direct rule removed the Museum from the 'narrow ground' of local political control at a time when the politics of identity had intensified in a cauldron of communal violence. The small section on the First World War was closed in the mid-1980s when the mezzanine on which it was located was closed to facilitate display plans that never materialised. In effect, this meant that the First World War and the Battle of the Somme were lost from the permanent gallery until the museum re-opened in 2009 following major refurbishment. In contrast,

Figure 10.5: View of the Local History gallery in the Ulster Museum, circa 1980, showing the section dealing with the Ulster Crisis to Partition. The 1916 Proclamation can be seen in the centre case (photo: with permission of National Museums Northern Ireland).

the Easter Rising was included in a section that focused on events in Ireland, covering the Ulster Crisis through to Partition. It was represented by the Museum's original copy of the Proclamation of the Irish Republic, the centrepiece of any interpretation of the Rising since the late 1970s.

For the period prior to the Troubles, the evidence of the Museum's Annual and Quarterly Reports does not suggest overt political interference either during the time of Belfast Municipal Museum and Art Gallery or the Ulster Museum, although unionist influence may well have been reflected though organisational culture and values rather than dedicated displays.[6] For much of the twentieth century, the diversity of exhibitions

[6] The experience of John Hewitt is often seen as an indicator in this regard. John Hewitt (1907–1987) was the most significant Belfast poet to emerge before the 1960s generation of poets that included Seamus Heaney, Derek Mahon and Michael Longley. From November 1930 to 1957, Hewitt held positions in the Belfast Museum & Art Gallery. In 1957, having been passed over for the directorship of the Museum, supposedly because of his left-wing views, he resigned his position as Keeper of Art/Deputy Director to become Director of the new Herbert Art Gallery in Coventry. www.newulsterbiography.co.uk/in dex.php/home/viewPerson/674.

reflected the encyclopaedic nature of the Museum's collections, along with a growing desire to reflect international trends, particularly in fine art. The Museum, with its preponderance of Irish archaeology, natural history, fine and decorative art, and ethnology, offered little cultural capital for the new Unionist state. Ulster's tribal politics, 'red in tooth in claw', could find little in common with the liberal sensibilities of the curators quartered in the genteel, leafy suburbs of south Belfast. The politics of Unionism was more powerfully and directly expressed in the built heritage of Parliament Buildings at Stormont, with its imposing statues of Carson and Craig, and the civic regalia of Belfast City Hall. These buildings – the two principal political power centres in Northern Ireland – were shrines to official Unionist memory. In regard to the City Hall, the inclusion in recent years of objects and symbols with significance to nationalists and republicans has been a central thread in the changing civic face of Belfast.[7]

In 1966, the year that marked the fiftieth anniversary of the Battle of the Somme and the Easter Rising, the Museum's principal focus was its major new extension. The foundation ceremony was held in mid-November that year and was performed by Lord Erskine, Governor of Northern Ireland, in the presence of the Prime Minister of Northern Ireland, Terrence O'Neill, the Lord Mayor of Belfast and other invited dignitaries. The Unionist ethos surrounding the Museum is evidenced by an event of this kind, so redolent of the ancien régime (although hardly surprising in the context of the time). However, in relation to exhibitions, the public face of the Museum, the report for the financial year 1965–1966 describes among its highlights an interesting example of North/South cooperation in an exhibition on 'Great Irishmen and Women': 'This exhibition of nearly 250 portraits of well-known or famous figures of Ireland's past came from many sources; it included works lent by H. M. the Queen, the President of the Irish Republic, Ministries at Dublin and Stormont, National and other galleries, colleges, learned societies and business firms in the Irish Republic and the United Kingdom.'[8] It was visited by over 10,000 people from 24 June to 24 July 1965. It seems reasonable to speculate that this exhibition was a cultural reflection of the political rapprochement between Belfast and Dublin associated with the

[7] www.bbc.co.uk/news/uk-northern-ireland-13726956.
    http://sluggerotoole.com/2012/06/05/new-mayor-seeks-to-return-belfast-to-unionist-past/.
    www.belfasttelegraph.co.uk/news/northern-ireland/sinn-fein-mayor-mairtin-o-muil leoir-gives-orangemen-pride-of-place-in-belfast-city-hall-parlour-29607658.html.
[8] Ulster Museum, *Ulster Museum Annual Report, 1965–1966* (Belfast: Ulster Museum, 1966), p. 3.

Prime Minister of Northern Ireland, Terrence O'Neill, and the Taoiseach of the Republic of Ireland, Seán Lemass, part of O'Neill's wider and ultimately unsuccessful attempts at political reform.

The following summer, the report for the year 1966–1967 lists ten 'principal exhibitions', nine produced by the Art Department with one produced by the department of Local History and Industrial Technology entitled 'Commemoration of the Battle of the Somme 50th Anniversary'. The report states:

> The highly successful Somme Anniversary exhibition organised by Mr Noel Nesbitt, Assistant Keeper, opened on 1 July and continued until 3 September. The theme of the exhibition was particularly the part played by the 36th (Ulster) Division in the initial attack on 1 and 2 July 1916. Exhibits included field maps and views of the area; insignia of the regiments and battalions; certificates and medals relating to officers and men of the Division, notably two of the four Victoria crosses won on that memorable occasion; relics found on the battlefield or otherwise associated with the battle; and material, including a model, relating to the Thiepval memorial ... The exhibition attracted a great deal of attention, owing no doubt to close and affectionate links which many Ulster people still preserve with men of the Ulster Division.[9]

Unlike the previous year's summer exhibition, North/South cooperation clearly did not extend to a collaborative approach to marking the anniversaries of the Battle of the Somme and the Easter Rising.

This temporary exhibition in 1966 remains the only time that the First World War has received a dedicated, singular exhibition within the Museum prior to the current centenaries. This is surely notable given its importance as a foundational myth of Ulster loyalism, and supports the proposition that the custodians of official memory lay outside of the Museum. However, during the Troubles and in the period following the Good Friday Agreement, the Ulster Museum staged a number of historical exhibitions marking significant anniversaries – notably *Kings in Conflict* (1990) and *Up in Arms* (1998). These landmark exhibitions marked, respectively, the centenaries of the Battle of the Boyne in 1690 and the Irish rebellion in 1798. These in turn were followed by *Conflict: The Irish at War*, which opened in 2002 to positive critical reception, and continued until the Museum closed for major redevelopment in 2006. In *Conflict*, the First World War found limited expression within a section entitled War and Rebellion 1912–1922, in an exhibition that spanned 10,000 years of human history in Ireland.

---

[9] Ulster Museum, *Ulster Museum Annual Report 1966–1967* (Belfast: Ulster Museum, 1966), p. 17.

The Ulster Museum that re opened in 2009 maintained the traditional mix of art, natural sciences and history, presented in refreshed galleries and augmented by a new suite of learning zones, a large white atrium and an expanded shop and café, relocated to the entrance of the building. The First World War and Easter Rising were contained within a small section containing two display cases. The Ulster Museum went on to win the UK Art Fund Prize in 2010, with recognition firmly situated within the narrative of 'post-conflict' progress: 'The transformed Ulster Museum is an emblem of the confidence and cultural rejuvenation of Northern Ireland.'[10]

With the power-sharing Executive stabilised through the St Andrews Agreement (2006), the Museum sought to adjust to new forms of accountability and scrutiny within the evolved political dispensation. However, the new modern history gallery, 'Plantation to Power Sharing', became the subject of controversy when a critical intervention on the new history and science galleries by the then Minister of Culture, Nelson McCausland, became public. However, the issue of the cultural representation of Orange and Green traditions (specifically, their absence) was ultimately overshadowed by the Democratic Unionist Party Minister's view that creationist beliefs should be presented along-side evolution.[11] The controversy nonetheless highlighted the particular sensitivities surrounding cultural representation that flowed directly from the Good Friday Agreement, which had established new structures of formal support for the Irish language and Ulster Scots language. A by-product therefore of the peace process was to politicise aspects of cultural heritage by institutionalising a version of 'the two traditions'.[12] However, this must be set within a context where the overarching theme of the devolved government was 'a shared future', most recently expressed in the policy 'Together: Building a United Community' (TBUC), published in May 2013, which aims to reflect 'the Executive's commitment to improving community relations and continuing the journey towards a more united and shared society'.[13]

---

[10] www.nmni.com/Home/News/Ulster-Museum-wins-top-UK-award.

[11] www.theguardian.com/uk/2010/may/26/northern-ireland-ulster-museum-creationism.

[12] The sensitivities surrounding cultural representation are evident in this criticism of the Museum's interpretation of the seventeenth-century Dungiven costume in the former 'Plantation to Power Sharing' gallery: http://clydesburn.blogspot.co.uk/2009/11/ulster-museum-part-two-ulster-tartan.html.

    A more extensive and nuanced interpretation of this artefact was developed for the new Modern History gallery, in collaboration with the School of Geography, Archaeology and Paleoecology at Queen's University, Belfast.

[13] www.ofmdfmni.gov.uk/together-building-a-united-community.

The tensions between 'shared future' aspirations and the political reality on the ground are a defining characteristic of 'post-conflict' Northern Ireland. Continued tension around flags and parades provides ample evidence of the deep-seated legacy of conflict, particularly in communities that continue to experience widespread social and economic problems. That said, it is important to note that an important element of the 'TBUC' strategy, the 'Urban Villages' initiative, is targeted on areas in Belfast and Derry/Londonderry that fall within this socio-economic framework, where many of the legacy issues are most directly experienced.[14]

The Decade of Centenaries 1912–22

The First World War is many things – terrible, epic, dramatic, tragic and compelling – but in Northern Ireland today, it is, perhaps most importantly, a barometer on our ability as a 'post conflict' society to deal with a complex and divisive period of our history. That is certainly the intention of local policy-makers in Northern Ireland, as evidenced by the priority attached to the so-called 'Decade of Centenaries 1912–22'. The Northern Ireland Executive released a statement on Thursday 15 March 2012 stating that, it had been unanimously agreed that the Minister for Enterprise, Trade and Investment and the Minister for Culture, Arts and Leisure will jointly bring forward a programme for a Decade of Centenaries project relating to the period 1912–1922. These significant events would be organised under the principles of: educational focus, reflection, inclusivity, tolerance, respect, responsibility and interdependence.

In 2010, the Community Relations Council and the Heritage Lottery Fund in Northern Ireland published four principles to 'help us all to steer through the complexities and sensitivities of remembering this decade'. These were:
(1) start from the historical facts;
(2) recognise the implications and consequences of what happened;
(3) understand that different perceptions and interpretations exist; and
(4) show how events and activities can deepen understanding of the period.
All to be seen in the context of an 'inclusive and accepting society'.[15] Underlying this is the concept of 'ethical remembering', an approach that

---

[14] www.bbc.co.uk/news/uk-northern-ireland-30299078.
   www.bbc.co.uk/news/uk-northern-ireland-30927466.
[15] Community Relations Council, 'Marking Anniversaries', www.community-relations.or g.uk/programmes/marking-anniversaries/.

emphasised flexibility and pluralism in narratives and hospitality towards the 'other':

> Ethical remembering is critical remembering. The succession of events during 1912–1922 changed Ireland in a dramatic way. It was a decade of change, but it was also a decade of horrific violence ... Ethical remembering is not about going back to the past in condemnation, nor to indulge in a blame game. Neither has any contribution to make to a desired and shared future ... Uncritical remembering is a failure to learn from history. Ethical remembering acknowledges the destructiveness of violence and its destructive legacy, and builds a different, de-militarised political future. Ethical remembering also underlines the need for hospitality, a generous openness to each other, to dialogue, hear each other and be prepared to walk through contested histories together.[16]

The Ulster Museum therefore approached the issue of remembering the First World War and 1916 within a 'post-conflict' political environment where culture can be the focus of fractious assertions of representation and entitlement, but within a particular policy framework around the Decade of Centenaries that emphasises tolerance and a 'shared history' approach. The expectations of museums more generally have also changed with new critical museology emphasising their role in interpreting and mediating complex contested history.[17] Significant too are the new directions in academic history that increasingly draw on cross-disciplinary approaches blending social anthropology and explorations of diverse forms of historical memory.

Frédérick Rousseau refers to history museums 'as hybrids, to the extent that they borrow historians' knowledge guaranteeing them a certain degree of veracity and thus legitimacy and authority to dispense knowledge'.[18] He has contextualised the narratives presented by history museums in the following terms:

> This explains why museum spaces are approached as being cultural, social and political objects; cultural as they are, due to their supporting role for history and representations, for memories and things forgotten; socio-political too because of the numerous different actors concerned with these spaces ...; around each

[16] J. McMaster and M. Hetherington, *Ethical and Shared Remembering: Commemoration in a New Context: Remembering a Decade of Change and Violence in Ireland 1912-1922* (Derry and Londonderry: The Junction, 2012), p. 7.

[17] See, for example, the two-volume series 'Radical Perspectives': L. M. Knauer and D. J. Walkowitz (eds.), *Memory and the Impact of Political Transformation in Public Space* (Durham and London: Duke University Press, 2004); and L. M. Knauer and D. J. Walkowitz (eds.), *Contested Histories in Public Space: Memory, Race and Nation* (Durham and London: Duke University Press, 2009).

[18] F. Rousseau, 'From Slavery to Hiroshima: Mankind's Museohistory of Painful Pasts' in M. Houdiard (ed.), *The Presents of Painful Pasts: History Museums and Configurations of Remembrance, Essays in Museohistory* (Paris: Michel Houdiard, 2012), pp. 5–13 (p. 6).

museum space, issues take form, fall together or apart according to the will of the players involved and the periods concerned; strategies are deployed, power struggles come into play; considering the duration, the museum space remains a living cultural and socio-political object; of course exhibitions 'go out of fashion' and suffer mutations, sometimes radical at that; the original promoters grow old, disappear and leave their place to the new generations of directors and to new authorities; here then, these spaces are examined as political objects, both witness to and receivers of ethical and/or civil projects, past or present, and often the bearers of a valuable lesson for today, tracing a path and line of conduct for tomorrow.[19]

This encapsulates how diverse expectations and policy pressures increasingly combine to force the pace of change within museums – deconstructing and reconstructing interpretations of the past within a nexus that encompasses present and future hopes and concerns. The challenges and opportunities presented by the Decade of Centenaries has led to the Ulster Museum re-developing its modern history gallery within five years of the Museum re-opening in 2009, with support from the Northern Ireland Heritage Lottery Fund. For the Museum, the current emphasis on 'shared history' and 'shared future' presents a potential tension in the presentation of history – that is the risk of shaping narratives to fit these aspirational agendas, while avoiding the more disruptive and difficult histories of sectarian division and violent struggles for power. The antidote sought to this has involved collaboration with the School of History and Anthropology at Queen's University, Belfast – perhaps an example of the need identified by Rousseau for history museums to borrow authority and legitimacy from historians. On one level, this pragmatically addressed the research gaps within the Museum, but it also provided the necessary external challenge within the interpretative planning process to inform a more critical treatment of the subject matter.

Exploring the First World War: objects and memory

National Museums Northern Ireland's approach to the First World War and the Decade of Centenaries, more generally, has included the development of a new Modern History gallery at the Ulster Museum; a series of temporary exhibitions and the development of new resources and activities for formal and informal learning. Underpinning this is a process of opening up the collections through research and recovery, leading to increased digitisation and online publication. Creative partnerships are also integral to the programme, most significantly, the Museum's

[19] Ibid., p. 6.

collaboration with Queen's University Belfast (QUB) and Ulster University (UU) to establish the Living Legacies First World War Engagement Council, one of five in the United Kingdom supported by the Arts and Humanities Research Council. Re-examining our collections has been akin to a process of excavation, and new research is recovering the meaning and significance of diverse items in the collection, located within multiple contexts ranging from personal/family history to broad themes of technology, social, political and cultural change, and commemoration. One element of the programme has been the development of an exhibition based on First World War posters entitled 'Answer the Call'. The Museum holds a collection of around 150 posters which cover recruitment and a range of campaigns encouraging support for 'home front' activities, including drives for war loans, war savings and war bonds. In all, nearly six million posters of more than 140 different designs were commissioned, with five large companies, including the Belfast-based firm of David Allen and Sons, supplying over half the market. Two posters in the exhibition were designed by the artist James Prinsep Beadle (Figure 10.6). Beadle was an academic painter who, unlike many of his contemporaries, did not make a living as an illustrator. The son of Major-General James Pattle Beadle, the artist, spent his early years in India, immersed in British imperial military culture, the inspiration for most of his artistic output. The South African Boer War (1899–1902) provided him with material for numerous canvases, along with scenes from the Napoleonic wars. However, from 1914, the First World War became his subject and he painted scenes either from imagination or sometimes with the help of veterans. In 1917, he exhibited 'The attack of the 36th (Ulster) Division on 1 July 1916' at the Royal Academy (Figure 10.7). Soon after, it was purchased to raise money for UVF War Funds. A committee chaired by Sir James Stronge was appointed to oversee the reproduction and sale of a thousand copies of the painting. Beadle arranged the reproduction and signed the artist's proof, free of charge. The profits were allocated to the UVF Patriotic Fund, the UVF Hospital for Limbless Soldiers and the Ulster Prisoners of War Fund. The Committee also decided to present the painting to the Belfast Corporation on behalf of the UVF. Sir James Stronge made the presentation at a ceremony during the monthly meeting of the Belfast City Corporation on 1 July 1918. The painting was unveiled by the Lady Mayoress and accepted by the Lord Mayor (Alderman James Johnston) on behalf of the Corporation. It has hung in Belfast City Hall ever since, with the exception of a period in 2006 when it was loaned to the Museum of the Great War at Péronne in France.

Figure 10.6: Scottish War Savings Committee, Poster No.36, printed H. H. Ltd., Edinburgh, signed and dated by the artist James Prinsep Beadle, 1917 (photo: with permission of National Museums Northern Ireland).

Figure 10.7: 'The attack of the 36th (Ulster) Division' by J. P. Beadle (photo: with permission of National Museums Northern Ireland).

Reporting the presentation of the painting to the Belfast Corporation on the second anniversary of the battle, the *Belfast News-Letter* described the painting as 'showing the troops proceeding to the attack in the teeth of a merciless cannonade from the enemy's artillery' and as 'a wonderfully realistic piece of work' giving 'a vivid impression of the gallantry and endurance displayed by both officers and men in their determination to reach the objective assigned to them'. Credit for the supposed accuracy of the work has been traditionally given to a young English officer from Liverpool who appears in the painting. Lieutenant Francis Bodenham Thornely, who had been commissioned into the Ulster Division and fought with them on 1 July 1916, was a month short of his twentieth birthday on the opening day of the Somme offensive. He was wounded during the battle and while recuperating was assigned to assist Beadle. This painting represents the defining image that underpins the myth of the Somme, showing soldiers in heroic pose going 'over the top'. It has become the dominant memory of the war for Ulster loyalists, to the virtual exclusion of other campaigns or branches of the armed services. All have been relegated in popular memory in favour of this potent image of Ulster's sacrifice for King and Empire. Perfectly rendered through the artist's imagination, it served in turn to fire the public imagination.

In contrast, the material being accumulated by the Museum during and after the war speaks to the scope of the war and the diversity of experience.

The accession register for 1916 records eleven acquisitions relating to either the 'European War' or the 'Irish Rebellion'. These include a fragment of glass picked up in Lincoln's Inn Fields in London following a Zeppelin raid; a German-made sea mine picked up off the North Antrim coast by a trawler; and a handbill and tramway poster made in connection with a bottle-collecting scheme by Belfast Boy Scouts to raise funds to provide a recreation hut for the soldiers at the Front. In relation to the Easter Rising, the Museum purchased two sets of commemorative postcards depicting scenes of 'damage and military occupation' in Dublin. The shell of a bullet found embedded in the wall of Liberty Hall in Dublin by a soldier on duty there was also donated. More generally, specimens acquired by the Museum between 1914 and 1930 include: Turkish pay sheets captured after the battle of Nablus 1918; a selection of stamps issued from 'German occupied Belgium, 1918'; a gas mask 'used by Bolsheviks'; a propaganda leaflet in English headed 'To the Worker's Soldiers & Seamen of England, France ... Etc.' and signed 'The Petrograd Council of Worker's, Soldiers & Peasants Deputies', from 'North Russia 1919'; eight machine guns of various types (later destroyed by police in 1929); a German bicycle and tricycle; a German flamethrower; a French gas alarm from 'Nr St Quentin'; a 1903 'Pfennig' copper coin 'taken from a German prisoner at Ypres'; a sniper's dress 'used to camouflage German sniper, Flanders'; an enamelled badge of the 'Queen's University Veterans Corps'; and a walking stick engraved 'Pretoria 1900 and France Belgium 1915.18', carried by Major-General Sir Oliver Nugent, commander of the Ulster Division. The process of locating the material within museum storage is revealing. It supports the view that many of the items have never been previously displayed. The clues are often in the manner of how they are found – for example, in an original box with an old label still attached, apparently undisturbed. Items that have been used for exhibitions usually show evidence of being conserved and re-housed in new storage materials, and labelled with more modern identification numbers. Around 250 First World War items are recorded in the registers from 1914 to 1930 and a selection of the most significant objects have been incorporated into the new Modern History gallery (Figure 10.8).

The centrepiece of the new Modern History gallery is a section entitled 'Home Rule to Partition'. This is introduced by two 'gateway' objects – the (Ulster) Division's base depot flag and an original copy of the Easter Proclamation. The Division's base depot flag was donated to the Museum in 1933 by Andrew Lorimer of Donnybrook Street, Belfast, a former quartermaster with the 9th Battalion of the Royal Irish Rifles. It flew on ceremonial occasions at the base depot of the 36th (Ulster)

Figure 10.8: The Modern History gallery in the Ulster Museum (photo: with permission of National Museums Northern Ireland).

Division in France and Belgium during the war. The depot received men on arrival from England and kept them in training while they awaited posting to a unit at the front. The Ulster Museum's collection also features an original 'Proclamation of the Irish Republic', which was handed to a Belfast man, Mr R. McMillan, on business in Dublin at the outset of the Rising. The poster was donated to the Museum in 1937 as part of a larger collection gifted by the Robb family of Castlereagh. The juxtaposition of these two objects in the same case, under the heading 'War and Revolution', deliberately connects and contrasts these two iconic objects. Visitors are invited to consider them as part of a larger inter-connected narrative that explores the impact of the First World War. More generally, the 'Home Rule to Partition' section of the gallery includes a selection of objects aimed at conveying the complexity of the period before, during and after the war. The Ulster Museum's collection has been augmented by carefully targeted loans from other institutions, notably the National Museum of Ireland, Dublin, and the Science Museum in London. The latter involved the loan of a prosthetic arm that was invented and made in Belfast by Surgeon T. Kirk and engineer Alexander Pringle (Figure 10.9). It serves as a poignant reminder of the

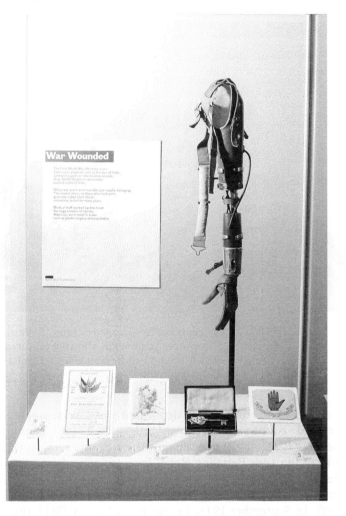

Figure 10.9: 'P & K Arm', made in Belfast, early 1920s (photo: with permission of National Museums Northern Ireland).

human cost of the war and the terrible injuries suffered by so many thousands of soldiers.

The subject of much recent research is a collection of photographs and diaries made by George Hackney of the Royal Irish Rifles. These had some limited public exposure in the past, primarily through illustrated talks, but nothing compared to the surge of interest that has been generated recently. George Hackney was born in Belfast in 1888. As a young

Figure 10.10: Photograph taken by George Hackney, Belfast, on 1 July 1916, the first day of the Somme campaign, showing captured German prisoners being led away from the Front (photo: with permission of National Museums Northern Ireland).

man, he worked at a Bible book depot and was a keen amateur photographer and countryside rambler. He joined the Young Citizen Volunteers (YCV) in 1912 and, along with many other Volunteers, joined the ranks of the 14th Battalion Royal Irish Rifles at the outbreak of the war. He was sent to France in 1915, where he saw action at the Battle of the Somme. He suffered from shell shock and DAH (disordered action of the heart). In September 1916, he was posted to Sheffield, then back to Ireland. He served out the rest of the war in Ireland and England. Hackney documented his own personal journey with both his pen and his camera, creating a record that provides a profound insight into the reality of war. This includes an incredibly rare photograph taken on the first day of the Battle of the Somme (Figure 10.10). In later life, George Hackney converted to the Baha'i faith, a Persian offshoot of Islam – the former frontline soldier had become a pacifist. George Hackney died in 1977, aged 89 years old. This collection has been the subject of a recent BBC documentary – 'The Man Who Shot the Great War' – which aired in

November 2014 to coincide with the opening of the Modern History gallery.[20]

Recent community engagement activities in the Museum have also recovered more complex memories that challenge the orthodoxies inherent in the mythology of the war. These highlight the value of personal accounts present within family histories. They are complex in the sense that they evoke the disillusionment, and even bitterness, of ex-servicemen at their treatment after the war, aligned to a sense of the ultimate futility of war itself. The inherent 'truth' of the lived experience of ex-servicemen as it echoes through family memory offers a stark contrast to the heroic narratives emphasised within forms of popular public remembrance such as Orange parades. The story told by Margaret Hamilton, in her nineties, about her father Alexander Hamilton is illustrative. Alex's parents died when he was young and he lived with his grandmother. During the First World War, he lied about his age and enlisted at the age of fourteen. She believed poverty was his main reason for joining the army. Initially, Alex was sent to France, before being sent to Salonika, part of modern-day Greece. He told her how he hated the lice at the Western Front, but how in Salonika ants ate the lice eggs, which meant they were never bothered by lice there. He survived the war without injury and returned home. Margaret spoke of her family hardships and her father's struggle to find employment in the years after the war. She also spoke of her father's disillusionment with the British Legion for failing to provide adequate help. As a result of this, he would never buy a poppy, even in later life. It was only with the outbreak of the Second World War that her father was able to find steady work at the Harland & Wolff shipyard. The Museum has also recorded the memory of William Hunter from East Belfast, who came to a Living Legacies community roadshow in October 2014. William had brought with him his father's war campaign medals. His father, also called William Hunter, enlisted in the First World War after a family row with his elder sister. He never knew the exact reason for the argument, but he enlisted in the Royal Irish Regiment. William survived the Battle of the Somme but the following year he was demobilised, having been disabled by exposure to mustard gas. He suffered stomach problems all his life as a result of this exposure. William spoke about how his father also struggled for employment after he returned home and his anger at the outbreak of the Second World War in 1939. Having lost so many friends during the First World War, he was profoundly upset at the thought that more young men would have to lose their lives in another round of conflict.

[20] www.bbc.co.uk/programme/b04pj7jq.

A possible glimpse of our 'post-conflict' future was offered through a recent project, *National Memory – Local Stories*, delivered by the Ulster Museum in partnership with the National Portrait Gallery (part of a wider UK-wide initiative).[21] This aimed to demonstrate how locally relevant objects from museum collections can engage young people and artists in responding to the First World War. Working with digital media and expressive writing, young people were encouraged to discover connections between local and national history through visual imagery, stories and experiences of the First World War. Project participants were introduced to a range of collection assets that reflected First World War experiences, both at home and abroad. These provided context for participants involved in researching their own family and community connections. Through structured discussion and activities, the young people developed new skills and were encouraged to deepen and extend their own understanding of the First World War as a precursor to producing a personal creative response to the themes and subject matter. Each participating museum worked with a practicing artist, who created his/her own response to objects from the museum's collection, and which in turn was integrated into the wider project. The workshop participants at National Museums Northern Ireland were eleven young people from the nationalist New Lodge area in North Belfast, aged between thirteen and sixteen. The local partner was New Lodge Arts, an organisation that provides innovative, educational arts-based activities across the community and political divide in North Belfast. The main collection resource used for the project was the diary and photographs of Private George Hackney. Workshops took place both at the Museum and within the participants' local area to enable interaction with curators and local historians, and the discovery of the 'hidden' First World War heritage within the local area. The work that was produced transcended traditional political and cultural stereotypes. Broader empathetic themes of human experience emerged around the concepts of 'community', 'communication', 'hope', 'fear', 'identity' and 'friendship' – and this was reflected in their creative response.

Conclusion

Walkowitz and Knauer highlight how political transformations serve as triggers or flashpoints for renewed struggles over the legacy of the past, and how political shifts often necessitate multiple and varied interpretations of history to engage with a changed present.[22] The history of the

---

[21] www.npg.org.uk/whatson/national-memory-local-stories/home.php.
[22] Knauer and Walkowitz, 'Introduction', pp. 1–18 (p. 4).

Museum's approach to '1916' is characterised by a shift from passive to active. For most of the twentieth century, the Ulster Museum remained largely detached from the politics of identity. Since the inception of the 'Peace Process' in the 1990s, however, interpretation and programming has accelerated in a conscious effort to contribute to the public policy agendas of 'shared history' and 'shared future'. The Ulster Museum's Decade of Centenaries programme rests on a deeper investigation of the collection to recover a breadth of material that reflects diverse human experience, both shared and contested. Locating this material culture within multiple contexts, local and international, and within a weave of personal stories, has enabled a more nuanced and critical interpretation to emerge. Critical insights have also been deepened through the active involvement of academic historians in the development of interpretive content. This in turn has enhanced opportunities for public engagement, stimulating new conversations with our visitors. The prison-made Connolly plaque and Somme painting lie outside the scope of the new Modern History gallery, but fall within the future development of the Troubles gallery. Given the present intersection of 'shared history' and 'shared future' agendas, the experience of the Decade of Centenaries indicates that these potent commemorative objects must be located within an inclusive and complex interpretation that challenges narrow ideological viewpoints and exclusive versions of history.

Part IV

Troubled memories

11 Reframing 1916 after 1969: Irish governments, a National Day of Reconciliation, and the politics of commemoration in the 1970s

Margaret O'Callaghan

I

This chapter looks at Irish government efforts to control the politics of commemorating the 1916 Easter Rising after 1969. It begins by looking at how the Irish government dealt with the attempt by militant republicans to claim ownership through commemoration not merely of Irish republicanism and the memory of the Rising, but the Irish Republic as it existed in state form.[1] The dramatic particularities of the Provisional Sinn Féin Commemorations of 1976 in Dublin and Belfast have been looked at elsewhere.[2] Here, the focus is on commemoration as a component of the northern policy of the 1973–1977 Fine Gael–Labour coalition government and, secondly, on Fianna Fáil's analysis of this policy in 1978 and its decision effectively to retain it. Material hitherto not in the public sphere illuminates the northern policy of the coalition government, and the important, if not pivotal, role of Conor Cruise O'Brien in formulating

---

[1] For broader studies of British and Irish government policy in these years, see Paul Bew, Peter Gibbon and Henry Patterson, *Northern Ireland 1921–1994; Political Forces and Social Classes* (London: Serif, 1994); Michael Cunningham, *British Government Policy in Northern Ireland,1969–2000* (Manchester: Manchester: Manchester University Press, 2001); Caroline Kennedy Pipe, *The Origins of the Present Troubles in Northern Ireland* (London: Routledge, 1997); Brendan O'Leary and John McGarry, *Understanding Northern Ireland The Politics of Antagonism* (London: Athlone Press, 1996), Ronan Fanning, 'Playing it Cool: The Response of the British and Irish Governments to the Crisis in Northern Ireland, 1968–9', *Irish Studies in International Affairs*, 12 (2001), 57–85; Martin J. McCleery, *Operation Demetrius and Its Aftermath: A New History of the Use of Internment Without Trial in Northern Ireland, 1971–75* (Manchester: Manchester University Press, 2015); Thomas Hennessey, *The Evolution of the Troubles, 1970–72* (Dublin: Irish Academic Press, 2007). For the best study to date of the politics of commemoration in this period, see Diarmaid Ferriter, *Ambiguous Republic: Ireland in the 1970s* (London: Profile Books, 2012), pp. 221–254.

[2] Margaret O'Callaghan, 'The Past Never Stands Still: Commemorating the Easter Rising in 1966 and 1976', in James Smyth (ed.), *Remembering the Troubles: Commemorating, Constructing and Contesting the Recent Past in Northern Ireland* (Notre Dame, IN: University of Notre Dame Press, forthcoming 2016).

commemorative policy, particularly through the new National Day of
Reconciliation, later designated a National Day of Commemoration,
which was designed to replace all other government commemorative
events. The chapter concludes that, although reframing 1916 within St
Patrick's Day in this manner was never a popular success, it nonetheless
acted as a bridge into a very low-key commemorative acknowledgement
of 1916, a policy that endured arguably until 2006. Though it is acknowledged that the commemorative policy of the Irish government was ideologically linked to wider security policies, they are not explored here.[3]
New British counter-insurgency policies in Ulster after 1975 facilitated
new popular mobilisation and new commemorative practices in 'the
North', as republicans insisted on utilising the pantheon of Irish commemorative dates. Though commemoration is always protean, fugitive
and resistant to state control, the lesson of the mid-1970s is that Irish
governments could, through the state apparatus, partially refashion public norms in relation to commemoration. This was not possible in 'the
North'. In this sense, northern nationalist commemorations of 1916 had
their own, often factional, dynamics; they drew on shared 'Irish republican' cultural capital in radically different ways. Northern nationalist
commemoration, whether in 1966 or 1976 or now, is not an offshoot of
southern actions or conceptualisations. So, although the commemoration
policies of the Irish government were partly articulated in the language of
not encouraging northern violence, their real success was in reshaping the
public culture of the 'little platoon' of the Irish state.

II

Force is one medium through which states assert their claims to legitimacy, but almost all states have their origins in violence. Yet, governments usually contrive to mask the dead bodies and the bloody acts that
brought their states into existence. Ceremony and ritual are the veiling
mechanisms. On Bastille Day, the French state celebrates the Revolution
by displays on the streets of Paris and other French cities and towns. The
state does not flaunt images of the baskets of guillotined heads that
formerly occupied the space now renamed as Place de la Concorde. On
4 July, the United States does not seek to tell the tales of the defeated
loyalists or reconstruct the battles that marked the American Revolution.
But divided societies, states where the past is contested by present battles
about legitimacy, find it hard to celebrate and commemorate their origins

[3] I am currently working on a wider study of aspects of the security policy of the 1973 to
1977 coalition government where these connections are examined in more detail.

through such necessary acts of concealment.[4] Successive governments of the Irish state found themselves in such a predicament as they sought to commemorate the origins of the Irish state in the rebellion of 1916 in Dublin that proclaimed an Irish republic, but found that the illegal or 'subversive' Irish Republican Army wished to claim that same point of origin to legitimise a violent campaign to end the partition of Ireland.

The stubborn actuality of partition, the continued existence and revival of various manifestations of the IRA[5] and, after 1969, protracted armed conflict in Northern Ireland successively complicated and politicised sovereign Ireland's desire to celebrate or commemorate the past in the same fashion as other western democracies. Commemoration became a site of contestation for the meanings of republicanism and its ownership, both within government and among historians in Ireland. Debate about dealing with the commemoration of the rebellion of 1916 at that time became a key moment in the attempted revision of official Irish state nationalism.[6] It led to a hardening of the distinction between state and nation, and can be seen within the same context as the repressive legislation that the Irish government introduced against the contagion of northern violence.

On 5 May 1976, a Sinn Féin Ulster Executive spokesman issued a statement stating that 'the use of the men of 1916 by the British against the Republican Movement had been the strangest twist in the propaganda war against the Irish people'. He was referring to the use in anti-IRA propaganda of the words of the former Irish Deputy Taoiseach (Prime Minister), Sean MacEntee, a Belfast man and early twentieth-century revolutionary.[7] The spokesman described himself as 'amongst those who experienced what he called "a living hell in a British prison"', and insisted:

---

[4] See 'Irish Modernity and "the Patriot Dead"' in Mary E. Daly and Margaret O'Callaghan (eds.), *1916 in 1966: Commemorating the Easter Rising* (Dublin: Royal Irish Academy, 2007), pp. 1–17, for the limits of state capacity to control commemoration. For an important theoretical analysis of the relationship between commemoration and conflict, see Rebecca Lynn Graff McRae, 'Forget Politics! Theorising the Political Dynamics of Commemoration and conflict' in Daly and O'Callaghan (eds.), *1916 in 1966*, pp. 219–238.

[5] See J. Bowyer Bell, *The Secret Army: The IRA* (London: Transaction Publishers, 1997); Patrick Bishop and Eamon O'Mallie, *The Provisional IRA* (London: Corgi Books, 1988); Brian Hanley, *The IRA: A Documentary History, 1916–2005* (Dublin: Gill and Macmillan, 2010); Richard English, *Armed Struggle: The History of the IRA* (London: Macmillan, 2003).

[6] See Margaret O'Callaghan, 'Propaganda Wars: Contexts for Understanding the Debate on the Meanings of the Irish War of Independence', *Journal of the Old Athlone Society*, 2 (2013), 367–372.

[7] See Deidre MacMahon, 'MacEntee, Sean (John) Francis (1889–1984)' in James McGuire and James Quinn (eds.), *Dictionary of Irish Biography*, 9 vols. (Dublin: Royal Irish Academy and Cambridge: Cambridge University Press, 2009), vol. 5, pp. 995–998.

As the British have been put k in seize, upon Sean MacEntee's remarks we, in direct reply to their question about the Republican movement   are they the heirs of the men of 1916 – state we are . . . In the words of Sean MacEntee and his fellow men of 1916 we proclaim 'the right of each people to defend itself against external aggression, external interference and external control'. It is this particular right that we claim for the Irish people.[8]

Who owned republican legacies, memory and cultural capital in Ireland? After the outbreak of renewed violence in Northern Ireland in 1969, and especially after the military campaign of the Provisional IRA began – and particularly when it switched from defending Northern nationalists against attacks by loyalists and special constables in order to go on a self-proclaimed national liberation offensive in 1971 – Dublin governments were confronted by a critical question. Why had the 1916 insurrection against British rule been morally and politically correct, whereas the current campaign of the Provisional IRA was not? Deciding what Northern policy to pursue destabilised the governing Fianna Fáil party, led by Taoiseach Jack Lynch. Should the government peacefully support Northern Ireland Catholics who had been subjected to pogroms in West Belfast, or actively supply them with the means of self-defence? Should it prepare for possible military intervention? Disagreement, rivalry and volatility among ministers culminated in 'the Arms Trial',[9] in which government ministers, most notably Charles Haughey, the former Minister for Finance and the son of an Ulster IRA man, were found not guilty of conspiring to import and disseminate arms after a state prosecution, which damaged the credibility of the Taoiseach and his Defence Minister James Gibbons. For most of the next decade, the historically dominant party was rent by a faction fight between Lynch's and Haughey's supporters, and it did not end when Haughey replaced Lynch as party leader in 1979 – as late as 1985, a new party, the Progressive Democrats, was created by Haughey's principal surviving opponent from the time of the Arms Trial, Desmond O' Malley.[10]

[8] *The Irish News*, 7 May 1976.
[9] Justin O'Brien, *The Arms Trial* (Dublin: Gill and Macmillan, 2000). See the self-published memoirs of the Irish army-officer James Kelly, *Orders for the Captain?* (Dublin: James Kelly, 1971); also James Kelly, *The Thimble Riggers: The Dublin Arms Trial of 1970* (Dublin: James Kelly, 1999).
[10] The electoral collapse of Fianna Fáil in 2010, following the banking and fiscal crisis that began in 2007, has led analysts to debate the causes of that traumatic defeat. The party was electorally successful after 1973, forming a majority government in 1977–1981; a minority government in 1982, and between 1987 and 1989; and it led coalition governments in 1989–1992, 1992–1994, 1997–2002, 2002–2007, and 2007–2011. Yet, it never won a majority government after Haughey became leader, and arguably the role of the northern crisis in weakening the party's electoral hegemony has been underplayed. See, among others, Richard Dunphy, *The Making of Fianna Fáil Power in Ireland: 1923–48*

The arms crisis and party divisions contributed to the defeat of Lynch's government in 1973, and its replacement by a new coalition government led by Liam Cosgrave of Fine Gael and Brendan Corish of the Irish Labour party. Within that government, Labour's Conor Cruise O'Brien, Minister for Posts and Telegraphs (whose remit included broadcasting), became the most dynamic critic of the Provisional IRA. Meanwhile, a future prime minister, Fine Gael's Garret FitzGerald, sought to became principal policy-maker on Northern Ireland as Minister for External Affairs.[11] It has been argued that relationships within that coalition were based on personal affinities rather than party political allegiances. It may, however, be that the new alliances within that coalition can be seen as an amalgam of the personal and the ideological, and that with the dramatic exception of the Sunningdale negotiations, FitzGerald was a more representative guide to northern policy after 1982 than in that 1970s' coalition where the balance of the cabinet on northern policy did not lie fully with him.

In *States of Ireland*, O'Brien provided what is now widely recognised as a compelling narrative that defended the Irish state, accepted partition and criticised the irredentist aims of the Provisional IRA and other Irish republicans.[12] It is far better written, and had greater sales, international recognition and a more enduring impact than Garret FitzGerald's mildly revisionist and pluralist text published at about the same time.[13] The *States of Ireland* argument is a classic articulation of what can now be seen as a counter-insurgency reading of how terror is sustained in sympathetic ideological waters. O'Brien's thesis was that wider Irish nationalist and, in particular, republican cultures shared a common cultural and ideological basis. It was not enough for non-radicalised Irish citizens or politicians to proclaim that they did not support the IRA, or simply to condemn the actions of militant Irish republicans in the IRA, while ignoring the fact

(Oxford: Clarendon Press, 1995); Donnacha O Beachain, *Destiny of the Soldiers – Fianna Fáil, Irish Republicanism and the IRA 1926–1973: The History of Ireland's Largest and Most Successful Political Party* (Dublin: Gill and Macmillan, 2014); Stephen Kelly, *Fianna Fáil, Partition and Northern Ireland 1926–71* (Dublin: Irish Academic Press, 2013); Catherine O'Donnell, *Fianna Fáil, Irish Republicanism and the Northern Ireland Troubles 1968–2005* (Dublin: Irish Academic Press, 2007).

[11] Conor Cruise O'Brien's memoirs provide his perspective on the relationships among the Labour members of that coalition. See Conor Cruise O'Brien, *Memoir: My Life and Themes* (London: Profile Books, 1998), pp. 341–359. See also Donald Harmon Akenson, *Conor: A Biography of Conor Cruise O'Brien* (Ithaca, NY: Cornell University Press, 1994). On the post-Sunningdale hiatus, see Michael Kerr, *The Destructors: The Story of Northern Ireland's Lost Peace Process* (Dublin: Irish Academic Press, 2011), pp. 289–326.

[12] Conor Cruise O'Brien, *States of Ireland* (London: Pantheon, 1972). See too W. J. McCormack, 'The Historians' Writer or Critic: Conor Cruise O'Brien and His Biographers', *Irish Historical Studies* 30 (1996), 111–119.

[13] Garret FitzGerald, *Towards a New Ireland* (London: Charles Knight, 1972).

that the whole public political culture of the Republic was irredentist. The wider Irish nationalist and, in particular, republican culture was a common space, one shared by the Irish state, wider Irish nationalism and the Provisional IRA. To condemn the actions of militant Irish republicans in the IRA, while ignoring the fact that the public political culture of the republic was irredentist, was not good enough. A cultural transformation in the public sphere, and in hearts and minds, was required.[14]

Central to the Republic's political culture was what O'Brien called the cult of 1916, the glorification of the rebellion that had been hailed as the foundational moment of the Irish republic and its charter document 'Poblacht na hEireann The Provisional Government of the Irish Republic to the people of Ireland', signed 'on behalf of the Provisional Government' by Thomas Clarke, Sean Mac Diarmada, P. H. Pearse, James Connolly, Thomas MacDonagh, Eamonn Ceannt and Joseph Plunkett. The proclamation contained certain fundamental statements about the nature of Irish historical experience. It proclaimed Ireland to be an ancient nation, regaining its freedom from a hostile power. It declared the right of the people of Ireland to the ownership of Ireland and to the unfettered control of Irish destinies, 'to be sovereign and indefeasible'. Further, it claimed 'the long usurpation of that right by a foreign people and government has not extinguished that right, nor can such a right ever be extinguished'. It declared that in every generation the Irish people had asserted their right to national freedom and sovereignty – 'six times during the last three hundred years they have asserted it in arms'[15] – and justified the Republic 'in the name of God and of the dead generations' through which Ireland was entitled to reclaim its 'old tradition of nationhood'.[16]

According to multiple governmental actions, the Proclamation was the founding charter of the state – officially named the Republic of Ireland in 1949.[17] As Mary Daly and Roisín Higgins have pointed out, on the fiftieth

---

[14] For a reading of the complexities of O'Brien's intellectual, ideological and emotional positions, see Richard Bourke, 'Languages of Conflict and the Northern Ireland Troubles', *The Journal of Modern History* 83 (2011), 544–578, and Diarmuid Whelan, *Conor Cruise O'Brien: Violent Notions* (Cork: Cork University Press, 2009). As Whelan and others point out, Conor Cruise O'Brien's volume *Herod: Reflections on Political Violence* (London: Faber and Faber, 1978) most directly questions the role of violence in politics. For a different and more critical reading of O'Brien, see John Regan, *Myth and the Irish State* (Dublin: Irish Academic Press, 2012), pp. 5, 86, 97, 151. See Frank Callanan, 'Conor Cruise Donat O'Brien' in James McGuire and James Quinn (eds.), *Dictionary of Irish Biography* (Cambridge: Cambridge University Press, 2015), http://dib.cambridge.org).

[15] O'Callaghan in Smyth (ed.), *Commemorating the Recent Past*.

[16] For an interesting reading of the 1916 proclamation, see Liam De Paor, *On the Easter Proclamation and Other Declarations* (Dublin: Four Courts Press, 1997).

[17] See Mary E. Daly on nomenclature of the Irish state: Mary E. Daly, 'The Irish Free State/ Éire/Republic of Ireland/Ireland: "A Country by Any Other Name"?', *The Journal of British Studies* 46 (2007), 72–90.

anniversary of the Easter Rising, the Fianna Fáil government, led by Seán Lemass, wished to domesticate and reshape for contemporary purposes that past. A new generation should seek to make a prosperous economic order to match its statehood, epitomised in the phrase 'every generation has its task'.[18] But the Provisional IRA and other 'subversive' republican formations also drew their political lineage from the Proclamation and sought to challenge British rule in Northern Ireland and the ownership of republican memory in the Irish state on that basis. They claimed to be the keepers of the republican flame, which, like a phoenix, could always rise from its own ashes, and like the 1916 insurrectionaries did not require a prior democratic mandate.[19]

The early years of the Troubles increasingly challenged the stability of the Irish state, existing improved relations with Great Britain, and raised again questions about the price of order and security within the achieved Irish state, as opposed to the bloodily-evoked potential future of the Irish nation.[20] The new coalition government of Liam Cosgrave in 1973 partly represented continuity with the Lynch and O' Malley axis within the Fianna Fáil government, but Conor Cruise O'Brien's presence in cabinet represented a dramatic opportunity to change the public culture of the south in relation to its former shaky republican consensus, at least rhetorically, on the north. As studies of the negotiation and fateful collapse of the Sunningdale agreement make clear,[21] Conor Cruise O'Brien did not win all battles in that coalition government, but he may in the short term have won a battle about commemoration. His strongest allies in that coalition appear to have been the more conservative Fine Gael members of the party: Cosgrave himself; Patrick Donegan, the Minister for Defence; and Patrick Cooney, the Minister for Justice. They took an unsentimental approach to what they viewed as the posturing of ' republican fellow travellers', sneaking regarders, armchair republicans, ballad-singing traditionalists and what they viewed as

---

[18] See essays by Mary Daly, Roisín Higgins, and Carole Holohan in Daly and O'Callaghan (eds.), *1916 in 1966* and Roisín Higgins, *Transforming 1916: Meaning, Memory and the Fiftieth Anniversary of the 1916 Rising* (Cork: Cork University Press, 2012).

[19] For northern claims on the proclamation, see Margaret O'Callaghan, 'From Casement Park to Toomebridge: The Commemoration of the Easter Rising in Northern Ireland in 1966' in Daly and O'Callaghan (eds.) *1916 in 1966*, pp. 86–147.

[20] For a mildly Anglo-centric perspective which, however, draws on the archives in three locations, see Anthony Craig, *Crisis of Confidence: Anglo-Irish Relations in the Early Troubles* (Dublin: Irish Academic Press, 2010), pp. 174–195. On the post-Sunningdale era, see Kerr, *The Destructors*, p. 326. For the position of John Hume and the SDLP, the former a particular *bête noir* of O'Brien, see P. J. McLoughlin, *John Hume and the Revising of Irish Nationalism* (Manchester: Manchester University Press, 2010).

[21] Kerr, *The Destructors*, p. 138, and Garret FitzGerald, *All in a Life: Garret FitzGerald, an Autobiography* (London: Macmillan, 1971).

ɯawkɪsh, one nation fuɪɪuɘlʁɪs O'Thɪ iɪ ɪɪ ꜱɒᴜght to reframe the terms of debate, with considerable success. As he saw it, the issue was whether or not the whole culture required changing if it was not to succumb to the lure of the 'sneaking regarders', that is, those in the South not prepared to fight with or actively support the Provisional IRA, but who were prepared tacitly to wish them well in what they saw as a final stage in the battle to win a thirty-two county Irish republic. For O'Brien, this broader Irish nationalist culture and its symbols, pieties, commemorations, narratives and fantasies provided the cultural capital and ideological sea in which the northern Provisional IRA campaign could swim. It was this culture that required transformation to prevent atrocities being perpetrated in the name of the Irish people, and to safeguard the independence and stability of the independent Irish state to which the IRA presented a fundamental threat, since it sought to present itself as the authentic government of the whole island.

O'Brien never fully succeeded in this push for change, but the coalition government arguably accomplished multiple policy initiatives that significantly squeezed the ideological ground on which the IRA stood in the Republic. This policy did not grow *ex nihilo* from O'Brien's undoubted talents in communication and public relations.[22] Arguably, his approach and that of the government recapitulated and refreshed the policy and aims of the Cumann na nGaedheal government during the Civil War, and the Fianna Fáil government before and during the Second World War, when the IRA threatened the government policy of neutrality. Both governments had seen their central object to be the maintenance of independent Ireland.[23] They had either accepted partition reluctantly, as the elder Cosgrave's government did in 1925 after the failure of the Boundary Commission, or they had looked to end partition through diplomacy with the British government rather than supporting violent insurrection.[24] The threat for the Free State government in the 1920s had been the republicans under de Valera, who would not accept the terms of the Treaty of 1921 that circumscribed Ireland's sovereignty; the threat to

---

[22] An Irish diplomat, he had previously worked with the then Minister of External Affairs Seán MacBride on the late 1940s/early 1950s Irish government campaign against partition, supporting the dissemination of Frank Gallagher's important book *The Indivisible Isle: The Story of the Partition of Ireland* (London: Gollancz, 1957).

[23] The phrase is Ronan Fanning's. See Fanning, *Independent Ireland* (Dublin: Helicon, 1983).

[24] See, among others, Kevin Matthews, *Fatal Influence: The Impact of Ireland on British Politics, 1920–25* (Dublin: University College Dublin Press, 2004); Deirdre McMahon, *Republicans and Imperialists: Anglo-Irish Relations in the 1930s* (New Haven, CT: Yale University Press, 1984); John Bowman, *De Valera and the Ulster Question, 1917–73* (Oxford: Oxford University Press, 1982).

Fianna Fáil in government during the Second World War came from former republican comrades, then banned and designated subversives, who sought to undermine neutrality as part of a wider aim, which was to end partition.[25] The primary aim of the 1970s' cross-party governmental cohort led by Cosgrave was the preservation of and maintenance of the 'little platoon' of the independent Irish state. The new threat came from northern violence and the Provisional IRA.

III

On 21 June 1972, Michael O'Leary TD, Irish Labour and future Deputy Taoiseach, questioned the then Taoiseach Jack Lynch on whether all national events of the period 1916–1922 could be confined to 'one annual event'. It was suggested in response that an 'announcement was imminent', but no such announcement took place and instead a partial answer was given. It was stated that Easter Sunday was the designated 'one day', and that in the 'very special circumstances' of 1972, 'the Defence forces were present at two ceremonies'. An elaborate commemoration of 1916 had taken place at Arbour Hill in 1972, and the Irish Army was also present at Béal na Bláth, the site of the death of Michael Collins, the pro-Treaty revolutionary leader, on 30 May 1972, for what was described, rather oddly, as the 'fiftieth anniversary of the start of the civil war'.[26]

The public political debate on new ways of commemorating – or rather restraining commemoration of – the rebellion or Rising of 1916 began with Michael O'Leary's parliamentary question when Fianna Fáil was still in power. In February 1973, in a 'Memo for Government from the Minister for Defence', the new Coalition Government Minister Paddy Donegan indicated his support for a National Day of Reconciliation. Conor Cruise O'Brien responded in April 1973 by proposing St Patrick's Day as the Day of Reconciliation, and the Department of Defence seems to have endorsed this suggestion on 9 April 1973. On 19 June, Cruise O'Brien wrote to Cosgrave with a view to getting the matter before cabinet, 'so that the government should have an early opportunity of considering the desirability of substituting a single day of national reconciliation for the various ceremonies that are

---

[25] Caoimhe Nic Dháibhéid, 'Throttling the IRA: Fianna Fáil and the Subversive Threat, 1939-45' in Caoimhe Nic Dháibhéid and Colin Reid (eds.), *From Parnell to Paisley: Constitutional and Revolutionary Politics in Modern Ireland* (Dublin: Irish Academic Press, 2010), pp. 116–138.

[26] Report on file on commemoration of events in 1972, Department of the Taoiseach files (D/T) 2010/53/255, National Archives of Ireland, Dublin (NAI).

now held. I have asked Paddy Donegan to arrange to have the matter submitted to the government as soon as possible.'[27] The Donegan agreement with O'Brien had clearly preceded the consultation with Cosgrave. Drawing on the files to summarise the position for a Fianna Fáil government some years later, a senior civil servant wrote that it was 'recommended that there would be only one day on which the state would participate in public commemorations, and the ceremonies were to include church services and two minutes silence for those who died for Ireland and for the victims of civil strife in Ireland as well as prayers for peace and reconciliation between Irish people of different traditions'.[28] The cabinet approved these proposals on 10 July 1973. It became clear that 'the Minister for Defence (i.e. Donegan) was considering a parade of unarmed soldiers' and that the Minister for Posts and Telegraphs (O'Brien) favoured a purely religious ceremony.[29]

Cosgrave was scheduled to make a statement about the new National Day of Reconciliation on the adjournment debate of July 1973 but, in the absence of such a debate, the 'matter was publicised by a press release on 15 August 1973'. In August 1973, Donegan wrote to O'Brien, 'I am wondering what department should take on the task of looking after the matter from now on. It doesn't seem quite appropriate that the Department of Defence should be actively concerned except as regards military participation in the ceremonies.'[30] He included a list of suggestions for the conduct of the proposed St Patrick's Day event: the main event should take place at the Garden of Remembrance with some military ceremony, and a reception at Dublin Castle. He also advised the 'discontinuation of state participation in Wolfe Tone, Easter, Michael Collins and other commemorations, liaison with the St Patrick's Day Industrial Parade'. But in his reply on 7 November 1973, Cruise O'Brien argued against state participation at either the Garden of Remembrance or at Arbour Hill.[31]

In January 1974, Dr O'Brien wrote to Liam Cosgrave, suggesting that the Garden of Remembrance was seen as 'exclusively Republican and Gaelic' and would exclude many who commemorated Irishmen who fell serving Great Britain in the First World War. He also viewed a separate event at Arbour Hill as a departure from the idea of one common day. The

[27] Conor Cruise O' Brien to An Taoiseach, Liam Cosgrave, D/T 2010/53/255, NAI.
[28] Memo, D/T 2010/53/255, NAI.
[29] In a related file, Diarmaid Ferriter has found evidence that O'Brien's objection to the unarmed soldiers was that their appearance could appear to indicate that the IRA was the army of the Republic. Ferriter, *Ambiguous Republic*, p. 233.
[30] Paddy Donegan to Conor Cruise O'Brien, 21 August 1973, D/T 2010/53/255, NAI.
[31] Minister for Posts and Telegraphs to Minister of Defence, 7 November 1973, D/T 2010/53/255, NAI.

Garden of Remembrance at the top of O'Connell Street in Dublin was a memorial garden specifically dedicated to those who had died in the fight for Irish freedom. Arbour Hill was a military barracks where the executions of the leaders of 1916 by British crown forces acting under martial law were annually commemorated by the Irish army. Almost all state commemorations of 1916, including the large-scale jubilee commemorations of 1966, had taken place under the direction of the Minister of Defence, because the Irish Army, Oglaigh na hEireann, was seen as central to them. Nicholas Simms, son of the Church of Ireland Bishop of Armagh and O'Brien's son-in-law through marriage to his daughter Fidelma, was appointed as his assistant in this and other matters. The senior civil servant, writing for Fianna Fáil some years later, mordantly put it that Nicholas Simms 'had been in contact with the Church of Ireland Archbishop of Dublin in advance of any other approaches to ecclesiastical authorities that might be made'.[32] He also pointed out that Dr Buchanan, the Church of Ireland Bishop of Dublin, raised with Nicholas Simms the question of the British Legion Commemoration Sunday in November and asked whether Cruise O'Brien would be prepared to meet with British Legion leaders before finalising any plans. Buchanan added: 'I think it would be right to attempt to solve this problem. Otherwise we – the bishops – might only be able to give a partial consent.'[33] Cruise O'Brien replied that this would not be a problem. He was primarily concerned with 'state participation'.

In February 1974, O'Brien proposed establishing a committee for the coordination of the new arrangements under the chairmanship of an officer of the Department of the Taoiseach and with representatives from the Government Information Service, possibly including the Head of the Government Information Service Muiris MacConghail,[34] and the Department of Defence, as well as Nicholas Simms. He also suggested that President Childers might give an address in St Patrick's Cathedral for the first commemorative occasion. The committee was set up under the chairmanship of Mr Dowd, Assistant Secretary of the Department of the Taoiseach; it met on 13 February 1974, with Mr Crowe, a principal officer from the Department of Defence, and Nicholas Simms present.

On 4 March, Liam Cosgrave wrote to Cardinal Conway, Roman Catholic Primate of All Ireland, Archbishop Simms, the Moderator of the Presbyterian Church, the President of the Methodist Church, the

---

[32] Memo by senior civil servant, 16 February 1978, D/T 2010/53/255, NAI.

[33] Most Rev Dr Buchanan, quoted by Nicholas Simms, D/T 2010/53/255, NAI.

[34] For the appointment of the talented Irish television director and intellectual Muiris MacConghail as director of the Government Information Bureau on the suggestion of Joan FitzGerald, see O'Brien, *Memoir*, p. 347.

Chief Rabbi, and the Head of the Society of Friends, referring to the decision to inaugurate a Day of National Commemoration and offering the suggestion that services on that day might include a special prayer, followed by a silence for all who lost their lives as a result of war or civil strife. The Taoiseach also notified them that President Childers would broadcast a message on radio and television on St Patrick's Day. The file simply states that the 'response from the church leaders was favourable'.[35]

The Department drafted the speech for President Childers and he delivered it on St Patrick's Day 1974. It included the statement: 'This year – and for the future – you are being asked to make St Patrick's Day a Day of National Commemoration – the day on which we remember all who died for Ireland and all victims of civil strife in Ireland.' The civil servant reviewing the initiative for the new Fianna Fáil government in 1978 wrote: 'It is probably a fair assessment to say that the decision to give a new dimension to St Patrick's Day had no particular impact in 1974 and has sunk without trace thereafter. No concerted effort seems to have been made in the years after 1974 to win public acceptance for the idea. It was, probably wisely, accepted that one cannot orchestrate a public response in such an artificial way.'[36] He then attempted to review government policy about commemoration over time, and stated that the 'other main reasons for failure are grounded in the notion that we have a proliferation of partisan commemorations throughout the year'. According to this brief, however, the latter was a mistaken view. He proceeded to litanise the 'rationale' for each singular event that Cruise O'Brien had sought so assiduously to amalgamate into one: 'St Patrick's Day is a national day, Easter has a particular association with 1916, Arbour Hill has an association with post-Rising executions, 11 July is Army Day and the anniversary of the 1921 Truce.' He went on to remember the significance of 12 July for Orangemen and then moved on to commemorations associated with places – Bodenstown for Wolfe Tone and Béal na Bláth for Michael Collins, who met his death there. He also referred to the national commemorations in November for 'the anniversary of the 1918 armistice'. Clearly, the dates all had commemorative significance, but the purpose of the National Day of Reconciliation had been to stop the drip feed of annual commemorations of the militant strain in Irish nationalism. The cult of commemorating republican violence had been that which the amalgamations had sought to close down.

The Fianna Fáil government's exploration of commemoration, following its return to office in 1977, was an attempt to placate certain of their

[35] D/T 2010/53/255, NAI.   [36] D/T 2010/53/255, NAI.

backbenchers who were apparently upset and restive at what they presented as the attempted marginalisation of the republican tradition
through several years of thin commemorative practices.[37] This unrest in
Fianna Fáil, and the pervasiveness of its earlier divisions, was now trans-
lated into a proposal by the Minister for Defence to return to major state
commemorations of 1916. The civil servant gingerly advised that in terms
of public opinion, 'the development of Easter Sunday or Monday' should
be presented 'not as a substitution but as a revival in face of failure to give
new dimensions to St Patrick's Day'.[38] In his memo, he emphasised that
the 'general interpretation of the former government's actions was a
desire to play down the Rising in an attempt to placate northern opinion'.
Therefore, he advised that the reinstatement of a large-scale state commemoration of 1916 should be portrayed as 'the restoration of a factual
historical perspective and not as any truculent defence of the physical
force element in past or present times'. The overall memo, entitled
'Easter Sunday as a Day of National Commemoration', is annotated by
Dermot Nally: 'Taoiseach. I think that it would be a pity if this became a
matter of controversy.'[39]

In a memo dated 16 February, the civil servant Frank Murray wrote: 'It
can be argued that if the state does not commemorate the anniversary of
1916 at Easter, by default it allows the initiative in this matter to fall into
the hands of subversive organisations, particularly Provisional Sinn Féin
and the Provisional IRA.' He also, however, minuted in a contradictory
vein: 'The existence of the Unionist community in Northern Ireland is a
constraint which has to receive consideration in determining policy on
matters such as this.' In defence of the latter view, Murray cited a recent
conversation he had with Sean O hUigin of the Department of Foreign
Affairs. O hUigin had said that in his recent meeting with William Craig,
the former Ulster Unionist Minister for Home Affairs and leader of the
Ulster Vanguard pressure group, the latter had expressed the view that the
Irish government did not appear to be interested in reconciliation in
Northern Ireland. There was also reference to the Taoiseach's call for
British withdrawal from Northern Ireland.[40] In light of these

[37] Programme/Clar, Ógra Fianna Fáil, Ard Fheis/Youth Branch, Fianna Fáil Annual
Conference, 1977.
[38] Memo by senior civil servant, February 1978, D/T 2010/53/255, NAI. This extensive
file, mostly worked through in 1978, appears be an amalgam of materials culled from
other earlier files to facilitate a review of commemoration policy under the previous
government and the preparation of advice to the new Taoiseach.
[39] Dermot Nally was assistant secretary at the Department of the Taoiseach from 1972 and
was perhaps the most important Irish civil servant of the last three decades of the
twentieth century.
[40] Briefing paper by Murray, February 1978, D/T 2010/53/255, NAI.

circumstances, the civil servants advised suitable military ceremonies at
the GPO and the Garden of Remembrance without a military parade or a
march past. They further advised that there be 'no announcement as to
next year'. The summary on file states that commemorations at Easter
were held up to and since 1971, consisting of a military parade and a
march past. For 1972 and 1973, it was alleged that 'due to heavy demands
on the Defence Forces, mainly because of security duties', the parade and
march past were not held. It claims that 'a suitable military assembly at
the GPO and the Garden of Remembrance were held on Easter Sunday in
these years'.[41]

IV

The year 1976 marked the end of the IRA ceasefire, the removal of special
category status, steady advances for emerging Irish government policy
against the IRA and a significant further shift in the Irish government's
attitude towards the commemoration of the Easter Rising. This went in
tandem with a new initiative by the Irish Department of Foreign Affairs to
push the Washington Irish Embassy to further marginalise Noraid and to
set up the Four Horsemen political initiative.[42] The Irish government's
policy directions were bound up in their post-Sunningdale interpretation
of the Northern Ireland problem, and their position in relation to the
commemoration of 1916 remained central. In January and February of
1976, the Irish government's case against the British government was
again brought to the European Court of Human Rights at Strasbourg.[43]
1976 was the second worst year of the Troubles, if intensity is measured
by the number of people killed. The Provisional IRA, which had arranged
a spectacle for the funeral of Michael Gaughan (who had died on hunger
strike in Parkhurst prison in 1974), sought to model hunger-striker Frank
Stagg's funeral on 25 February 1976 in the same manner, again challenging the Irish government. The previous year had appeared to indicate to
certain key southern figures in the leadership cadre of the Provisional IRA

[41] Review of commemorations, D/T 2010/53/255, NAI. Key civil servants at this time were
Dermot Nally, Wally Kirwan, Murray and Richard Stokes at the Department of the
Taoiseach. In the Department of Foreign Affairs, their counterparts were Sean Donlon
and Noel Dorr and later, at that level, Michael Lillis. Several of these spoke at the
Sunningdale and Anglo–Irish Agreement witness statement seminars held in University
College Dublin. See too, the Centre for Contemporary British History, Institute of
Historical Research, London witness seminar on British Policy in Northern Ireland, 11
February 1993.
[42] McLoughlin, *Hume and Irish Nationalism*.
[43] Ireland against the United Kingdom of Great Britain and Northern Ireland (Annexes 1
and 2 to the report of the European Commission of Human Rights, adopted 25 January
1976), Strasbourg, p. 288.

that the talks between the British government and the IRA might lead to some form of British withdrawal.[44] Viewed retrospectively, these were unrealistic expectations, though recently available material from the Duddy archive indicates how far the 'Southern' leadership of the Provisional movement was prepared to go in order to secure a settlement. Retrospectively, their hopes look naive. After Sunningdale's failure in 1974, a variety of British government options had been considered, including withdrawal.[45] The failure of the Convention, reasonably clear at the beginning of 1976, represented the closure of any possibility of a renewed devolved administration in the medium term. In January 1975, the Gardiner Report, which had been set up to recommend powers to deal with terrorism in Northern Ireland, had opposed the continuation of special category status in the prisons. By March 1976, a new prison regime was in place in Northern Ireland, ending special category status. The ending of internment in 1975 paved the way for Diplock courts and convictions without jury trial.

As *The Daily Telegraph* obituary of Sir David House, appointed as British Army General Officer Commanding in Northern Ireland in January 1975, states:

The Secretary of State, Merlyn Rees, sought with Lt General Sir David House and other security chiefs to marginalise the terrorists through a policy of 'Ulsterisation' and 'criminalisation'. They advocated the disengagement as far as possible of the Army's non-Ulster regiments and replacing them with the Royal Ulster Constabulary and the UDR ... If the number of army casualties could be reduced, Rees felt, the pressure in Britain for withdrawal from the province would diminish. The strategy was also designed to change perceptions of the conflict from a colonial war to a campaign against criminal gangs.[46]

Before Rees and House could make much progress, the deteriorating situation led House to call up Ulster Defence Regiment reservists over Christmas 1975 and place extra troops, the SAS, into the 'bandit country' of South Armagh. Weeks later, the IRA ended its ceasefire.

On 25 April 1976, the Provisional Sinn Féin staged an Easter commemoration march in Dublin on the sixtieth anniversary of the Easter

---

[44] It also clearly marked the effective end of the so-called old-style Southern Command. But the notion that more concessions and naiveté were displayed by that older Southern leadership among the IRA has been shown to be inaccurate: see Robert W. White, *Ruairi O Bradaigh: The Life and Politics of a Irish Revolutionary* (Bloomington: Indiana University Press, 2006).

[45] For the threat of British withdrawal, see Garret FitzGerald, 'The 1974–75 Threat of a British Withdrawal from Northern Ireland', *Irish Studies in International Affairs* 12 (2001), 57–85.

[46] 'Obituaries, "Lieutenant-General Sir David House"', *The Daily Telegraph*, 9 August 2012. House was GOC Northern Ireland from 1975 to 1977.

Rising.[17] This was a clear challenge to the authority of the Irish government. Banning the march testified to the intention of Liam Cosgrave's coalition government to cease any ambiguities in relation to the IRA. Addressing the crowd from a 'tri-colour covered lorry platform', Mr Dáithi Ó Conaill said that 'those who set out to defile Easter Week merit nothing but contempt'. He said Britain had spurned two opportunities to establish a lasting peace and had sent 'professional assassins into South Armagh'.[48] Liam Cosgrave pursued a more aggressive policy towards the IRA that built on the banning of their 1916 commemoration in that year. The murder of the British Ambassador Christopher Ewart-Biggs[49] and Judith Cook, killed by a land mine as they left the residence at Glencairn in Sandyford on 21 July 1976, added to the challenge of the Easter performance on the streets of Dublin, intensified Irish government determination to disassociate the Irish state from militant republicans.[50]

In early May 1976, the *Irish News*, the key mainstream nationalist newspaper in Belfast, reported the occupation of their front offices in Donegall Street by the Provisional IRA on the previous day.[51] The IRA's own newspapers circulated primarily among the converted, so the *Irish News* was an important public platform for it in a variety of ways. Fifty protestors denounced what they called the lack of coverage of the 'plight of our imprisoned people' and condemned the acceptance by the paper of 'advertising from the RUC and the Northern Ireland office, in particular advertising which promotes employment for the sectarian RUC and for prison warders'.[52] If the *Irish News* was failing on propaganda grounds to satisfy the IRA in this regard, there was another area in which it was more compliant. The most interesting use of any Irish newspaper at Easter 1976 was the newly-established commemorative genre in the deaths and

---

[47] On the 1976 commemorations, see O'Callaghan, 'The Past Never Stands Still'. On the ceasefires and negotiations, see Niall O' Dochartaigh, 'Everyone Trying: The IRA Ceasefire of 1975; a Missed Opportunity for Peace?', *Field Day Review* 7 (2011), 50–77.

[48] See Brendan O'Leary, 'The Labour Government and Northern Ireland, 1974-79' in John McGarry and Brendan O'Leary (eds.) *The Northern Ireland Conflict: Consociational Engagements* (Oxford: Oxford University Press, 2004), pp. 194–216.

[49] For Irish government reaction to the killings, see 'British Ambassador to Ireland – assassination, 2/7/76–18/10/78', D/T 2006/133/708, NAI.

[50] Emergency Powers Act 1976 file, D/T 2006/133/580, NAI. This extensive file, a vital source for policy in this year, shows how the Easter commemorations, the issues of cross-border incursions, the murder of the British ambassador, and the perceived requirement for greater security, the near-constitutional crisis and the resignation of the president Cearbhal Ó Dálaigh are connected.

[51] *The Irish News*, 1 May 1976.

[52] For the new broad-based campaign to oppose 'criminalisation' in the prisons, see the important study by F. Stuart Ross, *Smashing H-Blocks: The Popular Campaign against Criminalization and the Irish Hunger Strikes, 1976–1982* (Liverpool: Liverpool University Press, 2011), pp. 20–41.

'in memoriam' pages of the *Irish News*. It was and, indeed, is customary in the 'death notices' section of that paper to insert notices of the deaths, commiseration and sympathy notices for the deceased by family members and friends, often invoking saints or Mary Queen of the Gael, and frequently accompanied by a poem in tribute to the dead. But by the mid-1970s, this practice was expanded and turned into a public commemorative space for the IRA Volunteers killed since 1969. Death notices in the ordinary manner covered dead Volunteers, but as time went on, a succession of local IRA units and Sinn Féin clubs inserted long patriotic tributes to their dead comrades, which functioned as a means of memorialising, inserting their comrades repeatedly in the consciousness of readers, and most significantly, linking them with the Irish republican tradition of commemoration. This living commemorative practice sought rhetorically to incorporate into the pantheon of the national patriotic dead those who had died 'in combat', through accidental self-immolation or through the actions of Crown forces or other state actors. By Easter 1976, this newspaper genre was a commemorative performance in itself, and further served as a messaging board for prisoners and their families and echoed and complemented the memorialising of new IRA republican plots in Milltown Cemetery.[53] But what these popular, communal and paramilitary commemorations in print perhaps more clearly indicated was how beyond the control of Irish government northern commemorative activity really was.

[53] Jim Smyth, 'Milltown Cemetery' in Smyth (ed.) *Contesting the Recent Past.*

12 New Roads to the Rising: the Irish politics of commemoration since 1994

Kevin Bean

Introduction: agreed history?

A visitor to the centre of Dublin on Easter Monday 2015 would have found the city *en fete* as tens of thousands accepted an invitation to 'Step into History' and experience 'the sights and sounds of the capital in 1915'.[1] The area around O'Connell Street had come alive with street theatre, music and vintage attractions as Dubliners in period dress promenaded past the General Post Office (GPO), the headquarters of the Rising, or joined walking tours of significant historical sites. However, if this was commemoration as a jolly family day out, there was also a serious side to the fun. Whilst some came along purely for a ride on the Edwardian carousel, probably just as many packed into venues like the Abbey Theatre or Liberty Hall to hear talks by leading historians about 'The Ideas of 1916' or discuss 'The Irish Language and the Cultural Revolution'.

The spirit of Dublin's 'Road to the Rising' reflected many of the strands in the official Decade of Centenaries programme launched in 2011 to commemorate key moments in Irish history between 1912 and 1922.[2] Speaking the language of reconciliation and peace-building, the Advisory Group on Centenary Commemorations proposed that the 2016 commemorations should acknowledge 'the complexity of historical events and their legacy, and of the multiple identities and traditions which are part of the Irish historical experience'.[3] Drawing on the discourse of 'remembrance, reconciliation and renewal', and stressing 'inclusiveness and mutual respect', these more conciliatory approaches seemed to stand in marked contrast to previous state-supported commemorations, which had been criticized for triumphalism and the glorification of revolutionary

---

[1] RTÉ, *Step into History*, 6 April 2015: www.rte.ie/1916/688257-rte-road-to-the-rising-site-launch/.

[2] 'Joint Statement by the Prime Minister David Cameron and Taoiseach Enda Kenny', 12 March 2012: www.gov.uk/government/news/british-irish-relations-the-next-decade.

[3] Ireland 2016, 'A Vision for Ireland 2016 Centenary Year': www.ireland.ie/about/.

violence.[4] As Anne Dolan observed in a recent essay on the relationship between history, memory and commemoration, 'when has commemoration ever truly been about history? The memorial events for the fiftieth anniversary of the Easter Rising told us more about 1966 than they did about 1916, and 2016's efforts are not likely to be any different.'[5] In this light, every commemoration since 1917 has held up a mirror to its own times and preoccupations, and every decade has had the 1916 commemoration it deserved.

However, the dominant discourse of parity of esteem and building a shared history amongst all the 'identities and traditions' of Ireland did not go unchallenged at Easter 2015. Just yards from the officially sanctioned festivities outside the GPO, participants in Republican Sinn Féin's traditional Easter commemoration turned their back on 'the sanitized pageant' going on around them, proclaiming instead their revolutionary continuity with the principles of 1916; whilst throughout Northern Ireland, militant republican marches also demonstrated a very different understanding of the continuity of history to that on display in O'Connell Street.[6]

Despite these differences, a fundamental thread of meaning linked all of these activities. From the politicians and the academics of the Advisory Group who had initiated and devised the Decade of Centenaries, through to the bank-holiday crowds and republican marchers, all shared a belief that history mattered as a subject of public interest and that the past maintained the power to shape both the present and the future. Much more than a foundational myth giving legitimacy and authority to the Irish State and the political class, for the people on O'Connell Street, the Easter Rising was above all part of a genuinely national story in which all could share and take pride. As Roy Foster has noted (after Koestler), commemoration is all about self-identification, and just as 'every US citizen has to feel as personally proud of the War of Independence as if he or she had fought in it ... [so] today's Irish citizens are equally proprietorial about their revolution'.[7]

However, this shared sense of the *importance* of history may not signify agreement about the history of the Easter Rising as such. The Rising, in its various representations, has long proved problematic in Irish public life, a battleground for conflicting opinions about the historical legitimacy of

---

[4] Bryan Fanning, *Histories of the Irish Future* (London: Bloomsbury, 2015), pp. 193–206.

[5] Anne Dolan, 'Commemorating 1916: How Much Does the Integrity of the Past Count?', *The Irish Times*, 2 January 2015.

[6] 'Easter Commemorations', *Saoirse*, May 2015; C. Young, 'Masked Man Fires Shots over Grave', *The Irish News*, 6 April 2015.

[7] Roy Foster, 'Ireland's Getting Ready to Forget the Real Easter Rising', *The Spectator*, 25 April 2015.

contemporary political projects, measured against their achievement of 'the ideals of 1916'.[8] Militant republicans, for example, have long asserted sole ownership of the legacy of 1916 against the claims of Fianna Fáil and Fine Gael whilst, since the 1960s, socialists and feminists have complained of the exclusion of the Labour movement and women's histories from the 'official' narratives of the Rising.[9] Controversies around legitimacy, exclusion and the inheritance of 1916 acquired a particularly sharp focus during the Troubles, not only for the Irish state but for constitutional nationalists and militant republicans on both sides of the border.

This chapter considers aspects of the public and political debates surrounding the commemoration of the Easter Rising since 1994, the year of the first IRA ceasefire, arguing that the peace process and the consolidation of the new dispensation in Northern Ireland have done little to lessen the destabilizing impact of these recurring questions of legitimacy and historical achievement in both Irish polities. Indeed, if anything, disputes about 'dealing with the past' have been reinvigorated and amplified by the ongoing crisis of authority at Stormont since the Good Friday Agreement was signed in 1998. The years from 1994 also marked a period of unprecedented economic growth, affecting major changes in the way both the Irish state and the people of Ireland defined themselves in relation to their history and place in the world. This chapter argues that the economic and political fall-out from the collapse of what has come to be known as the Celtic Tiger has had a profoundly disorientating impact on Ireland's sense of nationhood. Consequently, for the Irish state, the current politics of commemoration appear to be less about remembrance or even the fighting of old wars than attempts to resolve more immediate problems surrounding political authority, ideological legitimacy and citizen alienation, which will determine the future of Ireland as a nation. Through reconnecting with the mythology of the Rising, all sections of the political class, from Fine Gael through to Sinn Féin, appear to be seeking new narratives of legitimacy and meaning through which to consolidate their authority and re-engage with sceptical and increasingly hostile electorates throughout the 'island of Ireland'.

Revising the Rising: revising the nation

The politics of commemoration after 1994 were decisively shaped by two closely related influences: the peace process and the changing definition

---

[8] Fearghal McGarry, *The Rising: Ireland. Easter 1916* (Oxford: Oxford University Press, 2010), pp. 286–293.

[9] Diarmaid Ferriter, *A Nation and Not a Rabble. The Irish Revolution 1913–1923* (London: Profile, 2015), pp. 76–85.

of the Irish state's 'national project'. An invented tradition celebrating the heroes of 1916 and speaking to a popular attachment and a pride in the story of the Rising had been central to the state-building project after 1922, reaching its apogee in the fiftieth-anniversary commemorations of 1966.[10] However, the outbreak of political conflict and the militant republican campaign in Northern Ireland during the Troubles produced what has been described as a period of 'revisionism, remembrance and forgetfulness' for the Southern state.[11] Eager to distance themselves from a Provisional rationale for 'armed struggle', with a vision for national unity that partly drew on the example of 1916, successive Dublin governments abandoned traditional state military commemorations after 1971 as a way of sharply distinguishing the 'legitimate violence' of the Easter Rising from the 'contemporary terrorism' of the IRA.[12] This 'forgetfulness' was to reach its nadir with the rather muted and somewhat perfunctory official commemoration of the seventy-fifth anniversary of the Rising in 1991. According to Garret FitzGerald, 'the appalling violence in Northern Ireland ... shifted the balance powerfully against the case for 1916 ... [and] undoubtedly contributed to the deep-seated national reluctance [to] ... "celebrate"' in this period.[13]

This emerging 'reluctance to celebrate' reflected other key political, cultural and social developments in the late twentieth century. The restructuring of the Irish economy in this period was producing a more urban, secular and self-consciously modern society whose political class prided itself on its ability to throw off the shackles of the past and take its place in the world as part of the European mainstream.[14] Although the institutions of traditional, conservative Ireland such as the 'Civil War parties' and the Catholic Church still exerted considerable authority, the election of a liberal campaigner, Mary Robinson, as President in 1990 was symbolic of impending social and cultural change.

One of the most important ideological and cultural features of this transformation was the accelerating pace of the revision of the Irish state's

[10] Roisín Higgins, *Transforming 1916: Meaning, Memory and the Fiftieth Anniversary of the Easter Rising* (Cork: Cork University Press, 2013).

[11] Mark McCarthy, *Ireland's 1916 Rising: Explorations of History-Making, Commemoration & Heritage in Modern Times* (Farnham: Ashgate, 2012), p. 305.

[12] Garret FitzGerald, *1916 Easter Rising: Personal Perspective*, 28 October 2014: www.bbc .co.uk/history/british/easterrising/personal/pp04.shtml.

[13] Garret FitzGerald, *Reflections on the Irish State* (Dublin: Irish Academic Press, 2003), p. 5.

[14] There is an extensive literature on these developments. For a general introduction, see Diarmaid Ferriter, *The Transformation of Ireland 1900–2000* (London: Profile, 2010) and Terence Brown, *Ireland: A Social and Cultural History 1922–2002* (London: Harper, 2010).

national project. Although the commitment of successive Dublin governments to the ideals of a distinctive Gaelic society and the re-unification of
the Irish nation was arguably little more than political posturing, few,
until the 1960s and 1970s, were prepared to openly challenge the traditional pieties of fulfilling the national destiny.[15] Significantly, the first
major attacks on previously unassailable beliefs concentrated their fire on
representations of the Easter Rising, widely and popularly understood
throughout the twentieth century to be the essential foundation myth
both of the Irish state and of a distinctive national identity.[16] These were
the first shots in a growing academic and political debate about 'revisionism' and the contested nature of Irish history, which was to colour wide
areas of public discourse throughout the 1980s and 1990s.[17] The underlying assumptions of the revisionist project, combined with the impact of
the Troubles, long-established pragmatic attitudes towards Northern
Ireland and an implicit recognition of the legitimacy of unionism from
the 1970s, were to become key factors driving Irish government policy-
making during the peace-process years.

One of the most significant developments to emerge from this period
was the amendment to Articles 2 and 3 of the 1937 constitution, which
followed the signing of the 1998 Belfast/Good Friday Agreement. The
concomitant changes in the definition of the Irish nation following the
1998 referendum to amend the constitution marked a dramatic discursive
shift.[18] The claim of all-Ireland sovereignty was removed: re-unification
could now only be achieved 'by peaceful means with the consent of a
majority of the people, democratically expressed, in both jurisdictions in
the island'. The traditional definition of the Irish nation in purely territorial terms was replaced by a new pluralistic description of a collection of
subjective categories, 'in all the diversity of their identities and traditions'.
Although membership of the nation became an 'entitlement and birth
right of every person born in the island of Ireland', the new Article 3 was
an explicit *de jure* acknowledgement of what had long been the *de facto*
policy of the Irish state: despite the rhetorical commitment to re-uniting

---

[15] For two accounts of the contrast between political rhetoric and pragmatic reality in the
policies of successive Irish governments towards Northern Ireland, see Clare O'Halloran,
Partition and the Limits of Irish Nationalism (Dublin: Gill and Macmillan, 1987) and
Catherine O'Donnell, *Fianna Fáil, Irish Republicanism and the Northern Ireland Troubles
1968–2005* (Dublin: Irish Academic Press, 2007).
[16] Conor Cruise O'Brien, *States of Ireland* (London: Hutchinson, 1972).
[17] Ferriter, *A Nation and Not a Rabble*, pp. 65–75.
[18] Tom Garvin, 'The Fading of Traditional Nationalism in the Republic of Ireland' in John
Coakley (ed.), *Changing Shades of Orange and Green: Redefining the Union and the Nation
in Contemporary Ireland* (Dublin: University College Dublin Press, 2002), pp. 123–131.

Ireland in the future, its nation-building project was now formally limited to the twenty-six counties.[19]

This displacement of a universalist definition of the nation-state by more essentialist narratives of identity and tradition expressed shifts towards the acculturation of politics driven by ideas of cultural peace-building which permeated the Good Friday Agreement. At the same time, with its formal commitment to pursue Irish unification through 'peaceful means' alone, the Agreement called into question the legitimacy of the revolutionary aspirations of 1916. The new aspiration to reconstitute a shared community was most clearly articulated through the consocia-tional language of 'partnership, equality and mutual respect', which placed 'parity of esteem ... and just and equal treatment for the identity, ethos, and aspirations of both communities' at the centre of public life'.[20] Whilst promising to draw a line under the old, confrontational politics of nationalism and unionism, the Agreement instead placed new and con-tested understandings of culture and identity at the heart of politics.[21] The impact of these political, institutional and cultural developments cannot be overstated. They represented a fundamental shift in the intel-lectual framework of Irish politics, offering not only different historical narratives but also a radically new definition of the Irish nation and state.

The heirs of Pearse?

Whilst commemoration in Ireland had frequently been a battlefield where history, memory and politics met to fight over the significance of the past and the meaning of the present, the problem of how to manage contested histories is by no means unique to the commemoration of 1916 or indeed to Irish politics in general.[22] Throughout the world, all types of societies use a variety of public rituals to celebrate or remember the past, often as a way of legitimating and giving meaning to the present.[23] Frequently experienced as a performance of consensus, the actors in commemorative events 'dress up in the clothes' (sometimes quite literally) of the ancestors

---

[19] See: www.taoiseach.gov.ie/eng/Historical_Information/The_Constitution/February_2015_-_Constitution_of_Ireland_.pdf.

[20] See Kevin Bean, 'Leaving the Soundbites at Home? Tony Blair, New Labour and Northern Ireland' in Laurence Marley (ed.), *Labour and Ireland* (Manchester: Manchester University Press, 2015).

[21] See: www.gov.uk/government/uploads/system/uploads/attachment_data/file/136652/agreement.pdf.

[22] Guy Beiner, *Remembering the Year of the French: Irish Folk History and Social Memory* (Madison, WI: University of Wisconsin Press, 2007), pp. 313–334.

[23] Dominic Bryan, *Orange Parades: The Politics of Ritual, Tradition and Control* (London: Pluto Press, 2000).

and demonstrate their right to claim the inheritance of the past. For governments, the rituals of remembrance are important ways of bringing people together to strengthen and transmit shared historical and cultural narratives in opposition to others. Through their repetition, rituals of commemoration loudly proclaim a sense of tradition and reinforce democratic ideas of shared values and historical continuity, through which contemporary authority is legitimated.[24]

Whilst political entrepreneurs frequently mythologize and distort historical events, whether to establish or reproduce the state's hegemony or a party's political mandate, this does not automatically negate their authenticity.[25] As forms of folk history, commemorations can be rooted in a common sense of collective memory, expressing a shared culture and forms of popular history, which imbue them with a real meaning and radiate a sense of belonging to both the casual participant and the committed political activist.[26] However, sharing a culture of commemoration does not mean that all those taking part in commemorative activities necessarily derive the same meanings or have the same motivation for attending. Even within the same relatively coherent group, such as a political party, there can be very different or even contested motivations for participation in a commemoration.[27]

Despite the suspension of the state's military parade during the Troubles and the low-key official ceremony in 1991, other popular and political commemorations of the Easter Rising did not cease. If anything, the Easter marches and the related sale of Easter Lilies became even more important for republicans as a public demonstration of their continued hostility to 'the partitionist states that had overthrown the Republic in 1922'.[28] Republican commemorations in both jurisdictions were often occasions of conflict between activists and the security forces, especially when marches were banned or restricted, which only added to their significance as a public assertion of continuity with 'the men and women of 1916'.[29] After 1998, commemorations remained especially important to 'dissident' republicans as an assertion of their unbroken

---

24 Gillian McIntosh, *The Force of Culture: Unionist Identities in Twentieth Century Ireland* (Cork: Cork University Press, 1999).
25 Eric Hobsbawm, 'Inventing Traditions' in Eric Hobsbawm and Terence Ranger (eds.), *The Invention of Tradition* (Cambridge: Cambridge University Press, 2012), pp. 1–14.
26 Geoffrey Cubitt, *History and Memory* (Manchester: Manchester University Press, 2007), pp. 118–174.
27 Anne Dolan, *Commemorating the Irish Civil War: History and Memory, 1923–2000* (Cambridge: Cambridge University Press, 2003), pp. 1–5.
28 'Ruairi O'Bradaigh Summer School Takes Place in Roscommon', *Saoirse*, June 2015.
29 For a particularly controversial Provisional march that was banned in 1976, see D. Walsh, 'Cabinet to Discuss Sinn Féin March', *Irish Times*, 27 April 1976.

fealty to the Proclamation of 1916 and their opposition to the Good Friday Agreement.[30]

Significantly in Ireland, the language of ideological continuity and political legitimacy was one that republicans both shared and contested with the state and constitutional nationalist parties, especially Fianna Fáil. Competing claims for ownership of 1916 were at the heart of this political conflict because, as critics frequently argued, Fianna Fáil had constantly proclaimed its historical origins and connections with senior 1916 figures, especially Eamon de Valera. These connections gave the party an invaluable aura of historically sanctioned legitimacy and strengthened its claims to be a national movement rather than a mere party or faction. This long-standing competition for the legacy of the Rising became particularly intense after 1994, as Sinn Féin attempted to replicate its electoral successes south of the border. Its strategy initially was to attack Fianna Fáil's republican credentials and move into that party's 'constitutional republican' territory.[31] These electoral dynamics were to become apparent in the Fianna Fáil government's decision to reinstate the military parade at Easter 2006. Sinn Féin had gained five TDs in the 2002 general election and appeared to be on course to increase both its votes and seats at the expense of Fianna Fáil in the approaching election. Addressing Fianna Fáil's Ard Fheis in October 2005, Taoiseach Bertie Ahern argued that his party 'had a particular claim to be considered the true inheritors of the spirit of 1916':

The Irish people need to reclaim the spirit of 1916, which is not the property of those who have abused and debased the title of republicanism ... [this spirit] is our State's inheritance. We must protect it from those who will abuse it and from the revisionists who would seek to denigrate it ... Since its foundation, Fianna Fáil has rightly commemorated the heroic struggle of the men and women of 1916. But it is now time that we suitably recognise the self-sacrifice of our forebears. Many of those who fought in 1916 became the founding members of our party. We all know the names of de Valera and Markievicz. We are also the party of Pádraig Pearse's mother and sister.[32]

Whilst Sinn Féin was one obvious target of the speech, Ahern's barbed reference to 'revisionists' was another significant theme in Fianna Fáil's politics during this period. This part of the speech was directed towards

---

[30] E. McDermott, 'Illegal Dissident Republican March Through Derry Passes Off Peacefully', *Belfast Telegraph*, 7 April 2015.

[31] Irish governments also used the mythology of 1916 in their attempts to undermine the legitimacy of dissident republicans after 1998. See M. Brennock, 'Ahern Contrasts "Brave Leaders" of 1916 with "vile deeds" at Omagh', *Irish Times*, 23 April 2001.

[32] M. Brennock, 'Ahern Re-instates 1916 Easter Parade Past GPO', *Irish Times*, 22 October 2005.

two claims by former Fine Gael leader John Bruton: firstly, that 'independence was possible without 1916' and, secondly, that the Provisionals had justified their armed campaign by drawing on the 'respectable traditions of the Easter Rising'.[33] Ahern's aim here was to suggest that Fine Gael as a whole was unpatriotic, both in its denigration of the founders of the state and in its admiration for John Redmond's Home Rule party. These tropes, which remained important in the subsequent political and public debate about the planned ninetieth-anniversary commemoration in 2006, were to be repeated again before the 2016 centenary.[34] Throughout these controversies, members of Fianna Fáil continued to present themselves as 'the true republicans' in opposition to a Sinn Féin tainted with a violent Provisional past and the fashionable revisionism of contemporary Fine Gael.[35] This argument especially suited Bertie Ahern's own political persona as an 'ordinary Dub', proud of his family's involvement in the independence struggle and someone who closely identified with Pearse because, in his words, 'we are his heirs. He has given us the right to fulfil our destiny. Without violence.'[36]

Changing the landscape of memory

From Easter 1998, Fianna Fáil politicians attempted to legitimate the peace process and the Good Friday Agreement by drawing on a particular vision of history that referred to the goals of the national project 'and the unfinished business' of 1916. In this reading,

the Agreement fulfils the ideals of all those in this and past generations who have worked for peace and reconciliation between the different traditions on this island, going back generations, to the founders of the State and the cultural revival, to Parnell and O'Connell, to Young Ireland and the United Irishmen. Let us resolve to make ... this day of commemoration the start of a just and lasting peace ...[37]

---

[33] P. McGarry, 'Independence Possible Without 1916, Says Bruton', *Irish Times*, 20 September 2004.

[34] For a good summary of this debate immediately following Fianna Fáil's Ard Fheis, see P. O. Muiri, 'Legacy of Pearse is Worth Commemorating', *Irish Times*, 28 October 2005. For an example of a wide-ranging debate on 1916 and its place in Irish history, see '1916 – A View from 2006', remarks by Mary McAleese, then President of Ireland, at a conference 'The Long Revolution: The 1916 Rising in Context', University College Cork, 27 January 2006 (http://cain.ulst.ac.uk/issues/politics/docs/poi/mmca270106.htm), and the subsequent debate in Letters to the Editor, *Irish Times*, 31 January–27 February 2006.

[35] For a flavour of these debates and the positions adopted by the various parties, see Dáil Éireann Debates, Private Members' Business – Irish Unification: Motion, 2 November 2005: http://debates.oireachtas.ie/dail/2005/11/02/00022.asp#N181.

[36] D. Lynch, 'A Pearsing Light on Bertie', *Irish Independent*, 15 April 2001.

[37] Bertie Ahern speaking at the Fianna Fáil Easter commemoration, 26 April 1998, quoted in R. Graff-McRae, *Remembering and Forgetting: Commemoration and Conflict in Post-Peace Process Ireland* (Dublin: Irish Academic Press, 2010), p. 62.

In so doing, Fianna Fáil was, albeit opportunistically, identifying itself with the nation, and showing that having struggled to achieve the Agreement, they were now going to win the Peace Process. It was, as Graff-McRae has suggested, an appropriation of a single narrative that 'marks the ending of one history and the beginning of another'.[38]

However, it would be wrong to suggest that Fianna Fáil's plans for the 2006 state commemoration were simply a revival of old traditions or purely political posturing. The exuberant confidence of the Celtic Tiger and relative stability of the peace process, amongst other factors, contrived to give the ninetieth-anniversary events a very different character from earlier commemorations. The state commemorations in 2006 seemed to be genuinely popular events. Contemporary press accounts recorded 100,000 people watching the parade in Dublin and commented on the public enthusiasm and emotional commitment to the memory of 1916.[39] The attendance of the British ambassador and Sinn Féin TDs, along with invitations to unionists, was also regarded as significant in demonstrating the inclusive nature of the commemoration.[40] Taoiseach Bertie Ahern's speech at the symbolically important Kilmainham gaol combined traditional themes of sacrifice and historical continuity with the contemporary language of the peace process.[41] He argued that whilst the present should never forget its debts to the past, it was also necessary to embrace all traditions and look to the future.

Our generation still cherishes the ideals of the courageous men and women who fought for Ireland in Easter Week . . . we honour and respect their selfless idealism and patriotism, and that we remember with gratitude the great sacrifices they made for us . . . The potential for progress has never been greater. Independent Ireland is now in full stride and beginning to fulfil the hopes and expectations that all the patriots of the past knew we possessed . . . We must be generous and inclusive so that all of the people of Ireland can live together with each other and with our neighbours in Great Britain on a basis of friendship, respect, equality and partnership . . . we will continue to work for peace, for justice, for prosperity and for reconciliation between all who share . . . this special island.[42]

These themes of generosity and inclusion became an important part of the narrative in official commemorations during the 2000s. In particular,

---

[38] Graff-McRae, *Remembering and Forgetting*, p. 62.
[39] A number of plays, television programmes, exhibitions, educational activities and local commemorations reflected this popular interest in the Rising. See, for example, a review by Karen Fricker of 'Operation Easter', *The Guardian*, 29 April 2006.
[40] S. Collins, 'Easter Parade Attracts 100,000 and Wins Political Approval', *Irish Times*, 17 April 2006.
[41] S. Collins, 'We Remember with Gratitude the Great Sacrifices They Made for Us', *Irish Times*, 17 April 2006.
[42] Collins, 'We Remember with Gratitude'.

there was a growing awareness amongst policy-makers that this sense of shared history and respectful commemoration of events such as the Easter Rising could be useful bridge-building exercises between 'the two traditions'. The invitation to unionists (which was not taken up) to attend the 2006 state commemoration provides one such example. Other strands, which were becoming increasingly important, concerned the identification of the First World War as a shared history with a common narrative of sacrifice for both nationalists and unionists.[43] It was suggested that commemoration could be

a mutually respectful space for differing traditions, differing loyalties ... which would help ... to change the landscape of memory ... None of us has the power to change what is past but we do have the power to use today well to shape a better future.[44]

The Somme and the Easter Rising were frequently linked together in these new understandings of the healing power of the past.[45] Former Minister of Foreign Affairs, Dermot Ahern, argued in 2014 that both 'iconic events' must be 'acknowledged and honoured' because:

As we build a shared peaceful present and future on this island ... we can no longer have two histories, separate and in conflict ... We must acknowledge that the experiences of all the people on this island have shaped our present and, in some way, defined what it is for all of us to be Irish.[46]

However, if politicians had hoped to permanently fix the meaning of Easter 1916 as a shared history, they were very much mistaken. Far from reflecting a settled consensus, the politics of commemoration continued to reveal that the significance of 1916 remained as uncertain and contested as ever. Even before the Decade of Centenaries had started, the questioning and debate had begun.[47] As 2016 approached, the Rising, as an historical event, continued to be an infinite *tabula rasa*, capable of being rewritten and refashioned according to political taste, whilst the perceived ideals of Easter remained an unsettling aspiration against which

---

[43] For an influential historical account that added weight to this argument, see Richard S. Grayson, *Belfast Boys: How Unionist and Nationalist Fought and Died Together in the First World War* (London: Continuum, 2010).

[44] President Mary McAleese, speaking at the Messines Peace Park, 11 November 1998, quoted in P. McGarry, 'Armistice Day: Remembering the Past Differently', *Irish Times*, 11 November 2014.

[45] The recognition of the significance of the First World War and the Somme to unionists were to be important themes in the mayoral terms of Sinn Féin Lords Mayor of Belfast after 2002. See, for example, S. Breen, 'Maskey Lays Wreath for Victims of Somme', *Irish Times*, 2 July 2002.

[46] D. Ahern, 'Shared History Can Help Build a Shared Future', *Irish Times*, 11 November 2014.

[47] Ferriter, *A Nation and Not a Rabble*, pp. 75–96.

contemporary Ireland could be judged by critics and usually found wanting.[48]

Was it for this ...?

Superficially, the Ireland of the Celtic Tiger seemed to be turning its back on the ghosts of the past.[49] The phenomenal growth in GDP and living standards alongside the social transformation wrought by one of the world's most globalized economies appeared to have solved the problem of history.[50] Now Ireland's project looked solely to the future, more concerned with the problems of affluence and sustaining economic growth than looking back and keeping old traditions alive. If Ireland had previously defined itself as a victim of history, its transformation from one of Europe's poorest countries to one of the fastest-growing economies in the world became a source of pride and growing self-confidence for most of the population. Likewise, where Ireland had once defined itself in relation to Britain, it was now reinventing itself 'in relation to Europe: an association of nations in which it is recognized as an equal ...'.[51] By 1997, Ireland had turned the corner, from being a country with a long history of mass emigration to become a destination for economic migrants. *The Economist*, for example, praised Ireland as a 'shining example' of modernization:

Illiberalism, anti-individualism and a deep suspicion of economic freedom may be fading now as Ireland modernizes. As they do, the social consensus may weaken – but (such are the dilemmas of political economy) so too should the clientelism and corruption bred by a securely entrenched corporate state ...[52]

However, other voices were more critical. As one prominent commentator noted, 'The Celtic Tiger wasn't just an economic ideology.' It was a 'substitute identity', replacing nationalism and Catholicism with 'mad consumerism', 'arrogance towards the rest of the world' and a 'wilful refusal of all ties of history and tradition'.[53] Whatever the assessment of the radical transformation of the 1990s and 2000s, arguably no other European country rose higher or fell farther in the worldwide financial

---

[48] Ferriter, *A Nation and Not a Rabble*, pp. 376–408.
[49] J. Waters, 'Celtic Tiger Shut Out the Relevance of Pearse', *Irish Times*, 2 December 2011.
[50] 'The Luck of the Irish', *The Economist*, 14 October 2004: www.economist.com/node/3261071.
[51] 'Ireland Shines: Lessons and Questions from an Economic Transformation', *The Economist*, 15 May 1997: www.economist.com/node/149333.
[52] 'Ireland Shines'.
[53] Fintan O'Toole, *Enough is Enough: How to Build a New Republic* (London: Faber and Faber, 2010), p. 3.

crisis of 2008. This meant that the collapse of the Celtic Tiger not only produced a series of profound political and economic crises, but it also had a significant psychic impact on Irish society.

The most immediate and dramatic effects were felt on the economy and the living standards of the population as a result of government austerity policies introduced at the behest of 'the Troika' of the International Monetary Fund, the European Central Bank and the European Commission. The minimum wage and unemployment benefits were cut just as unemployment rose to nearly 15 per cent in 2011. The raising of the state-pension age, combined with cuts in public-sector pay and tax increases, had serious effects on salary earners and those dependent on benefits.[54] The loss of the state's AAA international debt rating, reductions in GDP and contractions in key sectors of the economy as a result of the wider European and international recession added to a deepening sense of crisis.[55] Politically, this was reflected in electoral volatility, widespread popular protests and a growing sense of disenchantment with traditional politics and institutions.[56] The 2011 General Election – 'the most volatile in modern European history' – produced a 'quite spectacular' breakdown in the Irish party system, with the resounding defeat of the Fianna Fáil–Green coalition government and the collapse of the Fianna Fáil vote to the lowest point since its foundation in 1926.[57]

This period also saw the electoral rise of left-populist parties, such as Sinn Féin, as well as various independent TDs opposed to the established political class. By-elections and opinion polls in the run-up to 2016 confirmed the decline in traditional party loyalties and identification with the Civil War parties, alongside the emergence of smaller 'anti-system parties' and independents.[58] This feeling of alienation and a breakdown of trust between the citizen and the political elites was further compounded by a series of public enquiries and tribunals that investigated the banking system's collapse, along with a number of financial scandals and allegations of corruption in planning and local

---

[54] P. Sweeney, 'My Experience with the Troika in Ireland', *Social Europe*, 13 February 2015: www.socialeurope.eu/2015/02/experience-troika-ireland/.

[55] OECD Data, *Selected Indicators for Ireland*: https://data.oecd.org/gdp/gross-domestic-pro duct-gdp.%20htm#indicator-chart.

[56] T. O'Brien, 'Thousand Attend Anti-Austerity Protests in Dublin', *Irish Times*, 13 April: www.irishtimes.com/news/thousands-attend-anti-austerity-protest-in-dublin-1.1359805.

[57] E. O'Malley, 'The Old Order and the New', *Dublin Review of Books*: www.drb.ie/essays/the-old-order-and-the-new.

[58] For examples of this continuing volatility, see R. Colwell, 'Labour Suffers Post Referendum Hangover', *Red C Polls*, 29 June 2015: www.redcresearch.ie/wp-content/uploads/2015/06/SBP-June-2015-Poll-Report.pdf.

government.[59] For many, the legitimacy and authority of the state and these entrenched elites were seriously being called into question.

Many of the economic and political characteristics of the collapse of the Celtic Tiger and the ensuing instability were common to other parts of the developed world, especially within the European Union.[60] However, a number of specifically Irish factors posed profound existential and moral questions about the future of the Irish state. For, unlike many other European countries, the questions facing Ireland turned on the nature of the state and the national project itself. Having begun to shed their history during the Celtic Tiger years, the contemporary crisis forced the people of Ireland to return to their past once more to confront the meanings of the country's modern history and the revolutionary origins of the state.[61]

These debates were not simply a reaction to the self-congratulatory hubris of the Celtic Tiger or a desire to find scapegoats amongst the political and financial elites, although these moods were powerful enough. Rather, they echoed older discussions about the purpose of the national project, the impact of partition and the incomplete national revolution; above all, what was the point of an independent Ireland that could not provide for its people?[62] A celebrated editorial in *The Irish Times* captured the extraordinary tenor of those times:

It may seem strange to some that *The Irish Times* would ask whether this is what the men of 1916 died for: a bailout from the German chancellor with a few shillings of sympathy from the British chancellor on the side. There is the shame of it all. Having obtained our political independence from Britain to be masters of our own affairs, we have now surrendered our sovereignty to the European Commission, the European Central Bank and the International Monetary Fund.[63]

Such references to the ideals and hopes of 1916 became commonplace, whether to invoke the sacrifices necessary to restore the economy or to

---

[59] Elaine Byrne, *Political Corruption in Ireland 1922-2010: A Crooked Harp?* (Manchester: Manchester University Press, 2012); S. Lynch, 'Ireland Must Do More to Tackle Corruption, EU Warns', *Irish Times*, 4 February 2014.

[60] R. Lambert, 'Now Ireland and Portugal, Too', *Le Monde Diplomatique*, May 2015.

[61] G. Ganiel, 'Joseph Ruane on "Ireland's Crises: North-South Intersections": From the Taming of the Celtic Tiger to the Rise of Sinn Fein in the Republic', *Slugger O'Toole*, 24 November 2014: http://sluggerotoole.com/2014/11/24/joseph-ruane-on-irelands-cri ses-north-south-intersections-from-the-taming-of-the-celtic-tiger-to-the-rise-of-sinn- fein-in-the-republic/.

[62] Jennifer Todd and Joseph Ruane, *The Dynamics of Conflict in Northern Ireland: Power, Conflict and Emancipation* (Cambridge: Cambridge University Press, 1996), pp. 232–265.

[63] Editorial, 'Was It for This?', *Irish Times*, 10 November 2010. A similar note was struck in the same period by a front-page editorial, 'Proclamation of Dependence', *Irish Examiner*, 19 November 2010.

criticise the harshness of government policy and the surrender of economic sovereignty. Taoiseach Brian Cowen was not alone in his frequent
references to the symbolism of the 2016 commemoration during the
crisis, especially in arguing that the country should be 'on the best
possible economic footing so as not to fail those whose sacrifice led to
the foundation of the State', and hoping that

we can say in 2016 when we get to O'Connell Street and look up at those men and
women of idealism that gave us the chance to be the country we are ... [that] we
did not fail our children but we did not fail our country either.[64]

Divided by a shared history

The electorate was, however, much less sanguine when called upon to
give their verdict on Fianna Fáil's stewardship of the inheritance of 'those
men and women of idealism'. Their assessment of the Celtic Tiger years
and the conduct of the political and financial elite was damning, revealing
a huge gulf between the Irish political class and its citizens.[65] A broader
battle of ideas was now being joined across all areas of public life, as
demands for fundamental reform and a new republic gave this questioning of society's values a deeply moral character.[66] Far beyond the narrow
point scoring of a discredited political class, questions about the significance of 1916 as a foundation myth and how it should be commemorated
have increasingly been coloured in the public imagination by the failure of
the Celtic Tiger and the stasis of Irish politics. As one cultural commentator suggested, 'the 2008 crisis represented a watershed moment ... an
opportunity to rethink the meaning of Irishness'.[67] For a wide range of
critics, the Decade of Centenaries was just such an opportunity to address
more fundamental questions and perhaps to give uncomfortable answers
about: 'What does it mean – what can it mean – to be Irish in the wake of
the Celtic Tiger?'[68]

Rather than using the commemoration of 1916 as a chance to take
stock, however, many politicians seem to prefer to cloak themselves in the

[64] H. McGee, 'Cowen Calls for Economic Sacrifices', *Irish Times*, 4 February 2010.
[65] As in so many other ways, Irish politics was in line with those of other developed countries
where political disengagement and citizen alienation was widespread and perhaps term-
inal. See Peter Mair, *Ruling the Void: The Hollowing of Western Democracy* (London: Verso,
2013).
[66] P. Kirby, 'The Irish Republic: A Project Still to be Completed'; paper delivered at 'The
1916 Rising: Then and Now' conference 21–22 April: www.theirelandinstitute.com/ins
titute/p01_kirby_completed_page.html.
[67] G. Smythe, 'Irish National Identity after the Celtic Tiger', *Estudios Irlandeses* 7
(2012), 136.
[68] Smythe, 'Irish National Identity', p. 136.

idealism of the past to mask the deficiencies of the present, re-engage with the public and restore the authority of the state. The Irish government's Ireland 2016 commemoration programme proffers a form of healing through remembering in which they hope all of the diverse and contra-dictory narratives of the children of the nation can be cherished equally. Thus, for Tainiste and Labour leader Joan Burton, the official events would be '[a] critical and open-minded exploration' offering 'an essential step towards lasting reconciliation between the different communities and traditions which share the island of Ireland', whilst for the Minister for Arts, Heritage and the Gaeltacht, Heather Humphreys, 'Ireland 2016 is designed to remember, honour and inspire ... while also looking to the future and asking ourselves where we want the country to go in the next hundred years.'[69]

Whilst it might be possible to stage-manage events like 'the Road to the Rising', combining state spectacle, family entertainment and elements of mediated public discussion, not everyone is convinced that the historical complexity of the Rising can be so easily and neatly packaged. Whilst politicians acknowledge the contested meanings attached to Easter 1916, as ever, it is the historians who are asking the most direct questions and presenting the most effective critiques. Roy Foster counselled against 'politicizing the past for the feelgood purposes of the present ... For all the well-meaning government rhetoric about "our shared history", revo-lutions are about antagonism, not reconciliation, and this is, above all, true of events a hundred years ago.'[70] As Diarmaid Ferriter, quoting Edna Longley, reminds us, the commemoration of revolution and war could also be contentious: 'By its nature, commemoration is divisive and if it is to be true to historical reality it cannot but be ... "Commemorations are as selective as our sympathies. They honour our dead, not your dead".'[71]

By referring to our relationship to the past, along with other aspects of the troubled relationship between history, memory and politics, these and other interventions by historians speak to more than an Irish condition. Whilst the debate about 1916 is inextricably bound up with the legacy of the Celtic Tiger and specifically Irish demands for political change, it may also tell us something about the nature of the contemporary political

---

[69] 'Minister Humphreys Joined by Taoiseach, Tainiste and MoS O'Riordain to Launch Ireland 2016', 13 November 2014: http://merrionstreet.ie/en/News-Room/Releases/Minister_Humphreys_joined_by_Taoiseach_T%C3%A1naiste_and_MoS_%C3%93_R%C3%ADord%C3%A1in_to_launch_Ireland_2016.html.

[70] Roy Foster, 'We Must Not Politicize 1916 for Feel-Good Purposes of the Present', *Irish Times*, 27 December 2014.

[71] Diarmaid Ferriter, 'Historian Ronan Fanning and Charlie Flanagan Conjure Up a Strange Vision of 1916', *Irish Times*, 28 February 2015. Ferriter is a member of the Advisory Group on Centenary Commemorations.

moment throughout the developed world. Peter Mair has characterised this condition as one in which the meanings and institutions of Western democracy have been hollowed out, whilst others have argued that all forms of political and social authority in these societies have been undermined by the collapse of self-confident belief in the possibilities of progress.[72] One response to these crises in Western societies has been a political retreat from dealing with the problems of the present and challenges of the future to seek solutions in the past. As Furedi argues, 'it is far easier to construct an idealised past than an ideal present'.[73] In the wake of the collapse of the Celtic Tiger, and the declining spiritual leadership of the Catholic Church, a return to the authentic certainties and moral authority of the past might be appealing to a troubled contemporary Ireland. However, it remains an open question whether such a return to the comfort of the past will indeed be possible or even desirable, given that 'Ireland', redefined and reimagined over the last two decades, remains a work in progress overshadowed by all the contradictions of its unfinished national revolution.

[72] Mair, *Ruling the Void*, pp. 1–16; Frank Furedi, *Authority: A Sociological History* (Cambridge: Cambridge University Press, 2013), pp. 403–409.
[73] Frank Furedi, *Mythical Past, Elusive Future: History and Society in an Anxious Age* (London: Pluto, 1992), p. 10.

13 Ghosts of the Somme: the state of Ulster Loyalism, memory work and the 'other' 1916

Jonathan Evershed

> The phrase that was developed inside the blocks was *Tiocfaidh ár Lá*. *Tiocfaidh ár Lá* literally means 'Our day will come'. So Republicans are looking forward to events, to change, to progress, to winning; however you term it ... And I think Unionism, sadly, is looking back to what it had, to what it was like, to what it was like then.[1]

A spectre is no longer haunting Ireland. A ghost has been exorcised. Grass-roots 'rediscovery' of those Irish Nationalists who fought for Britain between 1914 and 1918[2] has contributed to ending what F. X. Martin called Ireland's 'collective amnesia'[3] about its role in the Great War. Embracing this process of rediscovery and rapidly transitioning from the merely perfunctory to the openly celebratory,[4] state ceremonies of remembrance in the South – including the joint inauguration by the Irish President, Michael D. Higgins, and Prince Edward, Duke of Kent, of a new 'Cross of Sacrifice' in Glasnevin Cemetery in July 2014 – are seen as marking a new political 'maturity' in the Republic of Ireland and concomitantly, a more reconciled relationship between Ireland and the United Kingdom. Likewise, the involvement of both Sinn Féin and the Irish government in commemorative rituals in Northern Ireland is heralded as symbolising new forms of political accommodation within and between the North and the South.

There are, however, spectres that continue to haunt this new commemorative landscape. The emerging orthodoxy in Irish memorial narrativisation – that which was forgotten now, at last, is remembered – in the first instance is based on a selective reading of the history of First World War commemoration in Ireland.[5] More fundamentally, it denies that the

---

[1] Sinn Féin member, interview by author, Belfast, 5 September 2014.
[2] See, for example, *The 6th Connaught Rangers: Belfast Nationalists and the Great War* (Belfast: 6th Connaught Rangers Research Project, 2011).
[3] F. X. Martin, '1916: Myth, Fact and Mystery', *Studia Hibernica* 7 (1967), 7–126.
[4] E. Pine, 'Irish Memory Studies' (paper presented at 'Commemoration: Contexts and Concepts', University College Cork, 10 October 2014).
[5] See P. Yeates, 'No Poppy Please', *Dublin Review of Books*, 20 October 2014 (www.drb.ie/essays/no-poppy-please).

foundations of the twentieth-century Irish Republican project and the very roots of the Irish state itself are located in a *purposeful* rejection of an 'imperialist' war. Rejection is quite distinct from simply 'forgetting'. Ireland's relationship with the Great War is perhaps marked less by the passivity of F. X. Martin's 'collective amnesia', and more by Guy Beiner's (pro)active 'social forgetting'.[6] A protest banner, proclaiming in the hundred-year-old slogan of the Irish Citizen Army that 'We Serve Neither King Nor Kaiser', and accompanying chants of 'Shame on you!', haunted President Higgins' speech in Glasnevin. Despite (or because of) the social and political transformations engendered by forty years of conflict, the ghosts of 1916 that haunted 1966[7] continue to disrupt during this Decade of Centenaries.

But Pearse's are not the only ghosts of the present Decade. In a recent article in the *Irish Left Review*, Fergus O'Farrell suggested that

The first stages of the Peace Process allowed for a reinterpretation of recent Irish history, resulting in a new found appreciation of the role played by Irishmen in British uniform during the First World War. But the role of Ulster unionists, their motivations for enlisting, the sacrifices they made and their commemoration of the war are aspects of the Irish experience which are unknown in the south.[8]

Although the Somme often presents itself in Irish discourses as the 'other' 1916, a footnote in a story whose epicentre is the Easter Rising,[9] in Northern Ireland, its significance is equal and opposite. Here, the present decade is haunted *as much* by the ghosts of Carson, Craig and the Ulster Volunteers[10] as by those of the martyrs of Easter Week. These ghosts are figures of the Unionist establishment and have played a vital role in supporting the Northern Irish state, particularly in its infancy. They are also *agents provocateurs*, at work in justifications for Loyalist violence, or in murals that demarcate territory on Belfast's divided streets. As Kris Brown asserts, they are not 'insubstantial will o' the wisps, clinging to recent tombstones or

---

[6] G. Beiner, 'An Archeology of Social Forgetting and Remembrance in Ulster', *History and Memory* 25 (2013), 9–50.

[7] See M. E. Daly and M. O'Callaghan (eds.), *1916 in 1966: Commemorating the Easter Rising* (Dublin: Royal Irish Academy, 2007).

[8] F. O'Farrell, '1916, the Poppy and Ulster Unionism: A More Rounded Memory in the Decade of Centenaries', *Irish Left Review*, 17 November 2014 (www.irishleftreview.org).

[9] R. Graff-McRae, *Remembering and Forgetting 1916: Commemoration and Conflict in Post-Peace Process Ireland* (Dublin: Irish Academic Press, 2010), p. xv.

[10] At the root of the Somme's symbolic importance for Unionists is the evolutionary narrative that links the Ulster Covenant, the UVF and the 36th (Ulster) Division. See T. Bowman, *Carson's Army: The Ulster Volunteer Force 1910–22* (Manchester: Manchester University Press, 2007).

Figure 13.1: 'In Memory 36th (Ulster) Division' Union Flag (photo: with permission of Dominic Bryan and Gordon Gillespie).

dog-eared history books',[11] but remain active agents in the politics of the present. In 2014, at a weekly 'flag protest'[12] at Belfast City Hall, one banner proclaimed that 'Our Forefathers, As We And Our Children, Will Never Surrender Our National Flag'. Next to it fluttered a Union Flag which had at its centre J. P. Beadle's famous depiction of those forefathers: the 36th (Ulster) Division leading the charge out of the trenches on the morning of 1 July 1916 (see Figure 13.1).

In the juxtaposition of its centenary with the ongoing project of reconstructing state and society in Northern Ireland (the project of 'peace-building'), the Somme's ghosts have the potential to be just as disruptive as those of Pearse, Connolly *et al.* in ways that are perhaps less well understood. In what follows, I will attempt to interrogate these ghosts

[11] K. Brown, '"Our Father Organisation": The Cult of the Somme and the Unionist "Golden Age" in Modern Ulster Loyalist Commemoration', *The Round Table* 96 (2007), 709.

[12] In December 2012, a vote was taken at Belfast City Council to restrict the flying of the Union flag above City Hall to no more than eighteen designated days. Protests outside City Hall on the night of the vote itself were followed by further protests which continued for several weeks into 2013. To date, a weekly protest is held each Saturday at the gates of the City Hall.

and those who follow them. Drawing on ethnographic research conducted in Belfast, I contend that commemoration by Loyalists during the Decade of Centenaries functions as 'memory work', what Spivak called a 'ghost dance', 'a prayer to be haunted'[13] through which the 'spectres' of the Somme are evoked. As Avery Gordon suggests, 'spectres or ghosts appear when the trouble they symptomize is no longer being contained or repressed or blocked from view'.[14] In a present defined by political and economic transformation and the 'rewriting' of historical narratives engendered by the peace process, this 'ghost dance' is about recovering a deferred eschatological promise, in the face of deep ontological uncertainty. Thus, Loyalist commemoration during the Decade of Centenaries is not exclusively, or even predominantly, about looking back, but about looking to the future. This future, I will argue, is defined in terms of a 'Golden Age': 'a past that has never been present, [and] always remain[s], as it were, to come'.[15]

Losing the war beneath the peace

'Politics', wrote Foucault, in an inversion of Clausewitz's famous maxim, 'is the continuation of war by other means . . . a battlefront runs through the whole of society, continuously and permanently'.[16] Post-Agreement Northern Ireland's permanent battlefront is clearly in evidence in this mural (see Figure 13.2) on Vicarage Street in 'Protestant' East Belfast. A litany of 'Loyalist' grievances on one side are plotted against 'Republican' 'gains' on the other. While murals come and go[17] in Belfast's always (however subtly) changing symbolic landscape, the sentiments expressed in this one have continued to fester in the Loyalist *zeitgeist*. 'Fuck the Peace', pronounced a prominent piece of graffiti that appeared in 2014 on another part of the Albertbridge Road.

It is clear that a vocal and substantive section of the so-called 'Loyalist community' believe that they are losing (or have already lost) Northern Ireland's Foucauldian 'war beneath the peace'. A survey conducted by Ipsos MORI for the BBC in 2013 found that 53 per cent of 'working class'

---

[13] G. Spivak, 'Ghostwriting', *Diacritics* 25 (1995), 78.

[14] A. Gordon, *Ghostly Matters: Haunting and the Sociological Imagination* (Minneapolis: University of Minnesota Press, 2008), p. xvi.

[15] J. Kirkby, '"Remembrance of the Future": Derrida on Mourning', *Social Semiotics* 16 (2006), 469.

[16] M. Foucault, *Society Must Be Defended: Lectures at the Collège de France 1975–76*, eds. M. Bertani and A. Fontana, trans. D. Macey (London: Penguin Books, 2004), pp. 15–50.

[17] At the time of writing, this mural has been removed and the building on which it was located has been redeveloped.

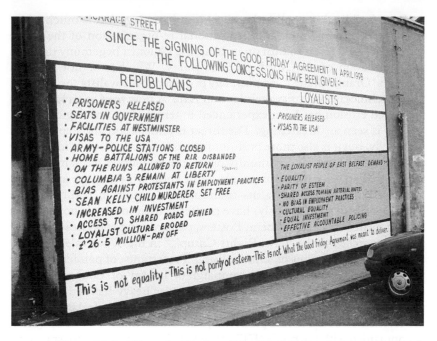

Figure 13.2: 'Since the Signing of the Good Friday Agreement' Mural, Vicarage Street, Belfast (photo: with permission of Pawel Romanczuk).

Unionists[18] believed that the current political system favours Nationalists over them. Perhaps more meaningfully, a narrative of loss is prevalent in everyday conversations with and between those who define themselves as 'Loyalist'. Many question whether the current settlement in Northern Ireland can really be described as 'peace' at all. In a recent report on the flag protests published by Queen's University Belfast, one 19-year-old interviewee, upon being asked whether she would describe the environment in which she had grown up as 'Peace time', responded,

Peace? I haven't grown up in Peace. You can't live in a peaceful society when your national territory is constantly under threat. When your identity is constantly under threat and when your life is subsequently under threat.[19]

---

[18] The full survey data are available at www.ipsos-mori.com/researchpublications/research archive/3126/. By 'working class', I am referring to those Unionists surveyed defined as belonging to the Ipsos MORI social grade bracket C2DE. See *Social Grade: A Classification Tool* (London: Ipsos MediaCT, 2009).

[19] Nineteen-year-old flag protester from North Belfast, quoted in P. Nolan, D. Bryan, C. Dwyer, K. Hayward, K. Radford and P. Shirlow, *The Flag Dispute: Anatomy of a Protest* (Belfast: Queen's University Belfast, 2015), p. 97.

'Peacebuilding' – a political and economic project that is much wider than the elite bargaining and institutional re-organisation of the peace 'process' – has served to turn on its head the Unionist hegemony that was the foundation of the Northern Irish polity. Whether or not Michael Farrell's 'Orange State'[20] ever *actually* provided for Loyalists the material and psychological security their 'community' is now seen as lacking,[21] its perceived erosion has been experienced in terms of an ontological crisis. 'Peace' is seen as threatening. The threat is understood and experienced physically, but it is also more profoundly existential: an issue of identity or of being. One Loyalist community development worker has lamented to me more than once that 'our people don't know who they are anymore'.

The state to which Loyalists traditionally (though in reality, always conditionally or ambiguously) have proffered their loyalty is now seen as having turned its back on them. Posters, placards and speeches at weekly protest marches to the 'Civil Rights Camp'[22] in the Woodvale routinely accuse state institutions of 'criminalising' Protestants; of pandering to (or worse, actively orchestrating) a campaign of 'hatred' of 'Orange Culture' as part of a 'Republican agenda'. Accusations of heavy-handed treatment of Loyalist protesters by the Police Service of Northern Ireland (PSNI) are levelled on social media platforms, and the moniker 'PSNIRA' (often accompanied with the prefix 'FT' – 'Fuck the' – or a warning to 'stay out') has been coined in graffiti in 'Loyalist' parts of Belfast. Concerns about educational attainment and deprivation in working-class Protestant communities are widespread, as are claims that 'Prods' can't get houses or jobs. The 'mainstream' Unionist parties – the DUP and the UUP – are accused of standing idly by or even of being actively complicit in this discrimination.

As the Queen's University report highlights,

[T]his rhetoric of discrimination – although no doubt deeply felt – refers to processes that are not, in actual fact, acts of discrimination but acts of *change*. It is to be expected, as in any post-conflict process, that a transition would take place in the rebalancing of power. In that sense, protesters are right to perceive a shifting balance of power – and they may even conceive this as a 'loss'.[23]

---

[20] M. Farrell, *Northern Ireland: The Orange State* (London: Pluto Press, 1980).

[21] See A. Finlay, 'Defeatism and Northern Protestant "Identity"', *The Global Review of Ethnopolitics* 1 (2001), 3–20.

[22] The 'Civil Rights Camp' at the junction between the Crumlin Road and Twaddell Avenue was established by members of the Ligoniel Orange Lodges and their supporters in July 2013 in protest at a Parades Commission decision not to allow a return parade to pass this volatile interface on the Twelfth of July. At the time of writing, the camp, nightly protests, and weekly attempts on the part of the Ligoniel Lodges to 'complete' their parade, all remain ongoing.

[23] Nolan et al., *The Flag Dispute*, p. 97.

Educational underachievement, deprivation and unemployment are very real problems facing both 'Protestant' and 'Catholic' working-class communities.[24] Their experience as a *loss* by Loyalists locates them in a broader 'Culture War' through which Republicans, in general, and Sinn Féin, in particular, are alleged to be paving the road to a United Ireland by stripping Northern Ireland of its 'Britishness'. Central to this so-called 'Culture War' is what is perceived, at least in part, to be a state-sponsored process of 'rewriting' history.

Re-orienting remembrance

Jay Winter has suggested that the unprecedented scale and horror of the First World War lent its memorials a certain political neutrality, providing 'first and foremost a framework for the legitimation of individual and family grief' and becoming *politically* symbolic only 'now that the moment of mourning has long past'.[25] However, it is difficult to see how the ascription of the label 'Glorious' to Britain's war dead in the engraving on Lutyen's Cenotaph was ever anything other than intrinsically political. War commemoration is 'a practice bound up with rituals of national identification, and a key element in the symbolic repertoire available to the nation-state for binding its citizens into a national identity'.[26]

Its coalescence with partition and the resultant search for new markers of national identification in the new nation-state of Northern Ireland meant that here, First World War commemoration was *unambiguously* political from the outset. As Loughlin asserts, Ulster Unionists were 'unique in the extent to which historical myth and the unresolved dilemma of their constitutional future provided an interpretative framework within which the meaning of the war was defined'.[27] In the volatile years between 1919 and 1921,

---

[24] In fact, according to data in the 2013 *Northern Ireland Peace Monitoring Report*, of the twenty most deprived wards in Northern Ireland, sixteen are predominantly *Catholic*. The 2014 report revealed that there is, however, an acute problem of educational underachievement among working class Protestant boys in particular. See P. Nolan, *Northern Ireland Peace Monitoring Report Number Two* (Belfast: Community Relations Council, 2013), pp. 92–93 and P. Nolan, *Northern Ireland Peace Monitoring Report Number 3* (Belfast: Community Relations Council, 2014), p. 97.

[25] J. Winter, *Sites of Memory, Sites of Mourning: The Great War in European Cultural History* (Cambridge: Cambridge University Press, 1995), p. 93.

[26] T. G. Ashplant, G. Dawson and M. Roper, 'The Politics of War Memory and Commemoration: Context, Structures and Dynamics' in T. G. Ashplant, G. Dawson and M. Roper (eds.), *The Politics of War Memory and Commemoration* (London: Routledge, 2000), p. 7.

[27] J. Loughlin, 'Mobilising the Sacred Dead: Ulster Unionism, the Great War and the Politics of Remembrance' in A. Gregory and S. Pašeta (eds.), *Ireland and the Great War: A War to Unite Us All?* (Manchester: Manchester University Press, 2002), p. 136.

some of the most characteristic phases of the Anglo Irish struggle for Ulster unionism coincided with war commemorations, allowing unionists the opportunity to
counterpoint any tendency of Westminster to 'betray' Ulster with a powerful
reminder of the province's sacrifice in the British national interest, and, accordingly a debt owed by Britain ... [I]t allowed them simultaneously to share
authentically in a profound British experience, and to address their own political
concerns.[28]

The symbolic reduction of the service of all 'Ulstermen' to that of the
Ulster Division was deliberate. Its utility for Unionists was expressed in
their sponsorship of the construction of the Ulster Tower at Thiepval,
which was opened in 1921. The first permanent battlefield monument, it
symbolised, 'in a clear and unambiguous form the contribution of the
North to the defence of Britain and an empire of which it was strenuously
asserted Ulster formed an integral part'.[29]

While the dominant memorial narrative of the new Northern state was
specific to Northern Ireland, the aesthetic of its ritual articulation was also
intrinsically and more broadly 'British'. The fiftieth anniversary of the
Somme was marked with both a 'pilgrimage' to the Ulster Tower led by
the Northern Irish Prime Minister Terence O'Neill and a state ceremony
on the Balmoral show-ground, attended by Queen Elizabeth II.
Commemorations of the Somme by the Orange Order and the co-option
of its symbolism by the newly (re)formed Ulster Volunteer Force (UVF)
from the late 1960s came to both reflect and contribute to rising sectarian
violence during the Troubles. But a state commemoration, hosted first by
the Belfast Corporation and latterly Belfast City Council, was held
annually at the cenotaph at Belfast City Hall for the duration. This
ceremony included representatives of the British state, first in the form
of the Governor, and then from 1976, the Secretary of State. A resolution,
passed every year at a special session of Belfast City Council and then read
by the Lord Mayor at the ceremony at the cenotaph stated,

That we, the Lord Mayor and Citizens of the City of Belfast, on the *nth*
Anniversary of the Battle of the Somme, desire again to record our feelings of
gratitude to the brave men of the 36th (Ulster) Division who, by their glorious
conduct in that Battle, made an imperishable name for themselves and their
Province and whose heroism will never be forgotten so long as the British
Commonwealth lasts.[30]

---

[28] Ibid., pp. 137–141.
[29] D. Officer, '"For God and Ulster": The Ulsterman on the Somme' in I. McBride (ed.),
History and Memory in Modern Ireland (Cambridge: Cambridge University Press, 2001),
p. 182.
[30] See J. Leonard, *World War Commemorations at Belfast City Hall: A Report Submitted to
Belfast City Council* (Belfast: Belfast City Council, 2003).

The shifting of the Armistice Day commemorations in Northern Ireland to the Sunday nearest to 11 November following the Second World War, and their expansion to incorporate the memory of members of the armed forces killed in more recent conflicts, were all also in line with broader British trends. Thus, commemoration of the First World War, in general, and of the Somme, in particular, has traditionally played a significantly symbolic role in maintaining and asserting Northern Ireland's 'Britishness', and its constitutional position within the Union. Of course, this in part explains the IRA's choice of a Remembrance Sunday service in Enniskillen in 1987 as a 'legitimate target'.[31]

Whether or not this convincingly adheres to claims about a 'Culture War', it *is* the case that 'official'[32] commemoration of the Somme in Northern Ireland has, in the era of 'peacebuilding', become less unequivocally 'British'. As it was put to me by a member of a 'Somme Society' in Belfast:

Thiepval Tower was given to the people of *Ulster*. Thiepval Tower was built for the *36th (Ulster) Division*. Then when Farset come on board they done all the work to get Thiepval Tower back into the way it was, 'cause it'd been lying derelict for so long. And then they set up the Somme Heritage Centre, and it was set up as the *36th (Ulster) Division Museum*. But over the years it's changed to the '*Irish*soldier. org' ... they're shying away from the 36th (Ulster) Division.[33]

The Community Relations Council, funding bodies, local authorities, cultural and heritage organisations (including the Somme Association), community projects and professional historians have all played a deliberate and active role in creating new 'official' historical narratives, in a context defined by a need for their 'cross-communal' re-orientation. In other words, the 'rediscovery' of the Nationalist war dead is not politically neutral. While recent scholarship, including the notable and rigorously researched contribution by Richard Grayson,[34] does paint a richer,

[31] H. Robinson, 'Remembering War in the Midst of Conflict: First World War Commemorations in the Northern Irish Troubles', *Twentieth Century British History* 21 (2010), 80–101.

[32] For more on the distinction between 'official' and 'unofficial' historical memory, see Y. Papadakis, 'The Politics of Memory and Forgetting in Cyprus', *Journal of Mediterranean Studies* 3 (1993), 139–154.

[33] Somme Society member, interview by author, Belfast, 24 June 2014. Somme Associations and Societies exist throughout Northern Ireland under the umbrella of a central '36th Ulster Division Memorial Association'. They co-ordinate commemorative activities including parades, talks and exhibitions, and facilitate visits to the First World War battlefields. For the sake of clarity, I have referred to 'Societies' throughout, reserving the label 'Association' for the organisation that manages the Somme Heritage Centre and maintains the Ulster Tower at Thiepval.

[34] See R. Grayson, *Belfast Boys: How Unionists and Nationalists Fought and Died Together in the First World War* (London: Continuum, 2009).

▓▓▓▓▓▓▓ and has Orange tinted picture of the Northern war experience, it is itself rooted in a particular moral and political paradigm; one which locates the foundations of a 'shared future' on the battlefields of the past. Fundamentally, there is an implicit suggestion that proof of their ancestors having 'fought and died together' in the trenches of 1914–1918 ought to mitigate historical (and perhaps, therefore, political) differences between Unionists and Nationalists in the 'new' Northern Ireland.

In part drawing on these 'new' histories, commemorations that emphasise the 'shared sacrifice' of the First World War, rather than those that see it as a uniquely 'Unionist' experience, are gaining dominance in the public memorial space. In 2010, the wording of the Somme resolution passed annually by Belfast City Council on 1 July was changed to incorporate the 16th (Irish) Division, while references to 'the Province' and 'the British Commonwealth' were removed. Since 2012, a representative of the Irish Government has participated in the annual Somme commemoration at the cenotaph. While, at the time of writing, a Sinn Féin representative has yet to participate in the 'official' ceremony at the cenotaph, Sinn Féin councillors have continued to lay a wreath during a smaller, more low-key event on the morning of 1 July each year since the precedent was set by Alex Maskey during his term as Lord Mayor in 2002.[35] All of these developments have been widely welcomed. But the plaudits belie ongoing tensions and political differences.

Commemorative contests

At its most reductive and politically expedient, the suggestion that there was no 'Orange and Green' in the trenches comes close to open celebration of a 'war that stopped a war'. Of this assertion, speaking candidly about his own role in the Decade of Centenaries, one public historian who is involved in a number of centenary projects said to me,

They all went off to the war together: the 16th and the 36th Division, we all went off, and you know what, we put aside our terrible differences and fought the Germans. This is not true. For a start, it's not true that they loved each other in the trenches. They didn't. But you know, what it turns its back on is the reality that here, during the war, it's quite clear that there was a lot of heading off in different directions. The war polarised, very, very, very much polarised opinion.[36]

---

[35] On 11 November 2013, Máirtín Ó Muilleoir became the first Sinn Féin Mayor of Belfast to participate in the Armistice Day commemoration at the cenotaph. To date, however, no Sinn Féin representative has participated in the 'official' state ceremony on either 1 July or Remembrance Sunday.

[36] Public historian, interview by author, Belfast, 4 July 2014.

In attempting to 'de-politicise' First World War remembrance in Northern Ireland, we forget, as Jenny Edkins has argued, 'that a complete, non-antagonistic society is impossible ... Too often what we call politics in the contemporary world is evacuated of antagonism. Most of what is accepted onto the agenda of discussion is already delimited to such an extent that it contains no properly political disagreements.'[37] As well as white-washing any meaningful debate on the war's causes or its wider morality, evacuation of 'politics' from its commemoration also negates that whether and how we choose to 'remember' is a marker of significant political difference. Where that political difference is both the cause and consequence of prolonged violence, the 'cross-communal' imperative is understandable and even laudable. It is nonetheless, to quote my historian friend, 'inaccurately emollient'.

Loyalist commemorations during the Decade of Centenaries serve as a counterpoint to these state rituals, which frame the current settlement and its imputed 'shared' historical narrativisation. On 1 July, the cenotaph hosts not only an 'official' state commemoration but also an 'unofficial' commemoration organised by the West Belfast Athletic and Cultural Society,[38] which functions to ritually (re)claim the Somme for Loyalism. In 2014, participants paraded into the grounds of City Hall in period costume, embodying a narrative arc that stakes a claim – via their 'forebears' in the original Ulster Volunteer Force and the 36th (Ulster) Division – on one of the most symbolically important places in Northern Irish politics. The symbols (the red poppy, the Union Flag), ritual forms (the Last Post played by a lone bugler, military-style marching to musical accompaniment, the raising and lowering of flags and banners, and the laying of wreaths) and vernacular ('At the going down of the sun, and in the morning, we will remember them') mirror and subvert those of 'official' remembrance. Concurrent to the WBACS commemoration at City Hall, the Orange Order's 1 July 'Mini-Twelfth' parade in East Belfast is a site of confrontation between both Loyalism and Republicanism and Loyalism and the state, particularly on the part of the route that takes it past the 'Nationalist' enclave in the Short Strand.

Underwriting the new commemorative dispensation in Northern Ireland, in general, and in Belfast, in particular, are contestational narratives: at times hidden and at times overt subscripts of resistance that make commemoration during the Decade of Centenaries one battlefront in the

---

[37] J. Edkins, *Trauma and the Memory of Politics* (Cambridge: Cambridge University Press, 2003), pp. 14–229.

[38] The West Belfast Athletic and Cultural Society was founded on the Shankill Road in 1998 by UVF former prisoners. It provides sporting facilities as well as programmes on culture and identity.

imagining 'Culture War'. It is a chief means by which Loyalists both
articulate and challenge the sense of loss and uncertainty engendered by
a peace process that, among other 'attacks' on their 'community', has co-
opted and corrupted 'their' commemorative traditions. Clearly, this
'[r]esistance can be regressive. That is, resistance doesn't have to be
counter-hegemonic to be resistance.'[39] On one level, Loyalism's commemorative resistance to new political realities in Northern Ireland represents a form of mourning, or even of melancholy, for the loss of the very
Unionist hegemony that was at the heart of historic patterns of discrimination in Northern Ireland. More fundamentally, however, it reflects that
that hegemony was probably never really experienced as such.
Furthermore, it points to a future in which the hegemony that 'was' in
the (imagined) past can be reconstituted.

The 'never-ending ought to be'

Simply put, remembrance is experienced by many Loyalists as an
obligation:

It's our duty ... It *is* a requirement to remember, but it's trying to get people to
realise that ... It's my job, this is the way I see myself, as an evangelist, for want of a
better term. Obviously I can't do very much because I'm working and I've family
and all the rest of it. But it's my job ... that's the wrong word, it's my vocation,
whatever you want to call it, to try and convince people.[40]

The past makes particular claims on the present. 'The tradition of all the
dead generations', wrote Marx, 'weighs like a nightmare on the brain of
the living'.[41] But this tradition, or 'inheritance', 'is never gathered
together, never at one with itself. Its presumed unity can consist only in
the injunction to reaffirm by choosing.'[42] The ritual act of commemoration proceeds precisely from this injunction: 'Lest We Forget'. On the
face of it, the imperative simply to 'remember' says nothing about why it is
or should be a collective, let alone, as the above quote would suggest,

---

[39] C. Gallaher and P. Shirlow, 'The Geography of Loyalist Paramilitary Feuding in Belfast',
Space and Polity 10 (2006), 150.

[40] Unionist Centenary Committee member, interview by author, Belfast, 4 November
2014. The Unionist Centenary Committee (UCC) was established at the end of 2009,
with the purpose of co-ordinating commemorative activities during the Decade of
Centenaries. It has played a key role in organising a number of the large-scale re-
enactments, including on 'Ulster Day' in September 2012.

[41] K. Marx, 'The Eighteenth Brumaire of Napoleon Bonaparte', *Marxists Internet Archive*,
accessed 5 February 2014 (www.marxists.org/archive/marx/works/1852/18th-bru
maire/).

[42] J. Derrida, *Spectres of Marx: The State of the Debt, the Work of Mourning and the New
International* (New York and London: Routledge, 2006), p. 18.

redemptive or salvational experience. The *act* of collective, ritualised commemoration contributes something to the Loyalist experience that is more complex or important than simply 'remembering'. In part through its collapsing of time linearity,[43] commemorative ritual is a means by which the present also makes particular claims on the past. Where this present is defined in terms of a 'crisis', 'the more it is "out of joint", the more one has to convoke the old, "borrow" from it'.[44]

The period since the paramilitary ceasefires in 1994 has seen a marked increase in Loyalist commemoration. In an historical moment of perceived political crisis, participants in these rituals 'anxiously conjure up the spirits of the past to their service, borrowing from them names, battle slogans, and costumes in order to present this new-scene in world history in time-honoured disguise and borrowed language'.[45] Commemorations in the present Decade of Centenaries have included a number of large-scale historical re-enactments, such as the one in 2012 marking the centenary of the signing of the Ulster Covenant at Belfast City Hall. At parades to mark the centenaries of the formation of the Ulster Volunteer Force at Craigavon House and their gun-running 'Operation Lion' in Larne, the same orations delivered one hundred years previously by Edward Carson were (re)delivered, *verbatim*, by Billy Hutchinson, the leader of the Progressive Unionist Party. Period costumes – the flat-caps, puttees and bandoliers of the original UVF, the gowns of the UVF nursing corps and the khaki of the 36th (Ulster) Division – have also been a predominant feature of these commemorations.

Increasingly, these period costumes have also wound their way into the other long-running commemorative traditions that define the Loyalist calendar. The sight of bandsmen in replica khaki uniforms or of colour parties containing one or more members in full 'historical' UVF attire is now a feature of most Orange parades in Belfast and of the Apprentice Boys' parades to mark both the beginning and the end of the 1689 Siege of Derry (in December and August, respectively). This is combined with the ubiquitous use of the symbol of the poppy on band uniforms, and the image of soldiers 'going over the top' on 1 July 1916 on drum skins and banners. All of the above are *also* a feature of paramilitary commemorations (see Figure 13.3). Traditionally the symbolic capital of the original Ulster Volunteer Force, the 36th (Ulster) Division and the Somme has been jealously guarded by the UVF,[46] but in recent years, attempts to

---

[43] See E. Tonkin and D. Bryan, 'Political Ritual: Temporality and Tradition' in Å. Bonholm (ed.), *Political Ritual* (Gothenburg: IASSA, 1996), pp. 14–36.

[44] Derrida, *Spectres of Marx*, p. 136.   [45] Marx, 'Eighteenth Brumaire'.

[46] See D. Bryan, 'Forget 1690, Remember the Somme: Ulster Loyalist Battles in the Twenty-first Century' in O. Frawley (ed.), *Memory Ireland Volume 3: The Famine and the Troubles* (Syracuse: Syracuse University Press, 2014), pp. 293–309.

Figure 13.3: Period Costume at 2014 Brian Robinson Parade, Shankill
Road, Belfast (photo: with permission of Jonathan Evershed).

stake a claim to it have also been made by the Ulster Defence Association
(UDA).[47]

The constant reiteration of these memorial tropes, and the accretion of
commemorative symbolism throughout the 'marching season' – which in
the era of nightly 'protest parades' has itself become increasingly
unbounded – subverts the liminality that customarily characterises commemorative ritual. The repetition of these same symbols on murals and in
memorial gardens in 'Loyalist' areas of Belfast serves to transform entire
streets into *lieux de mémoire*, where the boundary between ritual and
normal time is blurred. One set of murals unveiled in 2014 opposite the
Shankill Road's Rex Bar even commemorates the Centenary commemorations themselves (see Figure 13.4). One commemorator I spoke to
reflected on this unending memory work:

[47] See E. Viggiani, *Talking Stones: The Politics of Memorialisation in Post-Conflict Northern
Ireland* (New York and Oxford: Berghahn, 2014), pp. 150–171.

Figure 13.4: 'A Force for Ulster' Mural, Rex Bar, Shankill Road, Belfast (photo: with permission of Richard S. Grayson).

Sometimes I remember too often. You know . . . and then you get drawn back to the Menin Gate. And they have it every day. So if they have it every day, why can't we have it every day? So, I've always thought that the Prods, the Unionists, you know, remember too much, and then you say, well, they do it at the Menin Gate every day, so it can't be that bad.[48]

This endless commemoration means that the ghosts of the Somme are never at rest. Their 'sacrifice' is constantly recalled, reiterated and, thereby, projected forwards, propelled always and endlessly into the future. In this way, the Somme functions as the Loyalist equivalent of

[48] Unionist Centenary Committee member, interview by author, Belfast, 4 November 2014.

what Arthur Aughey has called Republicanism's 'never ending ought to be'.[49] As Beiner suggests, '[i]n representing their dead soldiers as political martyrs and turning military disaster into a promise for future triumph, Protestant loyalists may have unconsciously emulated the nationalist republican tradition of triumph of failure.'[50] The simultaneous expression in the public space of the contrasting narratives of past imperial glory and of victimhood in the unjust present 'proclaim[s] an imminent status reversal: though at present "we" are oppressed, shortly we shall be restored to our former glory'. It points towards 'a glorious destiny, stemming from the true nature revealed in and by [the] golden past'.[51] The ghosts of the 36th (Ulster) Division are the paragon of their ethnie, the exemplars of a deferred and 'authentic' essence to which the community ought to simultaneously 'return' and 'aspire'. Its recreation in a 'visionary future' provides a 'hidden direction and goal beneath the obscuring present'.[52]

This essence is, however, fundamentally irrecoverable, for there is a paradox in stressing the *unparalleled* virtue of the Ulster Volunteers (which in any case is imagined), while simultaneously insisting that it is something their descendants might reasonably be expected to live up to. They can do no other than fall always shamefully short. This is mirrored in the refutation by many Loyalists (including by many members of the UVF itself) of the idea that any continuity can be claimed between the organisation founded in 1913 and that which was (re)formed in 1965:

Sordid, incestuous and squalid: that's how you would describe this forty years in Northern Ireland. There was nothing honourable about it, nothing honourable. In fact, it was disgusting. And it's got nothing to do with the Ulster Volunteer Force who, number one, declared war on the British Army ... and also the men who went to the Somme and fought at the Somme. It's a world of difference.[53]

In the era of peacebuilding, when Loyalists see themselves as being in cultural and political retreat, this sense of inadequacy is compounded.

Thus, the sacrifice of the Ulster Division at the Somme represents an unfulfilled and, particularly in the era of peacebuilding, inherently

[49] A. Aughey, 'What Is Living and What Is Dead in the Ideal of 1916?' in M. Ní Dhonnchadha and T. Dorgan (eds.), *Revising the Rising* (Derry: Field Day, 1991), pp. 71–90.
[50] G. Beiner, 'Between Trauma and Triumphalism: The Easter Rising, the Somme, and the Crux of Deep Memory in Northern Ireland', *Journal of British Studies* 46 (2007), 382.
[51] A. Smith, 'The "Golden Age" and National Renewal' in G. Hosking and G. Schöpflin (eds.), *Myths and Nationhood* (London: Hurst & Co., 1997), p. 51.
[52] Ibid.
[53] Former Progressive Unionist Party member, interview by author, Belfast, 21 July 2014.

unfulfill*able* promise of salvation. James Craig's 'Protestant state for a Protestant people' – guaranteed with the blood of Ulster's Volunteers – is a political project that has only ever been on its way to completion. Even at the height of the 'Orange State', it was probably *experienced* more as aspiration than as lived reality. It is Loyalism's utopic vision: founded on a blood sacrifice that, by its very nature, cannot be emulated and to which return is impossible. Always elusive, 'parity of esteem' serves to place it that much further out of reach. That 'a home where's there no Pope of Rome ... and flute bands play the Sash everyday' is not in keeping with what is conventionally called 'utopic' and – more fundamentally – is incongruous with an historical moment defined by an obsolescence of utopic political projects, in general, only serves to emphasise its unattainability.[54]

The ghosts of the Somme therefore point to a future in which the insecurity of the unstable present can be overcome, while simultaneously demonstrating that it can't. For instance, a primary message of the Unionist 'Golden Age' for the present is one of *unity;* of a shared purpose across divisions including class and gender. The 'reclamation' of this Unionist unity is a central and explicit aim of those involved in planning and co-ordinating commemorative events. Reflecting on the centenary commemorations of the Ulster Covenant, a member of the Unionist Centenary Committee noted that

everything worked in the end and everybody walked and we were all, you know, part of one big happy family, which was really, really good ... you'd seen the whole Unionist ... *every* shade of Unionism walking: Orange Order, Apprentice Boys, UVF, UDA, *every*body! You know what I mean?[55]

But in its very attempt to reproduce the essential 'authenticity' of Unionist unity, commemoration also betrays its impossibility. Unity is not simply expressed or represented through memory work: it is imagined and constructed, its outward appearance belying a series of internal conflicts. As one participant in the Covenant centenary events put it to me:

On Ulster Day 2012, 100,000 Unionists put their feet on the ground ... 100,000 people bothered their arse to do something about it. So that's the positive. Now, if you want to go into the negatives: the UVF walked from South Belfast to City Hall, stood there like planks while row upon row of Orangemen walked past them ... The 36th Ulster Division Memorial Association and the UDA formed

---

[54] Set to the tune of 'Home on the Range', 'No Pope of Rome' is a popular marching tune played by Loyalist flute bands. Full lyrics available at: http://lyrics.wikia.com/The_Tho rnlie_Boys:No_Pope_Of_Rome.

[55] Unionist Centenary Committee member, interview by author, Belfast, 25 June 2014.

up in front of the Orange Order, who didn't want us anywhere near them, and paraded up to Stormont . . . Now we didn't go in the gates. They wouldn't let us in you see, to Stormont. They made sure the gates were closed.[56]

The same individual also went on to criticise the DUP for their (lack of) involvement in the centenary commemorations to date:

[I]t doesn't help when the major Unionist political party has no interest in the centenary events . . . they don't commit themselves in any shape or fashion to the centenary events. Now, they all turned up at the City Hall on Ulster Day 2012, to get their photographs taken . . . but put that all aside, did the DUP take much part in anything? No.[57]

At the same time, as it claims to have overcome them, commemoration reproduces division and contestation. These divisions function at multiple levels, within and between the various groups that constitute the so-called 'Loyalist community'. The conflict between Loyalists and Republicans, divisions between 'Loyalism' and 'Unionism' and between 'Unionism' and the British state are all also mirrored and replicated. Thus, 'commemoration functions as a fulcrum point, a hinge, in the discursive construction of conflict and *the political* in ways which serve to reproduce, re-write and deconstruct its accepted and acceptable boundaries'.[58] In sum, commemorating the Somme is a form of symbolic negotiation. The subject of this negotiation is the very subject of politics itself. Claims are made to moral authority and political legitimacy, and particular forms of cultural capital are mobilised to contest (or to reinforce) prevailing hierarchies. Memory work is not simply about who should be 'remembered' and how; it forms part of a properly *political* conversation about the shaping of the social order. This conversation is, by its very nature, difficult and disruptive. But it is nonetheless important.

The ghosts of the Somme will continue to haunt the present Decade, and it behoves us not to ignore but to engage with those who follow them. We must 'situate groups in relation to their own traditions, asking how they interpret their own "ghosts" and how they use them as a source of knowledge'.[59] Ultimately – and despite the risks it appears to represent to 'peacebuilding' in Northern Ireland – an empathetic engagement with the Loyalist 'ghost dance' and an understanding of its role in a communal politics defined by chronic uncertainty and discord may even be crucial in the pursuit of lasting peace. Understanding Loyalism as an *ongoing*

---

[56] Participant in Covenant centenary parade, interview by author, Belfast, 4 November 2014.
[57] Ibid.   [58] Graff-McRae, *Remembering and Forgetting 1916*, p. 15, original emphasis.
[59] J. Fentress and C. Wickham, *Social Memory* (Oxford: Blackwell, 1992), p. 26.

political project (or, more accurately, as a set of overlapping and often conflicting projects) guided by the ghosts of its imagined past allows for a deeper understanding of the (identity) politics of Ulster Loyalism and, thereby, the possibility of more meaningful conversations not only about (Northern) Ireland's past but more fundamentally about its future.

Index